"I COULDN'T PUT IT DOWN! . . .
as gripping as the most suspenseful novel, yet
brimming with humor, pathos, mystery, sex."
—Harold Robbins

•

WHATEVER HAPPENED TO . . .

The cheerleaders—the jocks—the "bad" girls that
were all part of our high school days?

Now 30 classmates talk freely about themselves and
each other, then and now.

The team quarterback who's now a Hollywood masseur
. . . the gangleader of "the Saracens" who's built a
million dollar business . . . the "most popular" boy
who committed suicide 7 years later . . . and all the
others.

We all knew them.

Some of us *were* them.
This is what happened to them.

•

"EXTREMELY ENGAGING . . . The authors do such a good
job of dramatizing their subjects' lives that in the end you
feel you do know them, almost as well as you knew your
own high school class." —*New York Times*

WHAT REALLY HAPPENED TO THE CLASS OF '65?

**Michael Medved
and
David Wallechinsky**

BALLANTINE BOOKS • NEW YORK

Grateful acknowledgment is made to the following for permission to reprint previously published material:

Time magazine: For excerpts from the article "Today's Teenagers," January 29, 1965. Copyright © 1965 by Time, Inc.

John Ciardi: For the poem "My Garden," by Janice Appleby
Succorsa. Copyright © 1959 by John Ciardi. Reprinted from
How Does a Poem Mean? (Houghton Mifflin, 1959).

Library of Congress Catalog Card Number: 76-10818

ISBN 0-345-27458-X

This edition published by arrangement with
Random House, Inc., New York

Manufactured in the United States of America

First Ballantine Books Edition: August 1977
Seventh Printing: January 1978

To our parents—
and the memory of Moshe Dove

It was the best of times, it was the worst of times, it was the age of wisdom, it was the age of foolishness, it was the epoch of belief, it was the epoch of incredulity, it was the season of Light, it was the season of Darkness, it was the spring of hope, it was the winter of despair, we had everything before us, we had nothing before us, we were all going direct to Heaven, we were all going direct the other way—in short, the period was so far like the present period, that some of its noisiest authorities insisted on its being received, for good or for evil, in the superlative degree of comparison only.

—CHARLES DICKENS

ACKNOWLEDGMENTS

Our thanks first of all to Nancy Medved, who did most of the transcribing for this book, and also to Flora Chavez for additional transcribing and typing.

The Dan Adams Archives provided invaluable material on the class of '65, and Michael Katz and Barry Oiffer provided indispensable photographic skills.

Many people deserve thanks for reading the manuscript in its various stages of evolution, and offering useful suggestions. We are particularly indebted to Sylvia and Irving Wallace, Len Hill, Ben and Harry Medved, Rabbi Manny Goldstein, Ruth, Larry and Ron Herman, Amy Wallace, and Sid Finster, wherever he may be.

We would also like to thank the eleven people we interviewed who are not included in the book. And last, but hardly least, we are grateful to our agent, David Obst (Culver City High, class of '64), and our brilliant and supportive editor at Random House, Susan Bolotin (Sharon High, class of '68).

Contents

Contents

Contents

Contents

"On the Fringe of a Golden Era"

The *Time* magazine article back in January 1965 was the biggest thing that had ever hit the Palisades. For weeks this quiet, comfortable corner of suburban Los Angeles was astir with controversy over what had been said, what had been implied. In the $100,000 homes, behind the broad lawns and carefully tended palms, the text of the article was debated over breakfast and dinner. And on the brand-new open-air campus of Palisades High School, the two thousand students chattered and worried and bragged, enjoying their place at the center of the stage.

For *Time* had selected this high school, and this senior class of '65, as the focus for its cover story on TODAY'S TEENAGERS. "In the mid-1960's," *Time* enthused, "smarter, subtler, and more sophisticated kids are pouring into and out of more expert, exacting and experimental schools." What better place to illustrate this trend than Palisades High School? The Los Angeles Board of Education had lavished $8 million on the construction of this stylish red brick facility in a secluded canyon overlooking the Pacific. The school was designed to attract the best teachers, and to service the most privileged students, in the city of Los Angeles. The neighborhoods that fed into Palisades High—Brentwood, Bel Air, Pacific Palisades—represented the sort of affluence that all America was striving to achieve. In one of the *Time* article's most

1

controversial passages, a member of the high school faculty commented sardonically on this rarefied atmosphere.

"These are the students' cars," says English Teacher Jeanne Hernandez, pointing to a fast collection of "wheels" ranging up to Jags, "and these are the teachers' cars," pointing to a sedate group of compacts and the like. "It's so lush here that it's unreal," she says. "After a while you feel like a missionary in the tropics. If you don't get out, you go native."

When we talked with her ten years later, Mrs. Hernandez was still marveling over the wealth of Palisades parents. "The principal at that time," she recalls, "was giving us the figure of forty-two thousand dollars for median income. I don't know how it was computed. But that's what he read to us at one of those new-term indoctrination meetings. It was so shocking that all you could hear was the concerted sound of indrawn breath."

It was only to be expected that this sort of background would produce a sense of isolation and security. Our Palisades classmates viewed the other stories in that January issue of *Time* as entertaining, perhaps, but hardly relevant to their day-to-day affairs. The big news of the week was the inauguration of President Lyndon Johnson, following his landslide victory over Barry Goldwater in the November elections. "The Great Society," Johnson declared in his inaugural, "is the excitement of becoming—always becoming . . . Is a new world coming? We welcome it —and we will bend it to the hope of man." Meanwhile, the Reverend Dr. Martin Luther King, Jr., announced that his 1965 civil rights drive would focus on the town of Selma, Alabama. Buddhist monks were demonstrating against the United States in faraway Vietnam. Winston Churchill had just died in England at the age of ninety, and *Time* devoted three pages to an article on his life. Hollywood marked the passing of another sort of greatness, as Jeanette MacDonald was honored with an enormous funeral. In sports, quarterback Y. A. Tittle of the New York Giants announced his retirement after seventeen years in professional football. And the newest hit of the TV season was *The Man from U.N.C.L.E.*, starring Robert Vaughan as the suave Napoleon Solo. Yet not even a discussion of this superhero could take our attention from *Time*'s detailed description of the social cliques, campus personalities and generational trends observed at Palisades High School.

There had always been a sense of celebrity and excitement about our group; we had known we were special even before *Time* told us so. Part of it was no doubt the Hollywood influence; the children of personalities such as Betty Hutton, Karl Malden, Henry Miller, Sterling Hayden, James Arness and Irving Wallace were highly visible on campus. Then there were the expectations of parents, teachers and now the press: we were part of the healthiest, most beautiful, best-educated and most affluent generation in the history of the world. We were, in fact, the natural leaders of that generation. Never mind *Time*'s dark hints about drinking, sexual promiscuity and unbridled hedonism in the Palisades senior class. We were the children of destiny, and we would make our way successfully through dangerous and uncharted seas. We were, as the article promised in its subtitle, "on the fringe of a golden era."

That era did not begin auspiciously. A month after graduation came the Watts riot, just fifteen miles from where we lived, and with it, America's first season of urban unrest. That same summer the Johnson Administration began the big American build-up in Vietnam. Then, in 1966, our old school was in the news again. It was *Newsweek* this time which did a special story on Palisades High, and the growing drug prob-

3

lem in the class that had followed us. Gone were the
balmy, tranquil days of '65. With the draft calls rising
and the first stirrings of student discontent, *Newsweek*
found "something clearly amiss in Paradise" and wondered, somewhat implausibly, whether the Palisades
might not become "a WASP Watts."

In the years that followed, through all the up-
heavals in sex, politics and life styles, our group was
always at the forefront, always riding the crest of the
wave. In the late sixties, when social commentators
around the country began hailing the pioneers of an
Aquarian Age, we had no question whom they had in
mind. In his best-selling 1970 book, *The Greening of
America,* Professor Charles Reich proclaimed "a great
change" among "the bright, sensitive children of the
affluent middle class." Specifically, this change centered on "the college class of 1969, which entered
as freshmen in the fall of 1965"—once again, our
class. "There is a revolution coming," Reich announced. "It will originate with the individual and
with culture and it will change the political structure
only as its final act . . . This is the revolution of the
new generation . . . At the heart of everything is
what we shall call a change of consciousness. This
means a 'new head'—a new way of living—a new
man."

Whatever happened to that "new man" who was
supposed to change America? After ten years of intense publicity, he seemed to have slipped from sight.
From the sober vantage point of 1976, how could we
trace the "revolutionary" history of our generation?

It was clear to us that the best course was to return to friends and acquaintances from our high school
class. There have been dozens of sociological surveys,
impressionistic studies and fictionalized accounts, all
purporting to show what happened to America's young
people over the last ten years. But what of the real

individuals who lived at the center of the storm? What has the last decade done to well-remembered individuals such as

—MARK HOLMES, Palisades High School's All-American boy, the captain of the football team, and voted Most Likely to Succeed. Did he follow the straight and narrow path to business success and a home in the suburbs?

—LISA MENZIES, the boy-crazy "bad girl" of the class, who received a ten-week suspension for stealing a history test in senior year?

—WILLIAM QUIVERS, the first—and only—black in a student body of 2,100. Painfully shy, he nearly succeeded in his desperate efforts to make himself inconspicuous. How had his life been affected by the dramatic currents in black history since 1965?

—LANY TYLER, a compulsive achiever, our head cheerleader, Homecoming Queen, Girls' League president, and winner of every citizenship award that the high school had to offer?

—ANITA CHAMPION, the plump socialite who said in the school annual that her life's ambition was to be a "good wife and mother"?

—whiz kid JAMIE KELSO, featured in the *Time* article as a "skinny near-genius." He was innocent, intense and a high school graduate at sixteen. What channels had he found for his passionate idealism?

Talking over our old times one night at three o'clock, we decided that tracking down these people, along with a score of others from our class of five hundred students, might provide a clue to the fate of an entire generation. Of course every high school is different, but in some respects they are all the same. Each class has its own leaders and pariahs, intellectual achievers and buffoons, intimidating tough guys and social queens and car enthusiasts and athletic heroes and quiet, pleasant ordinary kids.

The two of us had managed to maintain our friendship over the years despite widely divergent life styles, but neither of us had seen most of the people on our list since graduation. There were even a few names that we had known only by reputation in high school. We often had a difficult time locating these people. The high school keeps no alumni records and we had to operate entirely on our own. We relied heavily on gossip, letters, calls to parents or friends, and even chance meetings to make the necessary contacts. Nearly everyone we approached was anxious to help with our project, and without that help this book would have been impossible. In each of our tape-recorded interviews, we solicited comments about the other people in our book; we decided that the best way to recreate someone as he was in high school was to rely on the memories of his classmates. With only two exceptions, we have used the real names of the real people in this book; the history of our generation has already been blurred enough by fictions and generalities.

About ourselves we have been equally specific:

—David Wallechinsky (*né* Wallace), the son of novelists Irving and Sylvia Wallace, dropped out of UCLA during his first semester. He later attended San Francisco State, but dropped out again to join the hippie movement in Berkeley, where he experimented with drugs, film making, demonstrations and communal living. A devout vegetarian, he is the co-author of books on organic gardening and laughing gas, as well as the best-selling *The People's Almanac.*

6

—Michael Medved, voted Most Intellectual and "Really Radical" in the high school class poll, went on to Yale and graduated with honors in 1969. After a brief stint at Yale Law School he worked as a professional speech writer for candidates of all political persuasions, and dabbled in advertising, public relations and teaching. In the four years since his marriage, he has turned to traditional Judaism, keeping a kosher home and honoring Orthodox rules of Sabbath observance and daily prayer.

We have interviewed and written about each other and are both included along with our classmates as full chapters in this book.

At the beginning of this project we disagreed sharply on what we expected to find—and what we wanted to find—in studying our high school class. We agreed only to follow the stories wherever they led. In the end, none of the predictions or rumors we had heard prepared us for the revelations we found along the way.

November 22, 1963

•

As members of the class of '65 we felt we were the Leaders of Tomorrow and expected that we would someday change the world. We knew that the future of mankind hung in the balance. We had gone through the Cuban missile crisis together—many of us in our parents' fallout shelters—just weeks after arriving at Palisades High School. Yet our first real confrontation with the fact that all stories do not have happy endings, and that bright promises are not always fulfilled, came that moment in junior year when we heard that the President had been shot. It was a nightmare of brief duration, and after a few days we returned to our classes, dances, debates and football games. Yet that November day foreshadowed the difficult days that lay ahead, and our universe could never again be entirely secure.

•

Jeff Stolper:
I was in the eleventh grade. I had Study Hall third or fourth period—I can't remember which. I was in the library with a friend of mine. He had just ordered his new surfboard a couple of weeks before and was supposed to pick it up that day. He snuck out of the library, which you're not supposed to do, over to the phone booth in the administration building. He came back and said, "I just heard something really weird. Kennedy has been shot. You know, people in the attendance office are crying."

I said, "Naw, it's got to be something else. They must have been sneezing or something." Then one of the monitors from the administration building came in, and talked to us over to the side. She said, "Yeah, everybody in there is crying. He was shot." At that time you'd never heard of anybody being shot except on TV. You remembered that cowboys being shot would get up afterwards. You figured that he was probably shot, but that he'd recover.

Sure enough, the announcement came over the PA system from the principal that he had been shot. They didn't say how bad it was. I remember now that it must have been third period, because I had gym fourth period that year. By the time I got to the gym they were changing in the locker room, and the announcement came over that he was dead. Nobody in the gym could hear it. The rumors were that he died and Johnson had a heart attack and died. Then it was that he died and that Johnson had a heart attack but didn't die. No one knew what the story was until we got to lunch.

I remember Mr. Thomas was my gym teacher. He walked out of the gym office with a bag of basketballs and mumbled one or two words that no one could understand. He dropped the balls on the ground, went inside and left us out there on our own to do whatever we wanted to do. I didn't feel like doing anything. Most of the people I knew didn't feel like doing anything.

Then lunch period came around. Naturally, everybody was talking about what had happened and the possibilities of being attacked by Russia. You know, nuclear war and the whole bit. Later some people were joking around, but it wasn't the time to joke around. It was a sad event. It was something that the whole country experienced together. You know, that people *do* get killed, people *do* die. Life can be hard. I guess it was probably the first time that everybody in that high school experienced one feeling together.

Sally Lobherr:

I remember it perfectly. As a matter of fact, that same date eleven years later was the day of my second wedding, and I thought about it that day too. It was the Friday of our homecoming. I was going to my first homecoming dance with my boyfriend. I remember that we were in girls' gym class. We were doing modern dance and we were inside. This thing came over the loudspeaker that President Kennedy had been shot. Everybody looked around like, "What is this?" We all got quiet and we heard it again; so we decided it must be true. Some people were crying. Some people were oblivious, they couldn't have cared less. Some real *assholes* said, "Oh, I'm glad. I really didn't like him anyway."

He was the first President I really ever knew. I liked to watch him and I liked what he had to say—of what I could understand then. I liked what he was doing for the people who didn't have it so well—I could see that through all of my obliviousness. I was sad. I was really sad when he died.

That weekend I watched television an awful lot. I was watching when Oswald got shot. *That* I couldn't believe. All these things were happening to my poor little unadulterated mind! You know, nothing had ever happened bad. All of a sudden these bad things were happening.

Jamie Kelso:

I guess we were in class and they announced it over the PA. We're talking '63. I would be fifteen years old. I was not a fan of John F. Kennedy. I think I felt the man was a charlatan. Emotionally, his death meant nothing to me at all.

I spent hundreds of hours studying the Warren Commission Report because it was so fascinatingly obvious. This was one of my first awakenings to the fraud and the sham of the media and the federal government in an attempt to manipulate the truth, à la *1984*. I have no idea what really happened. I don't imagine anyone will know in this century.

Gary Wasserman:

It was a very frightening day for anybody who had their eyes focused at all. I found myself wondering how this could happen, and what the fuck I could do about it, how I could cope with it. There's a funny thing that happens whenever a full panic breaks out around me. I usually become rather calm in comparison and try to help as much as I can. I found myself that day spending an awful lot of time just trying to soothe people I cared about, male or female. They had come apart like cheap watches in that respect. I was in a classroom with a teacher that did more harm in that moment than I think I saw in any other experience in school. She came apart. She was a little bit crazy. She said, "The United States has just fallen apart. Our government has obviously failed. I see nothing but the imminence of being taken over." She was bananas. I remember watching most of the girls in the class bursting into hysterics, saying, "My God, our life is over. We won't ever leave this school."

Then I stood up and I nailed her. I categorically said, "Back anything up you have to say because you're creating a mania in this classroom, which is ridiculous. Your statements are not only hypocritical, they're crazy." She went on the whole period about this and it was terrifying people who had to listen to it. It was very frightening to me because she was still a teacher, one that supposedly is a guider of our destinies.

Anita Champion:

I remember the shock in the classroom when it came over the PA system. I was shocked and very hurt. I started to cry because I had remembered him as the type of person who everyone really liked. He was doing great things for our country. I remember leaving school when they let us out and I went to church that afternoon with a couple of my girl friends. We just went into the church and we lit a candle. We were kneeling and crying and saying a few words. Just feeling very bad.

Bob Searight:

I thought he was a nice President, but I didn't have any personal feelings about his Administration or anything. It was just kind of an eventful day. Now everybody has his own theory on what really happened, and big books are written about it, but only Krishna knows. Our Spiritual Master cites President Kennedy as making a mistake by going to visit Dallas. Also, he gives the example that no matter how important a man may be, one minute he's the President of the United States and the next minute he's just a lump of flesh. No one really knows where he actually goes, where his karma dictates his next birth will be.

Lynn Marble:
It was announced to us while I was in gym. I couldn't comprehend it or come to terms with it. I felt that I was looking to everyone else to find out what I should feel. I didn't know how to feel.

Suzanne Thomas:
It was an unbearable, horrible thing. I thought he was a wonderful President. Maybe nowadays people think he got us into a lot of things, like Vietnam, but I think the way he handled situations, and his diplomacy, were really great. All the countries liked him. I've never known much about politics. I'm just not that type of person. But as much as I thought about it then, I thought the country was running very smoothly. Every time that they had an article on him, there was no backbiting about him. Everything was just all good.

Mark Holmes:
It was Friday, and there was a football game that day. We were meeting in the cafeteria. I think we were going to another school. The announcement was made while the football team was together. Our first emotion was, oh, no game today. We'll have to change our schedule around. I had a responsibility at the time in relation to the football team, because there were certain functions I performed as a quarterback.

Lany Tyler:

Mark Holmes's reaction is such a vivid memory to me! I was in a complete state of misery and shock. I was walking down one of the corridors at Palisades and he came up and muttered something about it being a lousy reason to cancel a football game. I was horrified.

The assassination was probably the single most significant event of my awareness over all those years. It affected me more deeply than anything else that happened, personally or politically. I was in the principal's office at the time. I had gone down to interview the principal for the student newspaper. That was during journalism class. He came rushing into his office and he said, "The President has just been shot!"

My first response was, "The President of what?" It didn't even occur to me that it was Kennedy that had been shot. Then of course he told me and my mission to interview him collapsed and we sat there glued to the radio. He told me that the student body had not been informed of anything yet. I left his office right after that and went back upstairs feeling this incredible sense of terror and waiting. I didn't feel comfortable enough to say anything at that point—no one had been officially informed. Very shortly after that, the principal came over the intercom system and said that Kennedy had been shot and that he would keep the student body posted. I wandered around in a daze. I was in chemistry class when the news came that he died. I remember every detail of that day. The chemistry teacher just hung his head in sorrow and proceeded to give us a huge assignment of difficult problems. He did it just to get us occupied with something so we wouldn't fall apart. People started crying and he left the room. I think he went somewhere and started crying too.

After that, in French class, Mr. Pann made some talk about how this was a terrible tragedy but life had to go on as planned, that we had planned to sing that day. I thought it was the most wretched thing for him to put us through. He made us sing that day. To this day I remember the songs we sang. If I ever hear them I get a chill. It was so ghastly to be sitting there in that class, singing in French. The rest of the day was sort of a blur. I remember seeing my boyfriend at lunch and crying.

At the end of school, instead of the normal thing they played when they put down the flag, they played taps, very, very slowly. I was so horrified and miserable. I cried through all of that. I rushed home and my family was all home and watching television— the events of the assassination. They looked at me tear-faced and miserable. I ran away from them into my room sobbing. As I got into my room I looked at a pink frilly dress hanging outside my closet. There was a dance scheduled that night after the football game. I looked at that dress and it was an incredible moment of realization for me, just looking at that dress and thinking how my life had been so wrapped up in those meaningless high school events. I just remember sobbing all week and thinking about it. I wrote things in my diary of a more serious nature than I ever had before.

Mark Holmes: The Quarterback

•

Entry from Lany Tyler's ninth-grade diary:

Dear Diary:

You don't know how happy I would be if Mark liked me! My life would be complete. I would have everything I could possibly want.

April 28, 1962

Lany Tyler, 1975:
One of the most momentous events in my entire junior high school life was the night that Mark Holmes and I were going to meet at the Bay Theatre. I can remember taking a bath for about an hour before. Mark was very good-looking and sort of a plum. He was president of our class. He was a little bit shy and kind of charming. When the grand meeting finally took place, I was so excited that when he put his arm around me and touched me, I just fell apart. I got all tingly and twitchy and everything else. Everybody went to the Bay Theatre on Saturday night, and the rumor got around that we had "made-out at the movies." I remember being very happy about that rumor.

15

Sally Lobherr:
Oh, Mark! Our All-American Boy! He always looked like he'd just stepped out of a shower. He had a Pepsodent smile, and his eyes were just like little marbles. Really a nice boy. Just All-Around Mark Holmes.

Lynn Marble:
I remember that he looked like he wore shoulder pads all the time.

Margie Williams:
When I moved to Los Angeles in February of '62, I didn't know anyone—not anyone's name even. But he was class president. I remember sitting in the auditorium and just looking at him with my mouth open. He was a very good-looking guy with a great body. He was one of the few people that I wanted to go out with, because he was such a symbol.

Gary Wasserman:
I respected him as much as anyone. He was an obvious leader in a very subtle way. He was a fine athlete, a strong, principled individual who was able to experience a lot of things without a lot of stress and strain on his mind.

Reilly Ridgell:
I think he looked down on me at the time; thought of me as a wimp, or whatever. I remember one time we were working out in preparation for the Junior-Senior football game, and I was on the defense. We were just doing tag, and I made a tag on him. As he went back to the huddle he said: "Goddamm it, you know who got me? The worst guy out there!" He was saying it loud enough for me to hear it, and I thought, well, what a lousy attitude. He may have been quarterback of the football team, but he wasn't even that good at it.

Mark Holmes: The Quarterback

Judy Tomash:
There was no way I was ever going to get to know him.
He was just too popular, too good-looking.

•

For ten years we heard nothing of Mark Holmes until
we ran into him in the men's room following a "Cosmic
Mass Celebration" at the Santa Monica Civic Auditorium. He didn't recognize us, but we cornered him by
the urinals and tried to set up an interview. He seemed
willing, but said that he would be extremely busy for
the next three weeks. He was organizing the annual
"Conference of Grace" for the Movement of Spiritual
Inner Awareness, a local group of which he was a
leading member. We asked him what the Movement
was about, and he told us of Mystical Traveler Consciousness and "getting in touch with the Mystical
Traveler, who has the ability to absolve karma and to
help you on all levels: physical, astral, causal and
etheric." We decided that attending the conference he
was planning would be a good way to get reacquainted
with Mark.

Three weeks later we drove thirty miles to the San
Gabriel Civic Auditorium. In the lobby, M.S.I.A.
members were selling books and pamphlets, all of
which were sealed in cellophane so that no one could
touch them except the purchaser. This policy was intended to "insure that the book's energy is pure, and
unadulterated by casual browsers." Inside the auditorium the audience watched a succession of maudlin
testimonials and amateur musical groups which ranged
from light and pleasant to loud and terrible. We fidgeted in our seats, waiting for the climax of the
conference and appearance by the Movement's much-
heralded leader John-Roger Hinkins.

Finally the curtains closed and, after a few minutes,
reopened to reveal a pudgy middle-aged man with an
elegant goatee. He was dressed in deep purple, and

seated on a lavender throne above a purple dais. Behind him were two pretty blond boys in purple turtlenecks and sports jackets who played inspirational songs on their guitars. The audience applauded enthusiastically. After a moment of silence John-Roger smiled complacently and launched into a long, rambling, unfocused monologue in which he compared himself to a computer which "scans the consciousness of his followers until he finds someone who is seeking his aid . . ."

As much as we wanted to hear what he had to say, our boredom got the better of us. After ten minutes of John-Roger, even the smoggy San Gabriel air tasted good to our lungs. We waited outside the auditorium until the program ended, and when Mark Holmes emerged from backstage we approached him. He was full of energy and feeling very high: he was obviously in his element. Physically, he had changed very little since high school. He still looked as if he wore shoulder pads under his shirt, and seemed, if anything, even more athletic.

We stood together in the sunlight and discussed our proposal for an interview. Mark told us he didn't like to talk about the past because "reminiscing is bad for the spleen. The emotion associated with spleen and stomach, which are paired husband-and-wife organs, is reminiscing. I have a weak spleen-stomach, so I endeavor to stay out of a reminiscing area." Nevertheless, he agreed to make an exception in order to help us with our project, and we scheduled an interview for later that week.

Mark lives in a small Hollywood home which he shares with another member of the Movement. As the sun went down one June evening we stood in his living room and waited awkwardly while the one-time quarterback hurried around the kitchen feeding his dog, Genji, and concocting an appropriate herbal tea for the evening. Finally he lit a candle and a stick of incense from a Tibetan monastery, and sat down at the dining-room table. When we asked about the candle he told us that "the frequency of light from a candle is high enough so that discarnate entities cannot enter into the immediate area." We made ourselves comfortable, turned on the tape recorder, and began the interview by asking Mark about his enormous popularity in high school. He answered us in a calm, self-assured and good-natured manner.

•

Ever since elementary school, whenever I was in a baseball league or football league, I was always voted Most Valuable Player, or this or that. It was just part of what was going on. My mother once told me, "You can't always live on your charm." I agreed, but I didn't think I was charming. I was just sincere. I think people felt my sincerity, and that's why I got voted Most Likely to Succeed.

For me, Palisades High was great. You know, who could have it better! I remember one weekend when two friends and I went surfing on Saturday morning, sailing Saturday afternoon and skiing Sunday. At Palisades everybody was healthy and intelligent, and everybody had enough money, so they didn't have to worry about working too much. My own father was a manufacturer of blocks and fittings for yachts and sailboats.

After high school I wanted to go to Annapolis and play football. My father went to Annapolis, but I guess my grades weren't good enough. So I ended up at New Mexico Military Institute, but I didn't like it at all. They shaved my head, put me in a uniform, marched me around and blew bugles at me. Even playing football got to be too much of a business and all the joy went out of it. Then I got injured and quit. It felt nice quitting. It took the pressure off.

My second year I switched to the University of Colorado, Boulder. It was very much a flip-flop from New

Mexico: lots of parties and ski trips and motorcycling in the mountains. School was secondary. My grades weren't good and they put me on a year's probation. So I changed schools again and went to Colorado State.

At that time, in the late sixties, there was a really big drug flow through Colorado, and I got into drugs a lot. I took speed to study with, smoked dope at night to come down, acid or mescaline on the weekends—just like that all year, everything short of hard drugs. At the same time I was training for some power-lifting contests, and I was taking steroids which are used to beef up cattle. I was building an external shell to feel secure. I had a Harley-Davidson at the time. Huge motorcycle, 1204 cc, high pipes, big ape-hanger handlebars—the whole thing. Maybe it seems weird to people who knew me in high school, but through all these trips I never felt lost; I always felt me inside.

One day my roommate came home with books from his philosophy class—Plato, Far Eastern religions—and there I was studying oceanography. So I changed my major from the sciences to philosophy. I went through a little bit of Hinduism and at one time I felt that I was a Zen Buddhist. I used to give tarot readings, and I was pretty good at it, too. I wouldn't let anyone touch my tarot cards. And then the *I Ching*. It was fun, but then it stopped being fun, because I couldn't make any decision without consulting the tarot cards or the *I Ching*. It was that bad.

I was living with a woman and when spring came we decided to go to Hawaii. My father told me that if I went, he would stop paying for school. I had some money saved in the bank, so I went anyway, and started paying for my own schooling. I split up with the girl friend because she put control patterns on me. I can't handle control patterns. I've lived with women two times since then and I've never felt "we" with a woman. It was always "me."

So I went to Hawaii and enrolled in school there, but the surf was too good, so I dropped out. You know, ever since I was young, male homosexuals have looked at my body and seen something that was attractive. So when I was in Hawaii I finally said okay, I'm going to go out and experience this thing. So I tried it, and I found it didn't work for me. I didn't feel it flowing. So it became balanced, and less and less people were attracted to me from a homosexual standpoint.

I went back to Colorado and I was thinking of going to California. I threw the *I Ching* and it said: "If you don't go now, you'll miss meeting a Master." So I came back to California and started working for my father. A friend came over one day and said, "Hey, there's this guy John-Roger, and you know, it really works." My friend told me that all I had to do was call his name and the right consciousness would be there.

That same summer, 1970, my mom and dad and I took the sailboat up to San Francisco. It was very foggy, and the northern California coastline is really treacherous. It was late afternoon one day and completely overcast. We needed a bearing. So all of a sudden I thought of my friend and tried it. I said, "John-Roger, just help." That moment the fog parted and we got a bearing. My parents were pretty negative toward the whole thing, but I did it five times and each time the fog would open.

When I got back to LA, I started going to seminars to develop my consciousness. I became a minister by studying for two years, using the precepts brought forth by the Movement of Spiritual Inner Awareness. So now I'm *Reverend* Mark Holmes, but I don't wear a collar or anything like that.

My parents came to a seminar once and they went from negative to neutral—which is really positive, right? They're afraid that I idolize the man, John-Roger. They're just not seeing clearly at all, because he doesn't get up on a pedestal.

•

This last statement seemed questionable to us as we recalled John-Roger seated on his purple dais, but we sat back quietly and let Mark continue.

•

The Movement asked the question: Why would you ever want to place your physical organ, or part of your body, in somebody else's body? Just why? What point? Where's the communion? You see a pretty girl and you say it turns you on. Look the other way. You see some food in front of you, like chocolate cake. Look the other way. You don't desire what you don't see. I get a lot of people on my massage table, and sex is the only reference point they have. They start getting grabby—and emotional—and they want to create. It's just energy, right.

For the last three years I've been making a living doing massage. I never graduated college. People in philosophy don't need to graduate. I've always liked touching people, so I went to massage school and got a license. I started getting jobs, and business has been good.

I've also made quite a study of healing arts. I went to Taiwan and studied for five months with an herb doctor. I also went to India and Nepal with John-Roger. The best part about it was the mountains. They were so pure and so clear—no one was interpreting the Word. In 1974 I graduated from the North American College of Acupuncture, but acupuncture is illegal in California, so I just teach classes at the Institute of Oriental Medical Studies in Hollywood.

Ten years from now I hope to be working in an M.S.I.A. healing clinic, doing acupuncture, herbs and also using magnetic light that comes through the body. Hopefully I'll be able to get to the Holy Spirit Light by that time too and be able to heal people without touching them.

When I look back, I know it seems like I've changed

a lot. But I like change. I like beginning. I don't want people to remember how I was. I want people to know what I'm doing now.

•

As Mark concluded his narrative he got up to brew another pot of tea and we spent the balance of a pleasant evening in small talk about various spiritual movements and personalities. When we finally got up to go, it was after midnight. Mark embraced us at the door and told us he looked forward to seeing us in a couple of months at the upcoming class reunion.

Mark Holmes had come a long way from his hero days at Palisades High School, yet his life contained elements of perfect consistency. Today, as in high school, he is preoccupied with his body and his physical well-being. As a masseur, he is definitely in a power position, controlling his patients in much the same way a quarterback controls the field.

In a sense, Mark has always managed to ride along with some of the powerful currents in our culture and to maintain his leading position. When football was important, he was the quarterback. When drugs were "in," he took them all. He drove a larger motorcycle—switched schools more often—traveled the world more fully—than anyone else. He experimented with homosexuality at precisely the time that it became acceptable to do so. In 1970, when the nationwide religious revival began to gain force, Mark got in on the ground floor and soon won credentials as a minister. In the last few years he has been a pioneer of the most fashionable healing arts and has managed to make a comfortable living as a practitioner. One could make the case that Mark has lived up to the high school prophecy of success, and that the distance he has traveled is only a measure of the distance our culture has traveled in the last ten years.

If those ten years could transform Mark Holmes from an athletic ladies' man to a mellow spiritual masseur, what had they done to people like Lisa Menzies, who already in high school showed all the signs of full-fledged rebellion? We set to work immediately to learn the answer.

•

Lisa Menzies: The Bad Girl

•

Suzanne Thomas:
Lisa Menzies—I remember who *she* was! She had kind of dark skin and brown eyes. She was always in some kind of trouble, and she didn't care what people thought. She was like her own boss—anything went that she wanted to do. She was kind of wild, and didn't stick to the rules or anything. People just kind of looked at her and thought, "Mmm, what's she up to today?" She was always doing something.

Jeff Stolper:
Lisa was the first person ever to be expelled for coming to school drunk. She put liquor in a perfume bottle and took it to school and got drunk. She was so loaded that she got caught. She was staggering around campus, putting her arms around everybody and saying, "I'm drunk, I'm drunk."

I recall one incident in the twelfth grade when rumors were going around that Lisa was going to fight another girl at the Hot Dog Show restaurant in the

Palisades. This was quite something because girls just don't fight at Palisades High School. So we went to the Hot Dog Show after school, and sure enough, Lisa was there and this other girl was there and a big crowd had gathered to watch them. Lisa called the other girl "a fucking Pachuco" in front of everybody—and this other girl wasn't even a Mexican! The whole crowd was behind Lisa, but someone came out of the restaurant and chased us away before they really got started.

Lisa was very much the flirt. It wasn't just friendly, either—it was walking up and putting her arms around the guy, and so forth.

She was definitely known to be screwing a lot of guys. She had a reputation. The other girls didn't want to get too close to her because of her reputation and the way she acted. Palisades High School had that snobbish sense and tended to look down on Lisa. But I always liked her a lot—I liked her spirit. There was nothing phony about Lisa.

Sally Lobherr:

I didn't know her very well but I think she was a fast girl. People used to say a lot of bad things about her. I was sort of in the frame of mind where I was so good and so pure that I condemned her along with everybody else. I think she was pretty brash and used a lot of four-letter words. Smoked in the bathroom. Always looked kind of sloppy with big sweaters and tight skirts that were short. Not particularly good-looking. No, I thought she was kind of ordinary, if not cheaplooking. She was just kind of unkempt. That type.

Lany Tyler:

I remember her being on the fringes. I felt that what Lisa did with her life was probably very different from what most of us did with our lives. I felt that she was much more sophisticated than I was in a lot of ways.

Gary Wasserman:

Lisa always had some very strange qualities about her. She was extremely aggressive and ballsy—much more so than the average lady. For some reason, she was always able to keep herself from falling into the slut category, but she obviously was very free and very active and very sex-oriented.

I happen to know that she had an extremely good home. Her father is a super dentist and we all went to him when we were young. My family knows her family, and it's a pretty tight relationship. I would have to say that probably she had a mother and father who were a little too strict. She was bright—probably too bright; that's one of her problems.

•

Lisa Menzies lives today on a quiet tree-lined street less than a mile from Palisades High School. In this particular corner of Los Angeles there are station wagons in nearly every driveway, and toys and tricycles on every lawn. Lisa herself has two children, the products of her three marriages. Her two-bedroom house is neat and comfortably furnished; the rent here is paid by Lisa's parents.

When we came to see her one Tuesday morning she was sitting cross-legged on the living-room floor making a new dress from a pattern in a magazine. During the four hours we talked she continued to sew and seldom raised her eyes from her work. With large round wire-rims and her honey-colored hair in a conservative bun, her appearance was plain and sedate: she was barely recognizable from high school. She wore a knee-length floral-pattern dress above stockings and black ballet slippers.

Her older child, Justin, is a handsome and giddy six-year-old, while Lyon is a soft-eyed mulatto of two and a half. The boys tried to amuse themselves by painting each other as Indians, watching television or running outside. It was a strange setting for our conversation about her wild times in high school.

•

You know, between the ages of sixteen and eighteen I actually counted how many men I went to bed with. I kept a running list. I counted four hundred and twenty-five, and then I stopped counting. In the summers I'd go to the beach. Maybe I'd ball two or three fellows a day. I'd have a date in the morning, a date in the afternoon, a date at night. Once I had two guys at the same time, but one of the fellows was a little reluctant. The male possessiveness seems to have interfered a lot.

It was a sport and I was very sports-minded. It was very satisfying physically. A workout. Like going to a gym and working out. Just isometric love-making —where you use all your muscles. I was popular at it. People liked to do it with me. I was a very violent lover. Very physical. Still am sometimes.

At that time I was coming up to kind of a peak in strength and still looking for communication with people. There wasn't anything else. What did we have, higher mental planes or something like that? Are you kidding? There was only one thing we had in common and that was sexual abilities. That was the only approach that most of the fellows took toward me. It was satisfactory. Like I say, what else do you talk about?

In school I was always getting into trouble. I'd smoke in the bathroom. I'd ditch classes. I'd try and break all the rules. I required a lot of excitement and a lot of stimulation. In senior year I was suspended for ten weeks for stealing a history final. It was just to do something exciting. I passed it out to everybody. Why not? I felt the school was so ridiculous. I'd seen a little more of life. The teachers were so dry. The students were so dry. I just wanted to spice it up. What good is it unless you do? I still feel that way.

A lot of times when I ditched school I ended up in Palisades Park, lying on the grass with some fellow. Mostly older guys who were just bumming around. One of them was always stealing booze from the liquor store because he delivered there. Sometimes he'd get stag movies. I cantered around. I messed around. I had a lot of fun. When I was fourteen I was going out with eighteen-year-olds. I enjoyed that.

Scholastically I was very far behind. My grades were just enough to pass, but I couldn't care less. It was dull and boring. I didn't even go through graduation. I left before that because I got into Shakespeare summer stock near San Francisco.

That first summer after high school was really fantastic. I played and I fucked a lot. I wasn't a very great asset to the summer stock, actually. I was introduced to pot up there.

When I got home I had several jobs and worked for my father for a few months. I've never held any job longer than three months. It was strange living at home, so I left and lived in an apartment. I was working in the Bel Air market as a short-order cook, making sandwiches. I was smoking a lot of dope by that time. Some people in the neighborhood would complain when I got loaded and parked my car up on the lawn—they didn't like that very much. So somebody called late at night and said that the police were coming. I had to flush all my dope down the toilet.

Shortly after that—I don't know how—my father got wind of it and said, "Well, move back in the house because it's too dangerous." My parents lived in a hundred-thousand-dollar house in Mandeville Canyon. So I moved back in, but then we got in an argument. I said, "Screw this, because I don't understand all of these 'morals' and why everybody is doing what they're doing." So I took my car and put gas in it. I had some money saved up and I went with this fellow down to Mexico.

When we got down there we met an LSD freak from Texas. He was jumping parole over the border and just wanted to read Kahlil Gibran and live his life. We looked very hippie and everything, so he shared his trailer with us. We went to Ensenada and picked up some heroin and I tried heroin. Got marks on my arm, and you can still see them.

•

Lisa proudly extended her arm and asked us to examine it. After we had duly noted two or three tiny black speckles, she returned to her sewing and her story.

•

Eventually the local authorities came out and searched our trailer; they found the dope and took us in. I was taken to Tijuana jail; two weeks in Tijuana jail. Actually, I had a fantastic time—in that jail it was very interesting. I met some American girls who were lesbians. And I watched a local gal go through heroin withdrawal in style. She just lay there with a cigarette hanging out of her mouth. She lay there and just held her mud. I respected her greatly for that. I became intimately associated with one of the head guys in the jail, so I was able to get out and watch TV and have a few extra privileges because of my intimacy with him. I had some good dope while I was down there.

Finally the American consulate got my name and notified my parents. I was very upset about it—I really didn't want them to know. I wanted to kind of disappear. So my parents procured a lawyer and proceeded to get me out. I refused to leave unless my friends got out with me, so my parents had to pay for them. My mother came and picked us up and took us back home. I hadn't bathed in three weeks and I'd gotten my period during that time, so I was quite dirty.

The night I came home there was a strange person at the house. My suspicions were that he was a psychiatrist and my father had him come by to check me out. I felt like I was under observation. So I called a friend of mine and said, "I've got to get out of here. I'm going crazy." I didn't fit and I didn't care to fit. So two days later I split again, and met up with my friends from Mexico. We hitchhiked up to San Francisco together, but then at the end of the trip they went their way and I went mine.

The next thing I knew I was hitchhiking by myself to Laguna. When I got down there, somebody pointed out a house where these people dealt in dope and maybe I would be welcome. I knocked on the door and they let me in and we talked for a while. They had some grass and passed it around. There were about four fellows living in the house. I remember they had an Afghan there that had just had puppies. Then around eight o'clock that night there was a big crash at the door and it was a bust.

We all had to get up against the wall and I was very stoned. Busted again! Taken in. I got out via the lawyer of one of the fellows who was there. He negotiated the bail because my parents wouldn't. After I got out I stayed at his home with his family, in the maid's room, doing a little baby-sitting.

Then I started taking LSD. A friend of mine had gotten hold of some really pure acid—little tabs—and we were taking them. One day I was hitchhiking on Chautauqua and Sunset—right near here—when I was picked up by a black Corvette. Inside was this very handsome young man, about six feet three, with black curly hair and deep-green eyes. I was getting tired of just tripping around, so I figured maybe I could work my way into this guy's life. His nickname was Bear, and he was a real mountain man. He was a good hunter, and he liked to live in solitude in the mountains. He was living up in the Malibu mountains when I moved in.

He was also very involved in acid. We had nearly a thousand tabs that we split between the two of us. At the minimum, I've ingested five hundred tabs of acid in my life. That's not counting the mescaline and other stuff I've taken. When you get up in that range, it doesn't matter. With Bear it was good acid, so it didn't hurt your body. We could eat on it, sleep on it. It was great stuff. So we proceeded, in the next four months, to party. Acid party. We did so until the money ran out and dope ran out and we had to leave.

We went back East to where he came from, to a small town in New England. His parents were very shocked that we weren't married, so we slept together in the barn. I didn't mind and we had a ball. We ate steak and peanut butter and it was fun. Then after a while we decided to come back here.

We got another place in the mountains, only this time near Agoura. In January of 1968, Justin was conceived in that little house. I wanted to get pregnant. I cared for my man very much. I cared for him enough to want something more of it. But by this time he had taken a great many drugs and started to flip out. When I got pregnant, I think it pushed him over the edge. So I spent a great deal of my time kind of nursing him.

I got a job as a dental assistant for a while. The fellow wasn't very nice to me, so I just quit. It was just too hard. When I was five months pregnant we got married. We got some unemployment and Bear bought a car.

We got busted and went to jail several times. One time it was for shoplifting. We did some carpentry work for this lawyer I already knew and he got us off the hook. Another time there was a roadblock and they busted us with some pot. But they had to let us go because roadblocks were rendered illegal or something two weeks before. One time it was grand theft. We stole furniture from a house. I really wasn't guilty—I was just along for the ride. So I've been in jail six or seven times.

When I was in jail I got hepatitis at the same time I was pregnant. I was in the waiting tank, waiting to go to court, when the DA noticed that I was very ill. He got me off the hook and I was released that night. But they didn't release Bear. I almost died waiting for him to be released. I hustled around and called his mother to get him out of jail.

At this point I was six and a half months pregnant and I loved this man very much. After he got out of jail he wanted to go back East again. He had a ride with a friend in a Corvette. I said, "Go. I'll hitchhike or I'll take a bus." I ended up hitchhiking. It took me one week and twenty-two rides, by myself with a dog and a sleeping bag and a knife.

Back East the baby was born. I almost died in labor. It took twenty-six hours. They had to shoot me full of drugs, and the baby was drugged and cold when he came out. They had to put him in a heater, and Bear had disappeared for a few days. So when I came home he was no help and I was in a great deal of discomfort. Two weeks after that, the water was cut off in our apartment, so I had no water.

Bear was taking drugs, and he started to flip out again. He collected guns. He was quite good with them. He did crazy things, like walking into restaurants with a cap-and-ball pistol and saying his name was Billy the Kid and waving it around. He started shooting at targets inside the house. It got to be just intolerable.

I was twenty-one and I really wanted to live a safer life because I had this little child. Nature took over my instincts and everything. But Bear didn't care to settle down. He kept flipping out. One day I just left. I had corresponded with my mother back and forth, and I came back here to live. Since then Bear has been in and out of mental homes, in and out of jail. Last time he was in trouble the police had to break his arm to subdue him. I was very unhappy when I left him because I still loved the man.

So I came home and my folks let me rest for a while. I was quite destroyed. I'd lost a great deal of weight. I stayed with my folks and then I started to work part-time. By now I was twenty-two. I met a man who was fifty-three—a lawyer in the area here. He and I became great friends. He wanted a sweet young thing. Of course I was. By that time I was living quite straight. I had sort of redone my whole life. As far as I was concerned, I was pretty much a virgin. So we got married, and stayed married for a year.

He had two children from another marriage. One of them was an unbalanced eighteen-year-old boy. I had quite a lot of trouble with him. My husband felt that I should give him a great deal of attention. Yet he didn't feel it necessary to give *my* son attention. I think he felt quite jealous that my little boy was together and his was not.

Anyway, it was a very turmoil-filled relationship. He used to listen in on my phone calls and go through the trash. Once I was having lunch with a girl friend and he came in and just took me out of the restaurant. He was quite paranoid. He also thought it was cute to make love in the living room and let his son walk through and see us. I'd say, "Why don't we go into the bedroom," but he'd veto that. He was strange—in my opinion.

So I filed for divorce. I went back and lived several months with my parents. But I still couldn't get along at home, so they offered to take Justin for a few months and let me live by myself.

I moved into a place in the heart of Santa Monica. I studied acting. I studied French. I studied music. I wasn't getting any alimony money because according to California law, being married a year isn't long enough. I was enjoying myself, anyway.

I met, through a friend, a black gentleman by the name of Gene Shaw. He was a musician and quite well known. A jazz musician. He used to play with Charlie Mingus. I have his albums—a couple of them.

•

Lisa went over to the cabinet under her stereo and got out the records for us to see. One of them was a solo album featuring Gene Shaw on trumpet. His picture on the cover showed a gaunt face with high cheekbones and magnetic eyes.

•

I'd never been involved with a black man before. Never. But Gene was different. He wasn't hung up about race. He didn't go, "Black Power! Yeah, Brother!" He was a human being. He was all races, I think.

We met, I believe, in March 1972. I became pregnant in June. Then in August we found out that Gene had lung cancer and was going to die.

There was pretty much nothing we could do. So we lived and wrote a book together for a year. It's called *Jazz: The Artless Art*. Gene sat in the back room and dictated stories. I would type them up and make comments.

The baby was born March 14, 1973, and that day Gene was taking chemotherapy at the Veterans Hospital. That particular dose rendered him bedridden for the rest of his life, which was five months. He had five months with Lyon. The first two months he held him and cared for him and loved him so dearly! But the last three months he never touched him. He didn't want to communicate that kind of feeling to him—the feeling of death.

In the last weeks we watched the Watergate faithfully on television. It was very stimulating recreation for him because he couldn't do anything else. He had to sit. I was getting welfare at the time because I couldn't work while I was nursing the baby.

Gene died in August '73. The last month I rarely slept. He didn't sleep—he knew he was going to die. He told me to watch—he wanted to describe what it was like to die. We had one very warm day, and then he died that evening at eight o'clock. He died in my lap on the floor, at home. Justin, who was four, was kind of flittering around the room like a moth—around the perimeters of the room, unaware of what was going on, although it was very obvious. There wasn't any violence in the death at all. He just stopped breathing. In his last words that I could understand he was trying to tell me what it was like. He told me he could see a beautiful woman. Then he stopped breathing. His eyes were wide open, his mouth was wide open. I revived him to breathing and he was in a coma. That was about for five minutes. Then he died.

I took a vacation because I felt I needed it. I went to Hawaii. After Gene died, the insurance came to me. I got ten thousand dollars, which I lived on for a while.

After I came back I spent most of my time with the children. I also worked on our book, polishing it for publication as best I could. Right now I'm still hoping for a publisher.

Lany Tyler:
About two years ago I discovered Lisa Menzies living across the alley from me in Venice. Our children became friends. I enjoyed seeing Lisa then and talking with her. We didn't see each other often, but I remember being struck by the amount of pain she seems to have lived through in the years since high school.

When I was living down in Venice there was a young man next door who befriended me and he moved in. He was twenty-one. He lived in the front and slept on the couch. One night we had a burglar—there was a great fight and the young man forced him out. A month later I moved here, and the young man moved with me. By then I figured I needed another vacation. He volunteered to take care of the children. So I went to Del Mar for the races. The week I was there I met a Korean gentleman and we became great friends. He moved in and the young man moved out. He's been living here up until yesterday. You might guess that he was a great gambler, and managed to gamble away twenty thousand dollars. He moved out yesterday. He just lived a different kind of life than I do.

Drugs don't have any place in my life any more. The only times I've even smoked pot in the last few years have been to intensify love-making. I drink more. I enjoy a couple of cocktails much more now.

Sexually, when I was liberal, everyone was conservative. Now when I'm conservative, everyone is liberal! I've gotten past that free, experimental thirst, that devouring of sex, where it was fun and games. It's come down to a much more serious, meaningful depth. Down to the roots of my life.

Although I was very scatterbrained to begin with, I know now what I really want to go after in life. I want to concentrate my energies to the point where I can make a good deal of money. Not just a living. I love life and I want to go out and see the world. I want my children to have whatever opportunities they will need. I've learned that it's time for me to go after the almighty dollar and to hell with everything else. I'm going to make it through my art. Either singing or acting. I've always been good at both. I'm writing some jazz music now—sort of old-fashioned jazz.

I will say that my mother has been very helpful financially. My parents understand. Like I told you before: I've never held a job for more than three months. I'm an artist.

I met a nineteen-year-old boy the other day when I asked him to baby-sit, and I'd say they're still as immature as we were. They still have the same laughable attitude about hiding marijuana in their bedroom while their mother is outside. You know, that same kind of giddy mischievousness.

I'm glad all that is over for me! I don't know what it's like today in high school. From what I understand, there are more drugs, more havoc, more everything. I might be dead if I went today—as crazy as I was! I think my crazy periods might have been even more extreme. It's a good thing I graduated when I did. I think it's a feat just going through what I've gone through and being here to talk today.

•

During the final moments of our conversation, Lisa's mother came into the house carrying a bag of groceries for her daughter. A well-groomed, handsome woman in late middle age, she seemed surprised that Lisa had company and did her best to ignore us during the five minutes she was there. Watching the friendly exchange between the two women, we couldn't help looking back on Lisa's story and thinking of the enormous pain she must have caused her family over the years. In certain respects her life was a paradox: she had run away from home many times, but not yet learned to support herself financially. Despite her hammer blows against convention, she had always been dependent on her parents—to get her out of jail, to shelter her in times of stress, to support her habits and nurture her ambitions. For all Lisa's rebellion, she had won little independence.

•

Reilly Ridgell: The Outcast

•

Lee Grossman:
Poor Reilly. He had droopy eyes, droopy jowls, a droopy walk. He looked like a Walt Disney cartoon of a dog. I remember in tenth-grade English class, we would be having a class discussion, and Reilly would say something that was not so much dumb as it was a *non sequitur*. It just didn't fit in. The whole class would stop and look at Reilly and think, "Why did he say that?" Finally, after this had been happening for several weeks, I remember turning to him and saying, "Shut up, Reilly!" Eventually it got to the point that whenever he would raise his hand, as soon as the teacher called on him and he started to speak, the whole class would shout out, "Shut up, Reilly!" This went on for about three years. In senior year, people were still doing it. On one occasion Reilly raised his hand in the middle of a lecture and the teacher just looked at him with great disdain and said, "Shut up, Reilly!" The entire class burst into laughter.

Debbie Gordon:
I may have had some pleasant conversations with him, but mostly I remember him as mopey and unattractive.

Reilly Ridgell: The Outcast

Jamie Kelso:
Reilly always seemed to be straining to achieve some acceptance from somebody. He was a misfit in Advanced English class. It was incomprehensible how he had gotten in.

Bob Searight:
Our crowd centered around sports. Reilly wasn't that athletic, so he didn't fit in very well.

Lynn Marble:
A girl friend and I went through a period of extreme cruelty in our comments about other people, and Reilly often had to bear the brunt of it. He more or less became a laughingstock for us. I would tease Reilly and I think he mistook that for an interest in him.

Carol Shen:
He seemed to be a very unhappy person, due to the fact that life is pretty rough in high school when you're as unattractive as Reilly.

•

Reilly Ridgell now lives six thousand miles from Palisades High School on Truk Island in Micronesia. We were fortunate enough to catch him on one of his rare visits to the United States. We invited Reilly for lunch, and he came the next day with Esa, his roommate and star pupil from the islands. Esa had never before left Micronesia and he flipped through old issues of *Penthouse* and the *National Lampoon* while we talked with Reilly.

We were shocked at how much Reilly's appearance had changed. His hairline had receded drastically, and there were deep wrinkles in his cheeks and forehead. It was hard to believe he was only twenty-eight. He fidgeted uncomfortably in his baggy clothes and explained that he was used to wearing a thu—the loose-fitting loincloth traditional in the islands. As we sat down to lunch, Reilly leaned back in his chair and began exorcising some of his bad memories from high school.

•

Yes, I remember "Shut up, Reilly!" I didn't know whether to take it as a compliment or a put-down. I guess people got tired of me talking too much in class, maybe it was just, "Let's do it to Reilly." It could have been somebody else. But it wasn't—it was me.

I remember that I earned an athletic letter for working with the baseball team—taking care of towels and equipment and everything like that. They gave me a letterman's sweater and I used to wear it all the time. But it seemed whatever clothes I wore, I was still out of it. I remember one day I looked around and realized that I was the only guy wearing brown shoes. *Everybody* else had dark shoes on. I never touched those brown shoes after that—I refused to wear them. Heaven forbid! I had enough problems.

I dated as much as I could, and I went to the prom with a girl from the grade below us. We went to a party afterwards and it was crashed by some guys—they heard the music and just walked in. It turned out that my date knew one of these guys, so she split with him and left me there holding her shoes. I wasn't so sure of myself to begin with and then to have my date ditch me like that! For the rest of the night I stayed at the party and tried to keep up my façade—despite this crushing blow to my ego. I've always been plagued by weirdness when it comes to my relationships with women.

In high school I generally felt that I was clawing my way upwards. I was an Air Force brat, and that was part of the problem. We always moved around when I was growing up, and I never got to settle down with one group of guys.

After high school I went right into UCLA. I'm one

of the few people I know who went four years straight
without changing major or switching schools. I wanted
to be in a fraternity, but I wore braces and—well, the
big houses weren't interested in me. The house I finally
got into was on the verge of collapse, and two years after I graduated, it folded. But I really enjoyed it while
I was there. It helped me develop socially. I met my
girl friend at a fraternity party. It was the first involvement I ever had and it lasted for three years. It got to
be a hassle when she would date other fraternity
brothers. We fought a lot, but we clung to each other
for security.

So I graduated in political science and got accepted
to graduate school at UC Santa Barbara. I decided to
stick it out for a master's degree because that was supposed to help me get a job. I moved into a beach house
with four other guys and I had a fantastic time. That
was a radicalization year for me: I finally turned
against the war in Vietnam. At UCLA I had been in
Air Force ROTC, but when I got to Santa Barbara everyone I knew was against the war. Even today I
sometimes get confused because I can still see the arguments on both sides.

When I finished my degree I cut my hair, shaved my
mustache and tried to get a job as some type of junior
executive. But there was nothing. Zilch. Nowhere. It
turns out that a master's degree makes you "over-
educated." They assume you'll quit and go back to get
a Ph.D. So you can't win for losing. Once I did get an
interview with an insurance firm, and they asked me all
these questions about capitalism and the profit system.
I gave all of the answers they were looking for, so I
got to see the vice president. He told me that my side-
burns were too long. And he said, "We're in business
for a profit. We're in business to make money. If a
company we insure is polluting, that's their business.
We'll accept their money. How do you feel about that?"
I've never been able to lie very well. So they didn't hire
me. They said I was too much of a "radical."

Finally I did land a job: showing porno flicks at an all-night theater on West Pico in LA. I was projectionist, ticket taker, candy seller. It was a very tight operation. You'd come in the front door and you could choose—go to the left and see boys fucking girls or go to the right and see boys fucking boys. The biggest thing about that job was being hasseled by the vice squad. They'd flash their badges and you had to let them in. They'd sit in the theater and try to catch people beating off. They'd arrest these poor slobs for playing with their own equipment!

One time the cops came in and they wanted to go back to the projection booth. I told them I wasn't supposed to let them go into the booth, but they insisted. So what was I supposed to do? Get myself busted for this crummy joint? So I wrote in the log, "Cops came in and went to the back room. Hell if I'm going to argue." The owner didn't like that and he fired me before I knew what hit me.

After that I decided I'd apply to the Peace Corps. I always thought it would be neat to go off and live in some primitive place, and besides, there wasn't anything else that I wanted to do. I got accepted in 1971, and they sent me to Puluwat Island in Micronesia. The island is about half a square mile with five hundred people on it. It's a hundred and eighty miles west of Truk. And what's Truk? Truk gets a plane once a day, so there's mail. From Puluwat, communication with the outside world is really difficult.

During the first year I was a teacher there, the people didn't think well of me—I wasn't physical and I didn't fish enough. They're really proud of their sailing tradition. The men wear a loincloth and the women go topless and wear a wraparound *lavalava*. At first I liked that the women were topless because I'd always been interested in that part of the female anatomy. But after a while I got to wishing that I could see some leg— they don't show any.

I knew all the girls were doing it, but not with me

because I was a Peace Corps and so conspicuous. My only sexual experience that first year was in the bushes with one of the island whores. I'd been on Puluwat for months and I was horny! Here was my chance, but I couldn't get a hard-on. I was shattered by that, but then, later, things got better. The people started to be more friendly. There was even one girl who came to visit me at night in my grass house.

I worked in the Peace Corps for two years, and at the end of that time I came back and traveled around the United States. I visited all my relatives and old friends, but I knew I'd be going back to the islands. I prefer to stay out there because it's simpler, less hassle. So I signed up to teach at one of the government schools and went back to Micronesia.

You know, there are parts of that life I really love. One time I took a trip from Puluwat to another little island—twenty-two miles by canoe, and it took us sixteen hours. We had to go right upwind, tacking back and forth in the rain. I've never been colder than sailing that canoe at night with the rain. It was still seventy degrees out, but with the wind and the rain, I was freezing to death . . . and loved it. What can I say?

A while ago we had a food shortage. It was the first time in my life I'd been hungry. I mean, really, really hungry! I went out with the people and picked pumpkin tips.

Last year I moved to Truk, the main island, where you don't have that kind of problem. If you want to know what Truk is like, take the most primitive Hawaiian island and divide by ten. The work is okay, but I've been in Micronesia for four years now and I haven't had an emotional involvement with anyone. I'm looking for someone right now. I'm at a point in my life where I'm confused about myself and what I want to do. I keep putting off a decision, just making commitments year by year. Even if I wanted to come back to the States, it's just about impossible to get a job. I'm probably better off staying where I am. I've got no commitment to anything else.

•

Before Reilly returned to Truk he dropped by and brought us a gift. It was a large square mat woven from native fibers by one of his students. We were sorry to say good-bye and could feel Reilly's melancholy. At the end of our visit he showed us a brief passage from the journal that he had been keeping in Micronesia. "I really don't want to be doing what I'm doing," it read, "but I can't think of anything else I want to do. I really don't want to be here, but I can't think of anywhere else I'd rather be." Reilly still seemed to be searching for a place to fit in. He closed the book and shrugged his shoulders. "That about sums it up," he said. "And that's probably why I'm going back."

•

Lee Grossman: The Intellectual

•

Jamie Kelso:
I remember Lee as an intellectual with whom I could talk, one of the very few. He was also a real card. He

44

made me laugh. But it was a lonely humor, a sarcasm at the world, a cynicism at the world.

Skip Baumgarten:
I used to ride with Lee on the same school bus. He had a very large vocabulary, and I was impressed. His father was a psychiatrist and his mother was a writer. I remember her stories used to show up in *The New Yorker*. Lee was weird. On the way to school, he spent a lot of time talking about books.

Mike Medved:
In English class, Lee used to turn in book reports on books that didn't exist. He fabricated titles, plots, publication dates, the whole thing. It took a semester before the teacher finally caught on. At that point Lee wasn't penalized—he was just congratulated on the success of his fraud.

For a brief period Lee was my debate partner. His attitude toward debating was irreverent, to say the least. On one occasion he took a sandwich out of a paper bag and began munching it while he was speaking. The debate judge was furious and ordered him to put it away. Lee shrugged his shoulders, put down the sandwich, picked up a toothbrush and continued to talk.

Lynn Marble:
I always thought that Lee had a lot of pretensions. He was one of that group that was trying to be so intellectual. He thought he was funny, but it wasn't my humor. He seemed more like a tragic figure to me. Unhappy.

Debbie Gordon:
Lee was my date to the senior prom, and I think I knew him pretty well in high school. I remember the things he liked to do: clowning around, and playing bridge all the time. Socially, he was sort of a bumbler. He always seemed out of place and nervous, and he clearly was not comfortable with that.

Lany Tyler:

He was a character! He was sarcastic. He was kind of a prankster. I liked him a lot. I remember that Lee had a crush on me in junior high and he was the first person that ever asked me to go steady. We were at one of those afternoon dances where everyone went and danced together under severe restrictions on how many inches you could get together. I was dancing with Lee and all of a sudden he asked me to go steady. I said something nasty, like "Are you crazy?" It was only because I was really shocked. I wouldn't have considered going steady with anybody, it was against my principles. I didn't even want to go out regularly with Lee—I don't think I liked him in that way.

Six years later we ended up going to the same college and Lee finally got back at me for that nasty crack in seventh grade. In my freshman year I made a lot of new friends and was trying very hard to start my life over, to keep my high school career away from my more sophisticated college friends. One day as I was going across campus with a large group of people, Lee walked by jauntily and said, "Lany, say something to me in cheerleader." That was the most devastating moment of my college career. Part of me was amused because it was a very funny thing to say. But it was also extremely insulting under the circumstances, and I was hurt by it.

Reilly Ridgell:

I think Lee opened up a lot of people's minds to certain things. I never held it against him that he started "Shut up, Reilly!"

●

Because of numerous detours and personal difficulties, it has taken Lee Grossman ten years to graduate from college. Recently he has settled on a new career which he pursues with an intensity which he himself describes as "bordering on fanaticism." He allows himself few breaks, so it was hard for us to schedule an interview. We finally caught up with him one Sunday afternoon in the kitchen of his tiny bachelor apartment. He sat sprawled across an easy chair, his long legs dangling over its arm, and recalled some of his ups and downs from the decade just past.

•

One of the most incredible inhumanities that I can conceive of is high school gym class, in which some asshole redneck makes you run two miles uphill under a certain time. If you don't do it in that certain time, you run it again. You keep doing this until you throw up.

Then there was that Boys' Vice Principal who was a real ex-Marine. He was an old cracker. He was out there telling people whose hair was anything longer than a crew cut, "Why don't you get yourself a *he-man* haircut!" I understand he's the principal today.

I think the best thing that ever happened to me in high school was one report I gave in English class—a psychoanalytic interpretation of the poem "My Garden," by Janice Appleby Succorsa. I still remember that in great detail. I present to you the poem . . .

•

Lee straightened up in his chair, and with a broad smile behind his curly beard proceeded to recite the entire poem from memory—after ten years! We were astonished.

•

There's a faerie at the bottom of my garden
  I see her when the dew is on the rose
And the bumble bee is bumbling, 'Oops! Beg
    pardon'
  As he bumps along the shining iris-rows.

47

Oh, of course it's only sunlight if you say so
    Making spangled stars when it begins to rise
And shine on all my dew-drenched pretty flower
        show;
    But I can tell the shine's my faerie's eyes.

And oh, the happy hours we've shared together!
    And oh, the happy garden paths we've trod!
Year in, year out, in every sort of weather,
    Finding our way to Beauty—and to God!

Inspiring, isn't it? I think I tried to make the point that the poem was really about a homosexual tryst. "The faerie at the bottom of my garden" was a reference to a gay person in the region of the genitals. "I see her when the dew is on the rose," I think was lubrication happening. "The bumble bee is bumbling, 'Oops! Beg pardon'" was a suggestion that the guy was clumsy. Then there's a comment about the fantasy nature of it all. But "making spangled stars as it begins to rise" is a pretty clear allusion to excitement. "Dew-drenched pretty flower show" indicates a successful climax. That was about it, except they apparently get it on, to meet "Year in, year out, in every sort of weather."

My interpretation was well received in class in the sense that everyone was cracking up all the way through. Including me. I had a lot of trouble trying to maintain decorum when I couldn't keep a straight face. I think the teacher regretted that he ever let me bring up the subject.

If I had it to do over again, and it were up to me, I don't think I'd go to public school. Maybe I wouldn't go to school at all. There's a line from Ivan Illich to the effect that "school is the advertising agency that sells you on the idea that you need society the way it is." My memories of school are mostly in terms of being told to go back and *walk* down the halls, or being told to run a lap around the track. I tend to compare it to prison. I can't think of any institutions other than those two where you have to ask permission to go to the bathroom.

Graduation came as a relief. I knew I was going away in the fall to the Santa Cruz campus of the University of California. That school was just opening up and the public relations people were talking about it like Oxford. Very small classes, the emphasis on learning rather than grades. Actually, they couldn't live up to that kind of public relations and still be part of the UC system, but I was pretty much sold on it.

The biggest thing that happened to me my first year was getting involved with a woman up there. She was very strange. She had very few friends. She may be the first woman I ever pursued with some sense of self-assurance. In college it became an acceptable thing to be an intellectual. I had finally gotten to the point where I didn't consider myself completely nauseating to women. We were both virgins, though for months I denied to her that was true. I even gave her the names of other women that I'd balled. For references.

She was fairly tall, very thin. Wore no make-up and had short hair. Giant dark eyes. We wore the same clothes a lot because we were built about the same. We did strange and bizarre things together, like sleeping out on the highway when we found a hillside that we liked. Whatever we did, it had to be on impulse. We never did anything with advance planning because that took the spirit out of it somehow. We went together on and off from ages seventeen to nineteen.

I gave more attention to my relationship with her than to my studies. The people at Santa Cruz were less intense and competitive than the intellectuals at high school, so I felt it was a step down for me. I got into the habit of cutting most of my classes, and my attendance record for my first two years was somewhere between ten and fifteen percent.

I got to be friends with a guy who owned a motorcycle shop in Santa Cruz, and he turned me on to motorcycles. It was an unusually large step for me to get on a motorcycle, because I didn't even know how to ride a bicycle at the time.

One night in my freshman year I was playing cards at about two A.M. That was something I did virtually every night till sunup. Jack, the motorcycle man, was trying to make it with this woman and suggested we grab a couple of bikes and run down and get some hamburgers. We leaped on the bikes. My girl friend got on the back of mine. By the time we were coming back to campus from the town of Santa Cruz it was about four A.M. It was raining fairly heavily. Jack and his woman were ahead of us. We took the corner a little too fast and we went into a skid. I plowed into a parked car on the other side of the road. It was an amazing experience.

It seems that this corner was the scene of frequent accidents at Santa Cruz. It was the front of a house in which lived a family including a mother and three or four daughters, all of whom had gotten so used to accidents that they had a ritual they went through. As soon as someone smashed up out there, one of them went to get the blankets, one of them went to call the ambulance, the whole thing. There was the strangest battle going on over my head while I was lying in the gutter, about where to put the pillow, under my feet or under my head. I was telling them to put it under my shoulder because my shoulder was hurting. I was conscious. I was not exactly in pain. I must have been in some kind of shock. The rain was coming down, I guess. This cop came up and shined one of those nine-thousand-watt flashlights in my face and asked me if I was all right. It seemed sort of silly. I told him I was sober. The ambulance drivers showed up and asked what hospital I wanted to go to. I didn't know any hospitals in Santa Cruz. I said, "The close one." So they dragged me off to a place, now defunct, called Sisters Hospital. I think it was probably closed down by the Health Department.

Since I was a minor, they couldn't give me any medication until they got my parents on the phone. They kept going over me with one of those man-eating brushes they use to remove grit from wounds, and asking me the most inane questions. A lot of it had to do with Blue Cross and insurance. Some of it didn't seem to have to do with anything. I'd swear they asked me if I liked sports, at least once, maybe twice. They asked me what my religion was and I told them I was a Dravidian. I have no idea what that is—I think it's an early Indo-European cult. Anyway, they didn't take kindly to that. Keep in mind this was a Catholic hospital. Periodically they would ask me if I was going to take communion. Finally they got me medicated. My shoulder was my main injury and they were going to do some kind of surgery that involved wiring the bones together and removing pieces of things.

My mother, in a panic, flew up to Santa Cruz after the accident and arrived while I was in surgery. Apparently it was a fairly tricky business. I was in surgery for three or four hours and my mother was out there wringing her hands. My girl friend was there and talking to her. She said something like "I want to be around when Lee dies. I'm sure his death will be magnificent because his life has been so interesting." Picture my distraught, saintly mother sitting there and listening to this! My mother's reaction to that was to write a short story, which I didn't see until years later. I was horrified when I read it because I hadn't realized how angry she was.

By then I guess I was dropping out of school. Up to that point I had been experimenting with things that marked a departure from the way I'd been doing things. Then, finally, I was ready for one of the more dramatic, overt rebellions of my life. I decided, All right, I'm gonna fuck around. I didn't have a great time of it, but I had decided to take charge of my own life. For the next couple of years, things were really hectic. I was not sleeping or eating. I was generally in poor health. I was living out the fantasy of the Bad Boy.

I didn't look forward to anything. I didn't give a shit about what happened outside of my own circle. I didn't want to fit into American society, and considered it fairly noble to be an outcast.

In April of '68 I took off for Europe, and toured around for six or seven months. A lot of things happened that were kind of nice fantasies. I passed myself off as a blues musician when I was in Minorca. I spent a lot of time writing *very* bad poetry. But I didn't get less depressed, I just got depressed in a different way. All of the depression which I had been attributing to Santa Cruz now clearly belonged to me.

When I got home I really hit bottom. I was getting into a lot of sexual situations with any woman I could find, and it was no longer a satisfying thing. I finally ran out of things to do, and I just gave up. I remember sitting in a chair in my parents' home just frozen. My dad was trying to get some sense of what I wanted to do, but I didn't want to do anything. I was so depressed I even quit smoking. I had been a chain smoker, like three packs a day, but I quit at his point because I didn't have the energy to lift the cigarettes to my mouth.

At that point my dad helped me get a job at a psychiatric hospital, and things immediately started changing for me. My position was "activities technician" at a salary of three hundred and eighty-one dollars a month. That meant mainly that I was supposed to run activities for psychiatric patients. While I was there I got more and more into what was actually happening with people and found it fascinating, and not at all mysterious, which I had expected it to be. It all made sense to me.

One day when they didn't have enough people to run regular activities, I suggested that we try something special. I wanted to put together a group with all the most regressed patients in the hospital—the five or six people who were totally mute. This was a very off-the-wall thing for an untrained twenty-year-old activities tech to suggest, but my boss was very cool and went along with it.

So I sat down with this group and made some statement about the reason we were all together. Right away, things started happening. I made a gesture with my pencil and one woman flinched. I noticed that and commented on it. I put down the pencil. There really wasn't any direction to the group, other than that I was trying to notice what was making people anxious, and commenting on what I saw. I made some contact. One woman who had been just frozen for the month she had been there started crying. Another one who hadn't said a word the whole time she was there started to talk about how anxious she was in the group. Pretty soon everyone in the group was talking —which was a totally unexpected breakthrough. I suppose if I had to pick an event in my life that sold me on the kind of work I wanted to do, that was it.

I worked as a psych tech for nearly six years. I put most of my energy into running groups, and I'm good at it. I can't imagine an experience that feels better than being part of somebody coming into his own.

While I was working at my second hospital I started thinking about different ways I could get a "union card" to do therapy. I was getting a little tired of being a psych tech and getting paid psych-tech wages and having to take orders from incompetent people. I worked on one program where my boss was a guy I had trained in group therapy: he was a psychiatrist making six times as much as I was. So I investigated the idea of getting a Ph.D. in psychology, but I finally decided that basically what I was doing was trying to find an easy way to become a shrink. Suddenly it occurred to me that I now had the stamina to consider trying the hard way to become a shrink—and that meant medical school.

Before I could even think about med school, I had to finish my B.A. and take pre-med courses. So I bit the bullet and went back to school—this time at Cal State LA.

I kept on working while I went to school, and the work has been my one real joy through all of it. I didn't think I could even survive my first quarter. At Santa Cruz I had resolved never to take any science courses, and never take any class before eleven in the morning. Then at Cal State I found myself taking eight o'clock labs three days a week. I was absolutely sure I was blowing every class, but I always ended up with good grades.

In 1975 I applied to thirteen medical schools across the country. I got twelve rejections, and then at the last minute they let me in off the waiting list at UC Irvine.

Right now I'm in my first year there, and my outside life is more or less suspended. That's the way it has to be through the first two years. The other night I sat around in my apartment by myself and started remembering what I'd been doing a couple of years ago. And I realized that my universe has shrunk to almost nothing—that my concerns have gone from being at one with the universe to getting a decent grade in molecular genetics. I don't get much of a chance to relax. I don't have any deep relationship with any single person. I'd like to have one really close relationship right now—whether it was with a man or a woman—but I see my school situation as almost precluding that.

The next couple of years look rather bleak to me. I have to look further ahead to find something to look forward to. I'll be thirty-one when I get out of medical school. I might be facing a year of internship on top of that, and I know I'll be facing three years of residency. But I'll be a doctor.

I have a lot of fantasies about what I want to do once I'm credentialed as a psychiatrist. One of the things I'd like to do is put together a preschool. I have this tremendous sense of what school does to kids. I'd like to get there first.

•

Two days after our visit with Lee, we drove to his parents' comfortable apartment on Sunset Boulevard. He had suggested that a conversation with his mother would shed additional light on the course his life has taken in the last ten years. Sylvia Grossman is a brilliant, sharp-featured woman who speaks eloquently on almost any subject. She masks her good humor with a gruff and raspy voice, but the warmth of her smile gives her away. As we settled down to some milk and chocolate cake, we asked her if she was at all surprised that Lee had chosen to enter the same profession as his father.

•

No, I'm not surprised. My only question is why he didn't do it sooner. Obviously, he was born to be a doctor and he had all his leanings that way. At some place it stopped.

He had gotten very much alienated in that period. I remember we could hardly talk about anything without getting into these speeches, which I heard from the children of other people too, about stereotypes. We were accused of making them into stereotypes. The only great poet of the century was Dylan. Our values were all wrong. We had brought the world to the brink of disaster. Vietnam was our fault. There was a nucleus of truth in some of these accusations, so that it made it very difficult to be defensive about any of it. I remember some of Lee's friends coming in one evening and smoking pot in our living room. It seemed to me we should have been asked, "Is it all right?" They were talking and it seems they were thinking of themselves as a group of enlightened, forward-thinking, completely uninhibited free people, forced to take the hospitality of these slobs, these uncouth, unthinking, uncaring, warmongering fascists.

The late sixties were an incredibly difficult time for people to grow up. I have some basis for comparison. I had other children and I know how it was the generation before. I think the sixties were the most difficult time to be young that the world has ever seen. All values were falling apart. The bottom was falling out of everything. We were at war—in a perfectly horrible war. It was a terrible time. The only thing worse than being a child was being a parent in those days.

Lee Grossman: The Intellectual

Palisades High School

TIDELINE

Volume III   Friday, April 3, 1964 — Pacific Palisades, California   Number 13

PALI TOP TEN

Don't Bother Me	The Beatles
All My Lovin'	The Beatles
Can't Buy Me Love	The Beatles
Shangri-La	Robert Maxwell
Money	The Kingsmen
Suspicion	Terry Stafford
There's a Meeting Here Tonight	Joe and Eddie
Dead Man's Curve	Jan and Dean
Find Yourself Another Man	Righteous Brothers
That's the Way Boys Are	Lesley Gore

Dance to the Music

•

Lee Grossman:
In tenth grade I actually went out with Judy Tomash for a while. Once we went to a party together—a scandalous party. Most of the people there were socially advanced of me. They kissed girls on the mouth. They were public about such things. I felt very socially backward. I couldn't dance. I was very conscious of my glandular secretions. Whenever I had to dance I was preoccupied with how anxious I was and how I didn't fit in, so that I didn't really notice much else. I ended up feeling that I had made such a fool of myself at that party that I couldn't face Judy after that.

Lisa Menzies:
I loved to dance. I taught dancing in those days as one of my part-time jobs. Mrs. Paul Henry's Dance Cotillion. I taught dancing to the children of famous people. Charlton Heston's son. Karl Malden's daughter. Lloyd Bridges' daughter. I was a very good dancer always. I was very physical. I liked anything that was happening.

Carol Shen:
Sports Night was every Friday night, and it was a big thing. There was always one room of athletic sport going on, and then another room of high school dance sport going on, where there was a very loud band—

58

lots of loud music in a pitch-black room. It could have been the sixth-grade Valentine's dance for all the little maneuvers that went on. I hated Sports Night. I just remember it was a torturous situation of not being asked to dance.

Jon Wilson:

I remember the object of Sports Night was to pick up a girl. I used to go there, and I'd stand around like ninety percent of the other guys, afraid to dance and afraid to ask anyone. I'd always be with another guy, I never went alone, and we'd always discuss the ladies across the room and which ones we ought to ask to dance. Once in a while I'd get my courage up and I'd dance for a while, but I wasn't very good at picking up girls. I probably went to thirty Sports Nights and I maybe picked up three girls.

Reilly Ridgell:

I remember standing around, sizing up odds and figuring out what to do. I'd look at the girls who weren't dancing and eliminate the ones that were just too ugly, or whatever. I remember waiting for the next dance, and waiting for the next dance and finally getting up the nerve. After that first dance I'd sort of stand around and ask, "What grade are you in?" All those bullshit questions. If the girl liked me, she'd sort of hang around, and if I wanted to keep her, I'd dance with her the rest of the night. But usually she'd say, "Thank you very much," and just walk away.

I remember specifically when slow dances came, I would always move my wallet and my handkerchief out of my front pocket. I'd look for the girl with the biggest boobs, or somebody who would be really fun to squeeze. Some of the girls really loved to just grind it out, to let you get your knee in between their thighs and kind of chomp on it almost. I remember that very vividly, yeah.

Margie Williams:

I was a crazy dancer. At Sports Night I would start at one end of the room and dance to the other end of the room—usually losing my partner on the way. I loved to dance at Sports Night. I went crazy. Just moving around the room. I'd go alone, or with a couple of girls. I didn't like to go with a date. Then you got tied down to him and you didn't feel free to move around. I never had a free dance, anyway. I got very tired, and ready for a good night's sleep.

Mike Shedlin:

One night I was too drunk at Sports Night. I had saved up twenty-five or thirty little airline liquor bottles and I popped a whole bunch of them that night. I got busted by Mr. Weinstein, the history teacher. I can't tell you what a mouthpiece for the dominant ideology this guy was! He busted me. And I wasn't even puking. I wasn't driving a car. I was just flailing around on the volley-ball courts. I was dancing, laughing. But I mean, yes, I was drunk.

Jamie Kelso:

I only went to one party in that whole period. I didn't even want to go, but I was pressured into it because it was an old childhood friend who was giving the party. How insane! You know, your mother or your father drives the car while you and your date sit in the back seat. You're not old enough to drive a car. How horrible! At the party we went on a scavenger hunt, and then there was dancing involved. I didn't know how to dance. All these other people were just these real hip swingers. They had this close-in, hugging type dancing and all. I was petrified. I was sweating, dripping. I was losing a pound of water every minute. I just wanted to get through the evening. I wanted to die. I wanted the clock to turn faster and faster so that thing would be over and my parents would come pick us up and I could get that girl back to her parents' house, where she belonged.

To this day I can't dance. I refuse to because there is this posing, this gesturing, this hip-moving "look-at-me." It just seems too absurd.

Debbie Gordon:

I was good friends in the last part of high school with a girl who was half a year behind us, and I'd say that a significant part of our friendship revolved around enjoying the Beatles together. We went to that big concert at Hollywood Bowl. We were way up high. We weren't going to scream, oh no, but then we screamed. We screamed like everybody else. My friend won the KRLA Beatle-drawing contest—she did the best drawing of the Beatles and we drove up to the Beverly Hills Hotel and we were going to try and deliver it to them. We took it up to the guards at the gate but they wouldn't let us in. I think that we enjoyed being very childish and adventuresome about it. We thought they were cute. Whatever sexual feelings there were about it, that was more an unconscious thing, like good feelings from dancing.

Sally Lobherr:

My first memory of the Beatles was in the back of someone's car. I was making out passionately with my boyfriend, and I think the radio was playing "I Want to Hold Your Hand." My boyfriend was saying, "Wow, this is a bitchin' group!" or something like that. I thought, Who are they? That's how I got introduced.

I learned to dance from my boyfriend. I think he was probably one of the best dancers in the school. He taught me and I just loved to get out there. Just fast dancing. It was the Jerk. Sure, I danced that. Then another little thing where you jumped around a lot—it was the Watusi. I remember flying through the room. I was very flattered when someone would say, "Could you teach me that?" It made me feel important.

It wasn't sexy for me. When I got older it became that way. I dance now if I can find anyone to dance with me. That's the problem. As a matter of fact, before I was married to Neil I used to go to singles bars and places like that. I used to just love to dance. I just had more fun! I didn't care who danced with me, who he was or what he looked like, just so long as he danced, that was fine. I'm always ready to dance if I can find someone to cooperate.

Sally Lobherr: Best Dancer

•

Lany Tyler:
She seemed to be very fun-loving, flirtatious, kind of buoyant. I remember she used to work on the Annual, and she won Best Dancer in the class poll. She was a natural blonde, which was what everyone wanted to be in those days. I think blue was her favorite color, and she always wore clothes that matched: blouse, sweater, skirt, purse and shoes, all the same. And then a thick blue ribbon in her hair that matched everything else. She's probably married today, probably with children. Nothing terribly earthshaking.

Skip Baumgarten:
I remember her at all the school dances, with that long hair whipping back and forth. She was probably one of those "in crowd" girls, but you always had the feeling that she had to work hard to get there. She seemed a little bit insecure in her position, and she'd never be

caught in public talking with someone who was socially below her.

Suzanne Thomas:
She had blond hair, and was thin, and nice-looking. We were friends, but I haven't really kept in touch with her. Maybe she'd be a model or something today. She seemed a little more sophisticated than we were.

Gary Wasserman:
Sally was a very attractive little lady who was a little underplayed in comparison with some of the more outstanding ladies of the time. We always had a very good friendship relationship; that's really all it was. I would guess, based on how pleasant and how well-adjusted she was at the time, that if she were lucky enough, today she'd have a very normal kind of marital scene.

●

Sally Lobherr would be the first to admit that her life has been difficult over the last ten years. The hard times have begun to register in her face; her gray eyes seem soft and sad. When we interviewed her, Sally was seven months pregnant, and there was a notable weariness to the way she moved. The smooth blond hair that we remembered from high school was now a wood-toned brown, and we asked Sally about the change.

●

It was just normally lighter in high school. It was never bleached. I don't know what happened. When I was in Idaho with my horrible first husband, he made me bleach my hair. And I looked like a streetwalker. I don't even want blond hair any more.

In high school I had a pretty nice figure. I liked it.

People used to say I was busty, which I liked. That was fine.

I always felt like a woodwork person—just there, nothing special. It was okay being average because then you weren't noticed and you didn't have to perform. I certainly was no student. There were a few classes that I got through with just a smile—literally. For geometry I had Mr. Kay and I was really failing. I couldn't even cheat—I mean, it was impossible on a geometry test. One day the teacher said to me, "Sally, if you promise never to take another math class in your life, I'll give you a C." I would have promised him anything, and I got by.

What I lived for most in high school was getting out and starting all over again because I didn't like the way I was then. I was boring and I had nothing to say. I didn't read anything. I didn't care about anything. I just didn't like myself.

At home my parents expected a lot of my older brother, but I was a girl, so it didn't matter. It was really very sexist. My father is an engineer for a big aerospace company. He goes to Washington every other week. He goes to the Pentagon all the time. He's a very bright man, but he comes home and goes to sleep in his chair after a couple of mai-tais. That's the extent of conversation with Old Dad.

I was never turned on by my teachers in high school, but as soon as I started junior college, I just went crazy. I fell in love with school and I got into studying. I just loved it. I went off to UCLA and when I got there I found this little room in the law school and I used to stay there until about two in the morning, maybe four or five nights a week. I used to go there on Friday and Saturday nights because I wasn't interested in going out. Studying was my high. I was just completely changed from high school.

My parents were surprised. I was surprised. Everyone I ever talked to was surprised. I actually did very well. I had an overall B+ average, which wasn't fantastic, but for me it was certainly okay.

I graduated in 1969. I'll remember that day forever! It was very poignant for me. I just couldn't believe that I was actually doing this thing—graduating from the Big U—because I had always considered myself such a nothing.

After that I started teaching. I got a job at a Catholic school. I had forty-one ten-year-olds, whom I immediately fell in love with. They were Mexican-Americans mostly, and this was the first time in my life I'd ever come in contact with lower-income people.

I taught for a year, and there was this other girl who was also a fourth-grade teacher. She was single. I was just twenty-one and I had never been to a singles bar, so we went to one in San Fernando Valley. That is where I met the love of my life.

I'd always had this little fantasy that I would like to chuck it all, and not be the nice girl from the Palisades, and do some really racy things. I always did everything the way it was supposed to be, come hell or high water. The person I met at the bar was totally opposite. He was a high school dropout. Every other word was some outrage. He was a gambler, a drinker—you name it. He couldn't cross the street without betting on it. He was always out of money. It was his being different, and the fact that my parents just couldn't stand him, that turned me on.

That first night we were pretty much involved after forty-five minutes. After that, I was always chasing him. He was always pushing me away. When he got bored, he'd come back. I was also going out with some normal, "acceptable" people, but I kept coming back to him.

I was supposed to go back and teach for a second year, but over the summer I got a job in the LA stock market, at a trading desk. It was office work mostly, but with a racy crowd. A really fast crowd that drank a lot, spent a lot of money. Something that was just completely out of my league. But I kept saying, "Wow, I like this life style. I like being fast."

I started getting into some really heavy partying. I'd be at work at six-thirty in the morning, and then we'd leave around noon and go drinking. Strictly business, of course! Then we'd stay on until we closed the bars. There were whole nights I don't remember. Instead of driving home, I used to go back to the office and sleep on the couch so I'd make the opening at six-thirty. I'd wake up in the morning, have a Bloody Mary and then start all over again.

The drinking got to be pretty outrageous, so I'd have a hard time functioning as a normal person. At the height, I'd have maybe ten drinks a day. Double Margaritas, they were my favorite. I would say it was a serious problem, but it made me feel good, so I did it. It made me feel reinforced, pretty.

Naturally, my boyfriend was getting pretty disgusted with me. He'd say, "I can't stand the way you're living!" Of course, who was he to talk, because he was no prize!

So I went on a little vacation to the Midwest. I met this person out there through the friend I was visiting, and he and I got along really well. He came from a very nice family—they were sort of bluebloods in the Midwest. He had been to Vietnam and won medals there. He was an Olympic skier. He seemed just perfect for me. So, to make a long story short, I ended up following him to Idaho. He went to graduate school in psychology, and I got a job as a teacher. We lived together for a while, and then we got married.

The wedding night was really strange. I remember talking to his sister, and I said, "Isn't it interesting that your brother was shot down in Vietnam and he managed to come out of it?"

She said, "What are you talking about? He was never in Vietnam!"

I said, "What do you mean? He has all his little medals on the wall."

She said, "No. You're crazy."

I said, "Well, it is nice that he was an Olympic skier, isn't it?"

"Well, no. He was never an Olympic skier."

I was crying—who is this person I just married. Maybe he was just lying about everything. It turned out he just had this problem. After we were married he'd come to me and say, "I just told so-and-so that I did such-and-such. If they say anything, would you please back me up?" What could I say?

Sexually, our relationship was horrible. Just rotten. If I ever wanted attention for myself, I'd have to ask for it. And I was a pretty girl. You know, I hadn't gotten fat and ugly and sickening.

Every once in a while he'd have a drink, and then he'd want to do something. It really repulsed me because I knew it wasn't him and it wasn't his true feelings. So of course I was called frigid, and it was entirely my fault, as everything was. He had a much bigger ego than I did, and he was always belittling me. I was all alone in this little town in Idaho, and he really made me feel like a nonperson.

I got so strung out that I was just shaking. I was on the verge of a nervous breakdown. I never really considered suicide, but I thought it would be super if someone would do it for me. Finally I saw this psychiatrist and he said, "You're driving yourself crazy. You're going to kill somebody. You'd better get out."

So I flew home to LA. Right away I got back together with the Love of My Life—this gambler from before. I moved in with him, but things were never good. He was very undependable, and I started to drink like before. Sometimes we'd be getting along fine and then I'd drink and I'd ruin it. It was just because there was no stimulation there! We never talked about anything. I wasn't working. There was just nothing!

He finally left me because he couldn't take my erratic behavior. I was losing on all sides at this point. My ego was crushed and I was frantic. I started going with a girl friend to singles places. I just needed a little self-esteem, but believe me, that's not the place to get it! It was just the only thing available at the time, and I wanted to forget that I was unhappy. I drank there, and usually quite a few drinks.

The truth was that I was heartbroken. I would cry, I would throw up. I would have a temperature. Then I'd eat and I'd throw up again. I was a real case. The psychiatrist I was seeing didn't know what to do with me. He was afraid for a while that he was going to have to send me somewhere.

But in the middle of this, Jimmy came back into my life—my old boyfriend from high school! It had been nearly ten years, but he'd never given up. Even when he was in the Army, he'd always write my mother and say, "Is there any hope? Can I ever get her back?" He just adored me for some reason. It was just one of those things. You know, first love. He had a job doing PR for a little airline, and when he heard I was having trouble, he came back into my life. He started seeing me. He'd come over, and he was the only person in the world I trusted. I couldn't trust my parents because they were always imposing their will. But I trusted Jimmy.

One night he came over just to see how I was. He brought me flowers and gave me a hug. He had to fly up to Mammoth on his airline later that night, but he said he'd call me as soon as he arrived. I just desperately needed something. So I waited and waited. He didn't call me. That's not like him. When Jimmy said he would call me, he called. I thought, "Well, to hell with him." But I didn't mean it.

One of my favorite programs in the morning is the *Today* show. So I got up early the next day and I was watching when they announced that this plane had crashed in Mammoth. That just did it! That's the way I found out that Jimmy had died. It was so traumatic. Things were shitty and getting a lot worse. Just everything! I'd about given up on my sanity. I was just miserable. I wasn't working. I was living at home. I was sure that there was no way that I was ever going to be normal.

That was my only dream in life at that point—to be normal. I think that's really been my dream ever since high school. I remember my mother used to say, "Why do you want this particular dress?" And I'd say, "Well, everyone else has it." I thought I was kind of abnormal, and I really wanted to be normal. Then when my life started falling apart, it got to be even a bigger dream. I just wanted to be okay. I didn't want to be weird.

About a year ago I decided it was time to find a job. So I went to this place called Cadillac Plastics, in North Hollywood, and started working as a secretary. Things started getting better, and then I met Neil. He was an outside salesman at this same plastics place. I wasn't dating anyone at the time; I had decided that I didn't like men. But then they had an inventory at work that took a whole weekend, and Neil was my partner. When you're with someone that long, you break down the barriers and insecurities. So we started going out. Two weeks later he asked me to marry him, and I said "Okay."

•

Neil Simpfenderfer is a mild, chunky, well-groomed young man who showed a strong interest in the book we were writing. Nevertheless, Sally asked him to stay in the bedroom while we talked to her in the cramped dining area of their new Glendale apartment. The narrow living-room window looked across an alleyway on the wall of a drab stucco apartment building.

•

My life is as normal as I would like it. It's a middle-class life and it's okay. I think it's more than I had hoped for a year and a half ago. Neil is very hard-working, but I don't think we'll ever be rich. That doesn't bother me at all.

I became pregnant immediately after we got married, and I look forward to being a mother. I like being domestic. I love to cook and like what I do. I like making Neil happy, 'cause I guess to me, this is normal. And I'm trying to do all my normal things, and I really enjoy it. In the future I hope things are just okay. I hope to have another child. Nothing exciting. You know, I don't want to be a millionaire. And I don't want anything to be erratic.

•

Two months after our interview, at the time her baby was due to arrive, we called Sally to see how she was doing. She had given birth to a healthy baby girl, and on the telephone she seemed happy and extremely busy. We had been thinking over her story in the weeks since we last saw her, and one nagging question remained. In high school Sally had been an average well-adjusted girl; today she is a hard-working housewife who glories in her normality. But what had happened in the interim? Why had her last ten years been so unexpectedly difficult?

•

Actually, I think a lot of my problems had to do with the Palisades. There is no doubt in my mind that if I hadn't grown up in such a protected background, I would have been better off. I would have chosen something like Neil's background. His family is a little more ordinary, a little more middle-class. They have this feeling that at seventeen or eighteen you're grown up. You make your own decisions. With me, I was just a "nice" girl who never got into trouble and was never allowed to make any mistakes. So when I started making mistakes, or when I started just making decisions for myself, I went haywire.

●

It occurred to us that Sally, and the other members of our generation, had lived through one of the few periods in human history in which constructing a "normal" life was a genuine achievement. Yet surely there were some people—even from the class of '65 at Palisades High—who had lived pleasant and uneventful lives over the past decade. We leafed through our old senior annual one night, looking for likely candidates. We settled on Suzanne Thomas, the school's most respectable beauty, who was noted for her quiet, conventional behavior. She seemed as well equipped as anyone to have survived the years untouched, and we placed her name next on our interview list.

●

Suzanne Thomas: The Beauty

●

Margie Williams:
Suzanne was probably the prettiest girl in our class, but she always seemed very shy. I could never understand why. She kept to herself and a couple of close girl friends.

Lynn Marble:
I have an image of Suzanne Thomas as being equivalent to the runner-up in a Miss America Contest. Statuesque, blond, with legs of a colt. She seemed like something that had been taken straight from the pages of a novel.

David Wallace:
I ogled her and dreamed of her for years without ever talking to her. I naturally assumed she was a pretty hot person—sexually advanced and way ahead of me. It was only when I sat behind her in physiology class that I found out she was actually very shy. I began seeing her as one of those natual beauties who became beautiful without even trying. I remember she won Most Natural in our class poll, and I think she deserved it. In physiology, I always sat back and watched her while we were supposed to be reading our books. One day I became aware of the fact that in the half-hour we had been reading, she hadn't turned a single page.

Gary Wasserman:
Suzanne always got a tremendous amount of respect from me because she was so sincerely polite and pretty and kind. I even dated her a couple of times. Whenever she was around I would be very careful. You always wanted to be careful with Suzanne. You didn't want to pat her too hard.

Harvey Bookstein:
She was very attractive, but pretty much down to earth. I can't imagine her in any job. I think she'd make a good housewife and a good mother.

•

We got Suzanne's phone number from her parents, but hesitated several days before making the call. There was no logical basis for our nervousness, but old-time insecurities die hard. In high school, a call to Suzanne Thomas would have been totally unthinkable; she was too desirable, too mature, too far above us in the rigid social hierarchy. Our current project, however, provided us with an excuse that we lacked in high school, and we finally developed the courage to place our call.

Our interview was scheduled for early Sunday morning so that Suzanne would still have time to enjoy an afternoon at the beach. When we arrived, we found one of those enormous new apartment complexes with colored lights and palm trees clustered at the front entrance. Judging from the Sunday sunbathers gathered around the pool, this place made a special appeal to hip young singles in their early thirties.

In Suzanne's own apartment everything was new and clean and plastic, reminding us of the Model Home interiors you would find in a high-class tract. Even the antiques, plants and knickknacks seemed newly minted and fresh out of the box. Suzanne was dressed in a floor-length orange Hawaiian dress. Her blue eyes were as clear and brilliant as always, and her rich golden hair now reached all the way down her back. She sat at the edge of her sofa, erect and alert, and answered our questions with warmth and courtesy.

●

My father's from Illinois and my mother's from Virginia. My father's retired now, but he used to be Director of Design Technology for Douglas Aircraft. My parents have lived in the same house in the Palisades for about twenty-five years.

When I was in high school I was really sheltered. I couldn't wear make-up and I couldn't go to all the parties. My mother wouldn't let me go to the Bay Theatre on Saturday night when everyone else went, but one time I did go. I said I was going to a girl friend's house or something.

A few times I did get drunk, I'm sorry to say. It's not the greatest thing for a girl. Those rum drinks were just so good and I didn't really know how much was in there.

The summer after I graduated I went to the beach every day. I knew I was going to college. I just never even worried about my future. A lot of people have something in mind that they're going to do. Unfortunately, I just kind of live from day to day.

I went to the University of Arizona—I heard it was a fun school. I was in Phi Beta Pi sorority and everyone was superfriendly. My major was home economics. I specialized in merchandising and fashion commercials.

It was in my sophomore year that things really began to change. Drugs were definitely a part of it, and you could just see the change in attitude. It kind of made me mad because I really liked it when everyone was pretty nice and there were no drugs and all of these real hip types. Maybe I'm corny, but I think that life in the fifties was a lot nicer. I didn't go with the trend. I would say I was pretty untouched by all the uproar.

I graduated in 1969, and when I came home I didn't know what I was going to do. I spent another summer on the beach. Then a friend of mine opened up a business in Tucson and I went to work there. It was a bikini business. My father wasn't too happy about that, even though I wasn't modeling. I just worked in the store. After a year they got another shop in Newport Beach, so I came back to California.

In '72 I was hired by Pan Am. I really wanted to be a stewardess, but then the fuel crisis came up and they closed the training school. In the back of my mind that's still one thing I really want to do. My roommate now flies for Pan Am and she really has a great time.

Suzanne Thomas: The Beauty

Eventually I got a job at the Warehouse Restaurant in Marina del Rey, and I'm still working there. A real success story! I'm a cocktail waitress. I do well enough to earn a living, and I don't really have to work that many hours. But sometimes I kind of get depressed because of the customers. Sometimes they're not that great. You know, snapping the fingers . . . it's really kind of degrading.

Harvey Bookstein:
She's a cocktail waitress? Shoot! There go my illusions. I don't think I want to go over to where she works—I think I'd be totally disillusioned.

I'd feel really badly if I wasn't married someday, but I've never been that close to marriage. I've gotten some proposals but I knew they wouldn't work. Maybe I don't have the greatest life right now, but at least I only have myself to worry about. Later on I'd like to travel. I'd like to have an easy life. If I get married, I want it to be perfect, and that Prince Charming just hasn't come along yet. I'm sure things will change. And I cross my fingers.

I have a lot of free time right now, so I like to take little trips. On Monday I went to Laguna Beach and saw a lot of pretty coves. Then I had dinner down there and came back. A couple of weeks ago I went up to Santa Barbara with a girl friend. We took our bikes and went bike riding and had dinner. I love the ocean, and also I collect sea shells.

•

Suzanne showed us a mirror she had made for herself: imbedded in its border were hundreds of beautiful and brightly colored shells. It was a looking glass fit for a mermaid, and surely appropriate for the woman chosen Most Natural in our class.

We asked Suzanne if she was happier than she was in high school.

•

In high school, everything was more organized. I knew what I was doing and where I was going. Now it's kind of helter-skelter. I wish I had a better idea of what was happening! I don't want to be a career woman, but I want a little more meaning to my life.

I don't really like the way things are going today. Sexually, I think that people are a little too free. I mean, enough's enough. If you're really involved with somebody, that's great, but I think people should be a little more selective. When you drive past Palisades High School today and see the kids that go there, I think it's kind of shocking. I know it's bad to judge people by the way they look, but they all look and act so smart-alecky! If I had any children, I wouldn't want them going there. I just think it's a really bad influence.

I think I'm a little stronger than I was in high school, but I'm still pretty wishy-washy. Everybody else has changed a lot, but I guess I've pretty much stayed the same.

Gary Wasserman: Mr. Slick

•

Ron Conti:
Gary was a real wheeler-dealer. A smooth talker. Mr. Slick. He knew where he was at all times. I remember that '57 Chevy pulling in, black, with a big shine, forty-eight coats of lacquer paint, the real show wagon. He used to park it two blocks away from school so it wouldn't get a dent. He put a tarp on it. He wouldn't drive in the rain. It had to be perfect weather for him to drive his car. Gary was somebody all his own. There was no one to compare him with.

I know he was playing around sexually a lot. He was way ahead of me, I'll tell you that. The night of the senior prom he and Brock Chester got a motel room together where they could take their dates. I went over the next morning and walked in on them. There they were, their beds all ruffled, and they were showing me their trophies on the bed, showing me the come-stains on the sheets. Brock and Gary were pretty close. Balling partners. I don't have any idea where Gary gets his energy. He's a goer, and he just goes.

Suzanne Thomas:
He was always well-dressed, and everything was always immaculate. I mean, I guess it got him where he is today!

Anita Champion:

He was the first boy that ever kissed me! Of course that was years and years and years ago. I was in grammar school. He was in the cub scouts and I went to a cub-scout meeting with him. Afterwards I went over to his house and we had some Kool-Aid and cookies or something on that order. Somehow, he conned me into this closet off in the garage, and he kissed me on the cheek. His comment was "Cherry lips." He was eleven or twelve. I was surprised, I remember turning red. I wasn't offended. It was so simple and so innocent. Then we opened the door and walked out. That was it. Gary felt very proud of himself. We never dated later on in school.

Margie Williams:

He was a good-looking guy, with kind of greasy hair. He was always slouched in his chair, trying to get out of homework assignments or borrowing someone else's homework. He was always bumming around with the Saracens, wearing a Saracen jacket or Saracen medallion.

Mark Holmes:

Gary was the driving force behind the Saracens. He had the big idea, and he organized the club. I think it stemmed from his big brother having had car clubs. We had elections, and since Gary was the mastermind, he was the president. And, for whatever reason, I got voted vice president.

Jon Wilson:

I wanted to hang out with the big-shot guys. I wanted to hang out with the Saracens. I couldn't because I was in a different social position. A great percentage of them were on the football team, or the baseball team or the track team. They had big parties all the time. Most of them were good-looking and most of them had a lot of girl friends. They had those orange jackets

Palisades High School

TIDELINE

| Volume 3 | Friday October 11, 1963—Pacific Palisades, California | Number 2 |

TIME, MONEY, AND LOTS of good hard work is Gary Wasserman's formula for turning out one of the finest cars ever seen on the Palisades campus.
—Photo by Loren Dolman

Car of the Week

A new sight at Palisades High is Gary Wasserman's coal black 1957 Chevy. Gary has been working several months and has spent $1,350, but has been paid off with a very beautiful car.

He bought the car six months ago and immediately began working on it. His car is actually quite rare, for Chevrolet made only thirteen such cars of this type. Gary feels that one of the advantages of his car is that he can race his car in the stock class.

The engine is the most powerful stock engine Chevrolet produced in 1957. for the 283 cubic inches have 283 horsepower to match. The engine is equipped with Rochester fuel injection from the Chevrolet factory.

The car has been covered with two gallons of black lacquer with only one gallon of thinner, for an extra thick base and lasting beauty.

The "tuck and roll" bucket seats and interior have been covered entirely in forty-ounce black naugahyde with half-inch pleats. Gary removed the rear seat and covered the rear portion with a black rug.

The 15 inch chrome reversed rims hold 8:20x15 inch Inglewood slicks and new 6:70x15 inch blackwalls in front. The exhaust system is a stock cross-over type with new Michael mufflers and dual exhaust pipes.

Gary plans to take his car to the drags after adding a Corvette four speed transmission. Gary's time and money spent was well worth it, for he has one of the most immaculate cars in the area.

that said SARACENS on the back, and they were really proud of the fact that they were Saracens.

Sally Lobherr:
The Saracens were a bunch of guys who thought a lot of themselves, and wanted the recognition they thought they deserved for being neat.

Gary Wasserman was sort of the leader. Oh, he was hip, slick and super cool! He'd let you know it. He could cut you down with just a look. You didn't want to mess with him. You just didn't want to walk in the same hall with him for fear he might point you out and say something critical.

I think he felt superior. You can just tell sometimes by the way a person walks, and everything about him. He was always perfect-looking and his car was perfect. He was the only person in high school who bought a cover for his car. He'd park it and put the cover on it, and then sort of pat it. Sometimes at recess he'd go out and visit it. He was phenomenal. I remember the day that someone backed into it. This was his baby! I've never seen anyone that wild. He had a real wild look in his eyes. It was his image and someone had put a dent in it! A hole! His image had been marred!

●

● ,

When we drove up to the address that Gary had given us, we assumed there had been some mistake. The landscaped driveway curved up to an enormous Tudor mansion: this was hardly the home you would expect for a young man of twenty-seven. At the front of the house stood a private paddle-tennis court; to one side was a huge pool sheltered by a row of elegant cypress trees. At the end of the driveway we passed under a broad stone arch before pulling up to the main entrance.

The master of the house welcomed us graciously at the door, but we were still not sure that we had come to the right place. This new Gary Wasserman presented himself as a mellow child of the Aquarian Age. He wore a soft black beard, rounded tortoise-shell glasses, and moccasins without socks. His faded work shirt was open across the chest, and the only reminder of the old Gary was the stylish monogram stitched above the pocket.

We sat down in the den and Gary's tall blond wife brought us coffee on a china tray. Gary took one sip from his cup, then frowned and handed it back. "You know, honey," he said, "it's kind of cold. Why don't you go back and see if you can get it a little better?" Suzy nodded, picked up the cups and returned to the kitchen.

"We have just a fabulous, fabulous relationship," Gary told us. "Suzy is a stewardess. She flies for Continental Airlines. Not to justify her position, but it's a great position for a lady. Coming from a town of two thousand in Iowa, the freedom that she's had and the exposure that she's had are great. She gets along beautifully with people and enjoys helping them. She also enjoys the travel aspects of it. She's flying tonight, so she has to go out in a little while. But I'm glad you had the chance to meet her. Normally, she's away from home about three days a week. We're not threatened by that at all. She's not concerned by the fact that I'm alone here. I believe that Suzy and I enjoy the solitude that her work and my work avails us."

We certainly felt that solitude after Suzy's departure. We sat alone with Gary in front of a sputtering fire while the emptiness of that enormous house pressed in around us. Gary, however, was in his element. He found it intensely pleasurable to reminisce about high school, and his recollections of the old days were more positive than those of anyone else we talked to. "It was a good time," he said, "a great time." He kept us there until three A.M. listening to his story.

•

High school was just such a fabulous open period! We got a say-so in so many things that had been patterns for decades before us. There was a lot of challenge and a lot of traditions that we were setting up.

Take, for instance, the Saracens. I remember choosing that name myself. I had done a little homework. The Saracens were a certain band in history who, through unbelievable toil, had been victorious against much larger warring bands. They had that kind of charisma behind them. We decided to call ourselves the Saracens.

We were very much sports-oriented, so we would challenge other clubs to football games for big money. Sixty-dollar games. Grudge matches. Heavy-duty stuff. We were very seldom beaten. We had some very, very rough guys in the club.

It was pretty much football games and parties. Every once in a while there'd be little sporadic battles with some of the other clubs. There would be a party, say, in Beverly Hills, and we would crash. After twelve quarts of beer, one of us would be talking to someone. Something would be misunderstood, and the next thing you know, they're fighting. After that, we would find ourselves at some meeting place and we'd be having a rumble.

We were known as inseparable, and we really did love each other. We felt there was a certain presence about the club. We never had more than thirty-three members. If someone was recommended by one of the members, he would go through a formal probation term when he would spend time around the rest of us. Then, when the group voted, if he got three blackballs, he could not be initiated into the Saracens.

The initiation was in no way anything that would endanger anyone. There were no specific rites. Maybe we would have the new guy do something like take off his clothes, and put him in a shopping basket and run him through Hughes Market in the Palisades. At one point he had to run an obstacle course—which was us.

We'd have fun with pillows and swat boards and stuff, but in no way endanger anyone.

We had jackets that were orange melton, with cream leather sleeves. They had a woven medallion patch—a crest with a dragon on it. The back had the letters SARACENS, WEST L.A. There were some people who never took their jackets off. In my case, whenever I was going steady the girl usually wanted it. I would say that we were one of those facets in the Palisades that would be considered the elite. Right or wrong.

•

We asked Gary what would have happened if he had come to school one day and found a non-Saracen, and a social outcast, wearing one of the Saracen jackets.

•

I believe that the person would have been coerced into taking it off. It was a pretty cut-and-dried thing. We would have stomped on his foot till that jacket fell off. We would have said, "Look, we've worked to develop an organization. If you want to be part of it, then try to be. If not, then we're gonna take this jacket off because it is a misrepresentation." He would have had to take it off.

Most of us were not virgins by the time we got out of high school. I think I matured in that area a little quicker than others. When I was thirteen, I was dating a senior in high school. Her own exposure made it easier for us to have a physical relationship. When I was sixteen, I had a relationship with a *much* older woman. As a matter of fact, she was the mother of a peer. Her son wasn't in our exact grade, but he was very close. He never knew what was going on, because I kept all the facts very much to myself. I specifically felt that it was much too controversial, possibly destructive to many people.

On a regular weekend night we'd have a party. There would be the normal amount of drinking and laughing, screaming and dancing, and sexual involvements too. Everybody was on his own, to whatever level they were on with their lady. The evenings would be over around eleven o'clock, as most of the girls would have to be home at a reasonable hour. But for me, I perhaps wouldn't go home right away. I would leave the party and go over to see this woman. Not illicitly by any means, because it was the furthest thing from that. It was a relationship based on intellectual respect.

If I had to pigeonhole myself, which is not the thing to do, I believe I've always had an innate sense of responsibility. I am extremely honest with people. Too honest. I go through some tremendous pain for it. People don't really want total honesty.

In our school there was a great deal more drugs than most people were aware of. It was because of the affluence, and the number of things people had been exposed to. They'd been to Europe before they were even out of high school, for God's sake! They had tons of experiences that a lot of people never have. I think it was about eleventh grade when the first people in our club tried LSD. This was when the very first articles on LSD were coming out, and it was a fascinating thing. Today I suppose I'd be termed "a sociable doper" —dope meaning marijuana in that context. It's no more than a form of luxury to me, whether taking an edge off, up, down, or any other way. I don't believe that it's anything unorthodox. But it can be a serious thing if it's abused. It all depends on how responsible you are.

I am very fortunate in the fact that I have fabulous parents. My father was in the construction business. My mother is a housewife, and very involved in the community and with all my friends and myself. I would say that they are, by definition, upper-middle-class. By no means wealthy. Right after high school I went off to the University of Arizona, but just at that period of time my parents went through a financial problem. A tough financial problem which really hit them right in the face! They felt that it would be a burden to keep me in the university at that time, so I came back. It was no big deal for me.

When I got home, I started getting involved in some theatrical work. It just kind of fell into my lap. There had always been people around who felt that I really should apply myself to that area. These were working professionals. They thought that my kind of extroverted personality would come off that way. Believe me, I have a very shy side, but it comes off rather extroverted. So I became involved with a professional workshop. Mostly bit-part stuff and extra work, but it was interesting. I got a job on daytime soap opera. On ABC. I worked on it for about twenty weeks. I started to take it very seriously, but I didn't want to have to depend on it. I wanted something to back myself up.

So at the ripe old age of eighteen I decided. I loved clothes. I had always loved clothes, and I used to work very hard to have the special kind of look I wanted, whatever it was. So I decided that I would attempt to open up this boutique, this small men's boutique. From different avenues, I was able to generate a small amount of capital, through my cars I had bought and sold, through the acting. When I look back at it now, it was an absurdly small amount of money. If it were to be tried today, it would be very difficult. This was back in 1966. The store was called Gary's of Brentwood. We sold sport shirts, dress shirts, ties, belts, but not tailored clothing. The first employee I ever had was Brock Chester, and he worked part-time. It was really not because I needed help for the "masses of people" coming in, because if we had one customer there, we were lucky. But Brock and I were so close that we always felt that anything I had was his, and his was mine. So it was just natural. We liked to be around each other.

After a while the store started to move a bit. I was fortunate that it developed, but I went through some hellish experiences.

Jeff Stolper:
I remember Gary's clothing store, the one on Twenty-sixth Street that he started the year after high school. I remember a good friend of mine went into his shop one day to buy a sweater. Instead of him trying it on, Gary put it on himself and said, "See how good this looks? And now, if you buy this pair of pants"—and he went and put on the pants—"you'll look like this." Gary went and tried on everything. It was my friend who came in to buy the sweater! He did buy it, but he said it was the craziest thing he'd ever seen, to walk into a shop and have the owner try on all the stuff to show you how good it looked.

Eventually things built to the point where we went from Gary's of Brentwood to a much larger store called Gary's and Company down in Marina del Rey. When I got into men's wear on this larger scale, a lot of things started happening. There was a certain amount of destiny about that. I think honestly that our ability to grasp onto a truer sense of the evolution in men's wear has helped us a great deal. I've always loved the aesthetic and artistic sides of the business. I've designed a line that's sold exclusively at our stores. We've pioneered a lot of things that have been vehicles for the industry. We were one of the leading forces in moving shaped, tailored clothing. We've had a great impact in the slacks business. We've helped to develop that wider leg. Almost every part of it, we've made some important statement.

Two years ago we opened up another store in the financial district of downtown Los Angeles. I'm very proud of the fact that our stores have won architectural awards—which is part of my direct involvement in it.

We also got into the finals in a European competition for packaging.

Today we employ about forty people. In terms of volume, we do about one and a half million dollars a year. I'm the president of Gary's and Company. I own the majority share of the business, but I have two partners. I'm proud that one of them is my father, who joined the business about two and a half years ago.

I work six days a week, and usually put in eleven or twelve hours a day. The truth of the matter is that there are very few moments that I'm not involved with it in some way. Whether I was working in high school for the ability of owning a car, or working for the ability of having a nice pair of slacks that I wanted, I've always had to strive and fight for each level I've attained. It's by no means over. It may always be that way. But I've been able to meet the challenge, and do it.

Sally Lobherr:

I know what Gary does, because I used to work in Arco Towers, and we have one of Gary's shops in there. It's outrageous. The clothes are beautiful, but more expensive than anywhere else. Everything there is perfect. There is not a tie out of place. Every window is dressed beautifully. I don't think Gary has changed a bit. He's doing what makes him feel comfortable, which is being wonderful.

Suzanne Thomas:

You always knew he'd be pretty successful! I really haven't seen him, but his shops are always advertised and I know he does really well. He has this shop in the Marina near where I work, but I've never run into him. It's funny, I've been by his shop several times, but I never actually stopped in. You know, if you haven't seen somebody in ten years, you want to look your best.

We've worked our ass off for what we've attained and we've plowed all of it back into itself. The house is something that I think you have to take into consideration to overall priorities. If a home can bring to a person the kind of momentary tranquillity or serenity that this kind of house can bring to Suzy and me, then it's specifically all right with me. Nevertheless, you have to come up with the dollars, and it isn't easy.

Since I put in sixty or seventy hours every week, I don't have much time to mow the lawn. You saw the size of the lawn we have out front! It's not that I wouldn't like to have the time—I only wish I did. But we have to have gardeners, and the proper amount of them. We have three of them. We have a pool man. We found that to keep the house maintained the way this house deserves to be, we have to work hard at it.

A lot of the antiques you see around are things that I got into on my own, rather early. Before it became a fad. I was involved in helping to start an antiques store, which is now doing phenomenally well. When I look at what I have around, it kind of boggles me!

I've owned thirty-seven different cars in my lifetime. That '57 Chevy was my first car, and I had to work hard to pay for it. I was a busboy in a restaurant; you name it. I started working on the car before I was even old enough to drive it. A person who works on a car and makes it an extension of himself brings out his own personality. Right now we have three cars. A Mercedes 280-SE Convertible. That's a handmade car, and very rare in this country. Then my lady drives a Mercedes 250, and she deserves it. The car that means the most to me is a Ferrari 1963 Super America. There are only fifteen in the whole United States. It's a fabulous machine, around four hundred horsepower. Whenever I feel bad, I go out to the garage and start the car and just listen to it. It's a thing of beauty.

On the surface, people took me for an extrovert in high school. Quite honestly, I was a great deal more morose and conservative than most people thought. I have always been a thinker—right, wrong or indifferent. Today, my lady and I are very reclusive.

Ten years from now I hope I will be much further along in the institutionality of Gary's and Company. Now it's strictly a matter of time. There are only so many hours in the day and you have to do so many things. The business world is fierce, competitive, incredibly complicated. It is hell out there. I come home and I'm tremendously frustrated. I feel like literally I have clamps on each side of my chest. I feel like the amount of time and work and effort that I have to apply is probably shortening my life some. But I believe that it's worth it.

●

In the small hours of the morning we finally ran out of cassette tapes, and Gary escorted us to the front door. We stood there for a moment, looking up at the stars and breathing the fragrance of a warm California night. Then Gary found something else to tell us. "You know," he said, "I've got some more on my mind I ought to say about Brock. I really loved that guy! The girls we used to date would always throw at us the fact that we cared more about each other than about them. We were so close. If you're going to use him in your book, don't make any mistakes about what really happened. Come back soon, and we can talk about it."

●

Brock Chester: The Dreamboat

•

Lany Tyler:
I used to love looking at him. I'd say he was probably the most handsome male in our class. He had beautiful eyes, a creamy dark complexion, just beautiful black hair, sort of wavy, longish. I think his eyes were green. I remember his long eyelashes. He had perfect features. Of course I liked him, but I was always intimidated talking to him because he was so beautiful. He was very quiet, very sweet. He wasn't terribly bright as far as I can recall, but I don't think of him as stupid. He was so strikingly good-looking that you didn't so much notice the other things.

Ron Conti:
He had phenomenal athletic ability. He was a natural. He was into track. He was into football. He was All-Western League End for two years in a row. He was captain of the baseball team. He was great in every sport.

He was very popular, especially with the opposite sex. He was an image, walking around campus like he was a god, almost. I think that other people were jealous of him. I know I was. He seemed to have everything going for him. Everything.

Gary Wasserman:
Anita Champion was actually the catalyst that brought Brock Chester and me together to become the dearest

of friends ever. We both had a crush on her in junior high and she was in the middle and couldn't make a decision. At one of those Sock Hops they used to have, Brock and I met in the bathroom. Everyone thought we were going to fight to see who was going to get Anita. But the second that Brock and I laid eyes on each other, neither of us thought about Anita from that moment on. We just instantly became such close friends that we spent every moment of time together. You know, people kidded us about being gay, for that matter. Not from the standpoint of how we put out to people, but because we were just inseparable so much of the time.

Brock was about six feet one. He didn't have a tremendously big build, but he had a well-proportioned build. He had beautiful features. His hands were beautiful. Because these things mean a lot to me, I was extremely aware of them. He was, by definition, a man's man. He was a masculine, strong, extremely attractive guy.

Jon Wilson:

I knew Brock because he went to the same church I did. I had classes with him since probably the third grade. The first recollections I have of him are in Palisades Elementary School, because he was extremely athletic compared to the rest of the people. When we played kickball, he'd kick it over the fence. When we played baseball, he'd hit that over the fence. All the girls liked him because he was very handsome.

In high school, Brock was in a social group that was separate from me. But he was very friendly toward me and toward other people that were outside the group, whereas some of the other people weren't. I used to see Brock all the time riding his bicycle. Since I knew him from before, he always stopped and talked to me and was always really friendly. But I never actually made a point of getting together with him because I always thought I was on a lower social level.

Lee Grossman:
In the A-9 vs. B-9 basketball game, he was playing for the B-9 team and he scored a basket in the wrong basket. It was a junior high school game in front of the entire student body. It was a terrible blow.

Jeanne Hernandez, teacher:
I remember Brock as being a steady and thoroughly reliable personality. Good all the way through. Steady and hard-working. Careful about what he did and what he said. Wishing to achieve. A nice-looking boy. The kind that I necessarily would reach out to and want to help. I was very fond of him.

Jamie Kelso:
Brock was very much a lady's favorite. A he-man. He was going with Patty Findlater, who was supposed to be the sexiest girl in the school. But down deep, I think Brock was bashful. An extremely shy individual, and very self-effacing.

Anita Champion:
I was very much in love with him at one time. We were going steady—he gave me a St. Christopher's medal and the whole thing. Then he just told me that he wanted to break up. He was leaving me for another girl—because Gary Wasserman told him to do it. It was at my sixteenth birthday party, sophomore year. I was very hurt. I was crushed.

Brock was very much a gentleman. I think in the whole time we went together we actually made out only three or four times. We were both perfectly satisfied with sitting, holding hands, that sort of thing. What Brock cared most about was football. School was always really hard for him. He used to come over to the house a lot, watch TV, sit and talk.

My mother always used to kid me. She'd say, "Is Brock coming over with Gary?" It was always a known thing that Gary was like his Siamese twin. Gary, for quite a few years, gave Brock a little bit more backbone, which he needed. He was such a perfect image and yet he really had very little self-confidence. By Gary being so overconfident, he kind of helped. Brock always depended on someone else for his strength or whatever.

Debbie Gordon:
He was very good-looking. I don't know anything about his personality. I just sort of picture him standing there smiling and with everyone looking up at him.

•

The bare facts about Brock's death raised more questions than they answered. We realized that we could never know exactly what had happened to him since high school, but we hoped that conversations with the people closest to him would begin to explain the tragedy.

With this purpose in mind, we paid a return visit to Gary Wasserman. Gary, as always, was full of energy and opinions. As he tended the fire and served us drinks, his need to talk about Brock seemed as deep as his need to talk about himself during our last meeting.

•

We had a relationship that was just extremely close. When you have a relationship of a male to a male, there are certain areas and levels that you get to that you couldn't possibly get to with a woman, or a wife. It was also the period of time. At that point in your life you don't have as many defenses up. You allow yourself to open up and get closer. We weren't afraid to be that close.

Brockus Lee Chester

Young Bay TV Actor Dies During Trip

Memorial services f o r television a c t o r Brockus Lee Chester of Santa Monica Canyon will be held at 1 p.m. Monday at Pierce Brothers Santa Monica.

BROCKUS L. CHESTER

The actor, who was 24, died unexpectedly Wednesday while on a camping trip in the Monterey peninsula. Cause of death was not immediately known.

Chester was best known for his appearances in the TV series Bracken's World and was under contract to 20th Century Fox.

He was graduated in 1965 from P a l i s a d e s High School, where he played both football and baseball. In football, he was named All-Western League End and won the most - improved player award. He won the captain's trophy in baseball, and was voted the most popular member of his senior class.

Brock Chester: The Dreamboat

Monterey Police Department	VICTIM'S NAME (Last-first-middle. Firm name if business)		71-01968
MISCELLANEOUS COMPLAINT	BROCK, Chester Lee.		
OR CRIME REPORT	RESIDENCE ADDRESS Santa Monica		PHONE
WEAPON, FORCE, OR MEANS USED	NO. OF SUSPECTS	LOCATION OF OCCURRENCE Veterans Memorial Park	CLASS. Cas. Suicide
Unk.			
APPARENT MOTIVE Despondency		DATE AND TIME OCCURRED 4-27-71 PM to 4-28-71 AM	DATE AND TIME REPORTED 4-28-71 0800
TRADEMARKS OF SUSPECT(S) (Actions or conversation)		TYPE OF PREMISES Open Area, Campgrounds	
		DIVISIONS OR UNITS NOTIFIED AND PERSONS CONTACTED Lt. BLACK, Investigations Div.	
VEHICLE USED BY SUSPECT(S) (Yr.-make-body-col-lic. no. & I.D.)		LIST ANY CONNECTING RPT(S) BY CLASS. AND DR NO. None	VICTIM'S COND. (HBD, NORMAL, ETC) Expired

CODE: V-victim R-reporting party W-witness

VICTIM'S OCCUPATION—SEX—DESCENT—DATE OF BIRTH	CODE	RESIDENCE ADDRESS (Bus. add. if him)	CITY	RES. PHONE	X	BUS. PHONE	X
Actor WM 3-10-47	V	See above					
NAME PERRY, Jerry Lee	RP						

IDENTIFY SUSPECTS BY NO. (Name—address—sex—descent—age—ht—wt—hair—eyes—complex—clothing—other features. If arrested, bkg no. & charge)

1.

2.

(1) IDENTIFY ADDITIONAL SUSPECTS (2) RECONSTRUCT THE CRIME (3) DESCRIBE PHYSICAL EVIDENCE, LOCATION FOUND, & DISPOSITION (4) SUMMARIZE OTHER DETAILS RELATING TO CRIME (5) TIME AND LOCATION WHERE VICTIM/WITNESSES CAN BE CONTACTED BY INVESTIGATORS IF NO AVAILABLE PHONE NUMBERS.

BROCK, (V), found to have committed suicide.

V. found by City maintenance man PERRY (RP) at approximately 0800 hrs. sitting in rear of his 1970 VW camper bus, 225 BXS.

A seven page letter was found indicating his intentions.

Dep. Coroner SHAW was contacted, arrived and took charge of the scene. The Body was taken to Dorney and Farlinger Mortuary, and the vehicle was towed to Monterey Garage for storage.

There wasn't anything we didn't do together. Living through the experience of the newest girl we had just met, or the tactics we'd use in a sport. The newest thing we were doing on our car, the next party in line. We even experienced our fantasies together.

To give you an idea of how subtly striking he was, how good-looking he was, the kind of air he carried about him: one day he walked into my house when my mother had quite a few of her women friends around for a card party. It was apparent to me—but not to Brock—that when we walked in, the whole thing just stopped. They were obviously staring at Brock. Just staring at him. Whatever fantasies were going on, or whatever feelings of "Gee, what a darn attractive, well-mannered guy," Brock wasn't aware of it. He never even believed he was good-looking. He didn't have any confidence about that. There was no pretentiousness. The air was totally natural.

Brock had a mother that was an angel. It was a big family. Unfortunately, his real father had very little influence because of how young Brock was when he left. Brock was adopted by his second father.

Brock always had a self-confidence void. Academics didn't come easily. He'd work very hard. He really did apply himself as diligently as he possibly could. But he was probably most dedicated toward sports. He was just a naturally excellent athlete. I think given just a little more peace of mind, a little bit more self-confidence, he could have very well been a professional athlete.

After high school Brock went to Santa Monica City College. It's unfortunate that the athletic program there was rather depressing. I was there myself, so I know. I think with the pressure he was under as far as handling the academic side, combined with the disillusionment about how the whole sports side was coming together, he just gave up. He was there approximately a year, maybe a year and a half.

For a while he was working at Gary's of Brentwood,

and then the acting thing happened, very much like the old Hollywood success stories. He and I were members of a gym up in the Palisades. One of the members of the gym that we used to see almost every time was heavily involved in motion pictures and television. He picked up this very real, very warm quality that Brock had, and of course he felt the visual impact. He wanted to see if he could develop something with Brock and help him to get into the entertainment business. That's how it started.

Brock was very trepidatious about it because he was very shy. He didn't want to run into any kinds of built-in defeats. He went into it cautiously and carefully in that respect, and was developing, I think, really very well. He had done commercials, and he was doing some television. I thought his prospects were very bright.

Then one day in April of '71 I was going between the Marina store and the Brentwood store. I walked into the Brentwood store and my mother was there. It didn't take a genius to know that there was something really wrong. She started to say, "Sit down. I want you to sit down."

I kept saying, "No, what's the matter."

She said, "I don't know how to tell you this."

I said, "What is it?" I was really starting to get very panicky. I didn't know whether it was my dad or my brother. I knew there was something really wrong.

She said, "It's Brock."

I said, "What's the matter? Is he hurt?"

She said, "No. He's dead."

I didn't really accept it right away. I felt I had control of myself. But it was really some time before I had totally digested the fact that he died that way.

Why he killed himself—that's a big question. There's been literally billions of times that I've thought about that. There is no answer—just fragmentations of why. I think it was really because of his feeling of not being able to contribute enough to justify himself. I don't think he realized one thing that was so apparent to many people. That is how much he was taking away from us.

After he died there was a whole time thing for me that just went away. At one point I was sitting in a chair in the living room. I couldn't talk to Suzy. I was just too emotionally upset. I was crying and I was sitting and pounding on top of my legs. Apparently I didn't realize it, but this went on for about eighteen hours. I have no recollection of that amount of time. After it happened, the tops of my thighs were just black and blue, and I found I could hardly walk.

In the last four years there have been like three or four times when an emotional outbreak about him has come. Usually the emotional thing comes before the realization of why. It's the sadness, the sorrow involved in it. I feel very cheated in the fact that I can't have him as my dearest friend all my life . . . experiencing all the things I'm going through.

Whenever I'm really faced with a lot of difficulties, I go back to those feelings and thought patterns that have come down from that situation. There are some reasons to thank him for giving us the wisdom that was really laid out in front of us all the time, for helping us to realize what life's all about. How a lot of things we take for granted in junior high school, high school, our contemporary lives, can mean a hell of a lot more than the face value. It's well worth bearing in mind. I loved him.

•

Brock's mother, Mrs. Jacquie Stark, is a hearty, big-boned woman with an open and pleasant face. Everything about her—the warmth of her handshake, the ruddiness of her complexion, the steady concentration in her wide brown eyes—spoke of kindness and good spirits. It was easy to imagine her laughing and enjoying herself, but on this quiet weekday morning she was not laughing. We sat alone with her in the living room, distracted by a couple of noisy birds fluttering around the patio, as she focused her energies on memories of her oldest son.

•

Brock was born in Wichita, Kansas, but he's lived in the Palisades since he was four. The date of his birth was March 10, 1947. His real name is Brockus—which was my mother's maiden name—but I had always planned to call him Brock. I thought that was a nice solid name for a boy, and I didn't think anybody could do anything with it. However, I guess in grammar school, the kids started calling him "Brock the Broccoli Man," so I figured there's no way you can get a name where they don't give 'em a nickname of some kind. But it didn't stay long.

He was extremely well coordinated and he didn't go through a period of time like a lot of kids do of being uncoordinated—you know, when you have the rapid growth. I guess it was a question of natural ability, because he started out as a very sturdy, square little boy who could do all the physical things. Now, Brock was not as into the intellectual and maybe this was a balance. He had a good solid IQ but he just had a tremendous inferiority complex about his mental ability.

I really don't know what it was based on. Apparently, when he first started school he didn't do as well as the teacher thought he should. He happened to hit a very rotten teacher in the second grade whose solution to these things was to put the kids back a whole grade, just for one subject. This for some kids was a big embarrassment. And Brock was large for his age. And very shy. He hated to be singled out for anything— good or bad. I think this experience gave him a tremendous mental block about his abilities, because he always thought he was considerably poorer in academic work than he really was.

He didn't really enjoy school. He struggled terribly. When he had to get up to make a speech in a class, like a two-minute speech in English, he'd lock his bedroom door and he'd practice and practice. He'd be impossible to live with. He wouldn't talk to anybody. He'd be sick at his stomach. Just a real nervous wreck over a two-minute speech. This is why it was so astounding that he later went into acting. Astounding.

Brock had tons of friends, always. From the time he started school. He was very shy, but he liked people and he liked being part of a group—as long as he didn't have to be the leader. Basically, Brock had the old-fashioned integrity. If he was a friend, he was a friend and a friend and a friend. And because he was shy, he was gentler than some.

It's hard for me to say when Brock first started getting interested in girls. I can tell you more accurately when girls first started getting interested in Brock, because he had such a bad time. It was about the fourth or fifth grade. I recall so many things. Little girls standing behind the hedge that we had at the side of our house, waiting, hiding, until he came out to go to school. And he would get so embarrassed. He'd go rushing and dive over the fence to go through the canyon to get to school rather than see the girls. However, that did change. In junior high he kind of got dragged into the scene of girls a couple of years ahead, because Brock was tall. He had a couple of short friends who really dug the girls. They kept dragging Brock along because they'd get a double date on the promise that Brock would be there.

The thing that made Brock so attractive to girls was the combination—the combination of being fairly good-sized and good-looking and shy. That's the thing for women of any age, you know. Not only are you drawn to somebody who's physically good-looking, but then the mothering instinct comes out with the shyness. It's a tough combination to beat. I think it was an embarrassment for Brock until he got conned into going into acting. I think if he had a choice, he would have preferred not to have had that appeal.

100

Brock was very serious about the girls he went with. He cared a great deal and he got very involved. He was very emotional always. The whole family is very emotional. He didn't go with an awful lot of different girls. I know that Gary—well, a lot of the guys would try to get him to go with different girls. When he was having a fight with one girl, they'd try to get him to go out with somebody else, and he wouldn't. Part of that was because he was a one-woman guy. And also part of it was, knowing Brock, that it was hard for him to call on a first date. It was embarrassing. He had a hard time forcing himself to make a new relationship. He was more comfortable with an old one, where he'd already made the initial contact and they knew each other a little bit. It was very difficult for him to call a brand-new girl.

Patty Findlater was without question the love of Brock's life. I think he was sixteen when he fell in love with her, and he never fell out of love with her. They had a pretty rocky time. Originally, I think he was drawn to the way she looked. And also, she was shy. Then, after they started going together, she was really an obsession.

I don't think Patty was good for Brock. They were unhappy more than they were happy. They were both having problems of growing up. They both had great feelings of lack of self-worth, and that didn't make them a good team. They couldn't bolster each other when they needed bolstering. And then Patty had the pressure, the constant pressure, to break off with Brock. And sometimes she would. It would never last any length of time. They'd be back together again. But they were forever breaking up.

When Brock graduated from high school with all those honors and that popularity, I felt very proud. He was a lovely son. He really was. He was very thoughtful, very dear, very sweet. The fact that he never had an enlarged ego made it very easy for me as a mother to totally enjoy him and to give him all the praise a mother likes to give.

Brock was concerned about his future, and he talked several times about wanting to be a football coach. He was a C student and this bothered him. He followed a sister who was an A student. That's always hard. He went on to City College after high school, and I know he planned to play football there. But he had some conflicts with the coach, and I think he was bitterly, bitterly disappointed when the coach didn't use him that first semester. I think he was probably humiliated that he wasn't playing. At any rate, he quit.

It's very difficult, I think, for people who didn't know Brock well to understand his tremendous feelings of inadequacy inside. He needed those athletic things that boosted his feelings of worth, whereas some of us do not. We have our own feelings of strength. But Brock needed the outside show that he was important to somebody, or that he had a place in life.

Somewhere along in there, Brock was working out in gyms to keep himself in shape, when this guy came along and offered him money to go into acting. This fellow would pay Brock a hundred and fifty dollars a week to do nothing but study. He would help Brock along in his career, and then later work as sort of his agent and promoter.

I know that at the time Brock must have been thinking a lot about what he was going to do with his life, how he was going to succeed. I know he was pushed by the drive for money more than he normally would have been because the girl he was going with—Patty—had a ton of money behind her.

Brock said he would try acting, but he didn't think he could handle it. He went into it very slowly. He started out with private lessons because he couldn't even handle class sessions. It was almost a year before the drama coach felt that he was emotionally capable of going into classwork. Apparently he did very well. He could draw on the depth of his feelings about things, on his areas of problems.

The first work he got was some TV commercials. Not all of them were aired. He was paid for them, however. He was selling a hamburger in one. He also did an Air Force recruiting commercial, and he had to cut his hair.

It was then, I guess, that he got the part on *Bracken's World*. And he thought that was really going to be a jumping-off place for his acting. It was good money and it was great fun, great experience for him. Brock was playing one of the students in the acting class within the show. There were three girls and three fellows that were in this acting class. The original concept was that every once in a while one of them would develop into a special scene, and they would get better parts. However, the way it worked out, the three gals were developed and the fellows were not. Of course, Brock was very disappointed about that.

The next season, Brock wasn't on the show, and he didn't get much of anything, other than a few commercials. I'm sure he was beginning to be depressed about his career because Brock never could wait. He was not a patient person, and he wanted everything right away. He would never even stand in line in places. So the fact that his career was going slowly was not something that he could accept.

I think Brock was feeling tremendous tension as he approached twenty-five. He had some friends who were coming back and had graduated from college and were onto careers. He felt his career wasn't going as fast as he wanted it to go and it wasn't going up as high as he wanted it to go. He had such tremendously high, such *unreasonably* high goals for himself! If you think you're really not much inside, then you've got to prove to the world that you are. And you've got to do it with material things.

If Brock had gone on with his original idea of trying

to be a football coach, he'd probably be coaching today. Without a doubt, that would have been a happier career for him. The acting profession is so damaging to the ego, I think it's just horrible for somebody like Brock.

When he was growing up, he used to have tremendous frustrations and rages. Not at any one person, but at his situation. He put his fist through the garage wall, the outside wall. He put his fist through the dining-room wall, he put his fist through the bedroom wall. His little brother thought it was neat the way Brock would always smash his fist through a wall or something. So Mike tried it once and he broke his hand.

Brock had about a half-dozen car accidents over the years, some of them not so minor. One time he was coming home from football practice. He hit a cement pole—totaled the car. Then, on Mother's Day a few years later, he skidded on a corner, and then the car flipped over and plowed through a lady's ivy and tore up all her sprinklers. It was a horrible accident—Brock got tremendous amounts of glass in his eyes and he almost lost one ear.

The very sad thing for me personally is that all this time Brock and I had fought hard together with his problems, and I felt that he had finally come through, I thought he was beginning to establish some feelings of security, his own feelings of worth. I knew from what I'd been told that he could eventually make it as an actor, and I figured eventually things would smooth out for him and Patty. They were fighting frequently, but that was a way of life by then. Brock was very possessive, and there'd be fights about that, I'm sure. I know that Patty didn't like to have him working with Gary at the last. Marriage was certainly in Brock's mind, but he didn't want to marry Patty until he had money. I knew that money was tight with him. But he knew we would always help him. He has an aunt that has tons of money and sends him a check every once in a while, for whatever he might need. So that I just wasn't aware of the depth of his problems.

He came by the evening before he died. He was very upset, but at the time I didn't think it was anything unusual. Maybe he was having problems with Patty, and whenever they had problems he was irritable, grouchy, hostile, angry. It was always like that, so obviously I didn't think anything about it. He also came by the next morning, just before he left for his trip up north, but I had already gone off to work. If I had known how upset he was, I wouldn't have gone to work. I would have been there to talk to him—all sorts of things would have been different.

All I know is that he went up north to the woods by himself, which he likes to do, to sort things out in his mind. Things weren't going the way he wanted them to, so he went up there to look at the clear sky and the mountains and to think.

I have never been a big student of precognition or any of these things, and yet with Brock . . . we were just so close. The year before he died I was coming home one night from visiting my mother, and my husband was driving. I suddenly got this tremendous depressed feeling. I started to cry. And my husband said, "What's the matter? Are you worried about your mom?"

I said, "No. It's so strange that I don't understand it. I thought things were better with Brock, but I have this horrible feeling that something terrible is going to happen."

And I got home and called him. He was then living in his own place and he was okay, he was fine. But I really can't put into words the black horror that I felt at that time, just out of the blue, driving home.

Then the night Brock died I was on my way to a meeting. I was driving down Sunset and all of a sudden I started to shake and shake and shake—and I ran into a brick wall. Now, I don't have accidents like that—really. I've only had two car accidents in my whole life.

After I hit the wall, I just started to cry and I turned around and came home. But there was no way I could reach Brock. He had already gone up north.

It's interesting. You know that Brock was adamant about drugs. Adamant. He was very much against them. He gave his younger brother a lot of lectures about it. And yet that's the way he died.

He was sitting alone in his Volkswagen camper when he died. It was just after dark, about eight-thirty. I think he borrowed the barbiturates from different people. They said he took five pills, which is not at all necessarily fatal, but he was drinking wine, too. And that is not always fatal, either. I think it was the combination of the wine and the pills and the wish to go.

It was a beautiful setting. In the mountains. In the mountains with all the big trees around, overlooking some water, a lake up there.

He left a note. It was addressed to me. He just said he couldn't handle things. He said it over a few pages, but that's primarily it.

Once when he was younger, in a session with a psychologist, they asked Brock, "If you could come back in your next life as something else, what would you come back as?" And he said, "A rose, because they always die young and beautiful."

•

For the first time in our conversation, Mrs. Stark lost her composure. We turned off the tape recorder and suggested a pause, but she shook her head. She wanted to continue.

•

At the funeral a friend of my stepson's played the guitar, and he played all the Gordon Lightfoot music that Brock liked. Brock's ashes were scattered up in the hills near here. He liked the mountains. He liked the hills and the greenery. And it's peaceful and it's quiet up there. I go on his birthday and on the day he died, and talk to him.

On those same days I also put a rose by his picture.

•

Mrs. Stark took us into the den and showed us a little corner that was devoted to Brock's memory. On the wall was a large picture of her son, smiling broadly, and smaller photos showing him in action on the football field. There was also a brass plaque for athletic achievement. On a six-inch ledge below these mementos rested a copy of Kahlil Gibran's *The Prophet* and a string of Oriental meditation beads.

•

The Prophet was Brock's favorite book. He knew it word for word. He was also very much interested in meditation—transcendental meditation—and he was very serious about it. He seemed to feel it helped him. I'm sure it did, because Brock always had problems controlling his emotions, and his meditating—every day at the same time—I'm certain was a big help. He did it for three or four years, I think.

I think Brock's depression may have been a temporary thing. I often wonder. Brock was very impulsive. It often occurred to me after he died that I wanted him to get up and say, "Damn, now why did I do that?" Because often he would do things impulsively he wished he hadn't. He never really planned to put his fist through the garage wall, things like that. But he was impulsive.

Of course, it was very difficult for Brock to live up to his tremendous popularity in high school. To live up to being All-Western League End, baseball-team captain, guy voted Most Popular on Campus—that's almost impossible. I think the fact that he wasn't as important to other people after he got out of high school had to have mattered to him. It would have mattered to anybody. You can't stay in high school forever, and things change. And yet, if you have that in your background, you have to go beyond it, or recognize it as a particular era, a lovely growing time, but just one era in your life.

I think the most important thing to come across is that Brock did the best he could with what he had. To my knowledge, he never knowingly cheated or hurt anyone. And he did his very best to be . . . Well, I have a poster of his that sums it up. It says, "If I cannot do big things, let me do small things in a big way." He did his best. He really tried very hard.

Patty Findlater: Foxy Lady

•

Lee Grossman:
Oh, she was beautiful! Absolutely stunning. I don't think I ever exchanged two words with Patty Findlater and she was in my homeroom. She was absolutely the most beautiful woman I had ever seen. She had the most incredible green eyes and the most incredible red hair.

Ron Conti:
Patty Findlater? She was a fox! That's my idea of a fox! She was something special. She was a girl that I was always afraid to walk up and talk to. She was too good for me. How could I possibly entertain somebody

like that? It was something I was reaching for, but I knew I would never get there. Brock was always going out with Patty, anyway. They had a thing going.

Lany Tyler:
I guess Patty was among those girls whom I envied because they were beautiful and all the beautiful men liked them. I never knew her terribly well, and I always felt a little funny around her.

Bob Searight:
She went with Brock Chester. She was really pretty. She kind of knew it. It just rings a bell that there was always some kind of rumor going around about her, but that didn't make her any less desirable. It made her more desirable, probably.

Anita Champion:
I was always jealous of her. She had the clothes, and all the guys wanted to date her. She was a beautiful girl. I don't think she was too good in the grade department. Her parents had a lot of money. They still do. I don't think she was intentionally a snob. Maybe through being as quiet and shy as she was, sometimes she appeared to be that way.

The only reason that Brock ever asked Patty out, from what I remember, is that Gary more or less pushed them together. Brock was basically so shy and unsure of himself.

Margie Williams:
Patty wasn't much of a personality. When she was in a group she was just usually standing there, never having too much to add to the conversation. I remember everybody else saying, "Look at that gorgeous red hair!" I remember her eyes as being such a light, light color. You could almost see through them. When you looked at her, the eyes were almost missing, they were so light. It really bugged you to look at them.

Gary Wasserman:
She plays a pretty important role in my life. I knew her from grammar school all the way through. I dated her for a while. Her involvement with Brock was the most important aspect of any of the relationships I went through with Patty.

She had a natural beauty that was incredible. She had a lust for getting out and finding out what was going on. I think she really possessed this type of magnetism. I have to think of it as negative magnetism, though. She'd be involved with a lot of things at all times—a lot of people, a lot of guys. She kind of skated along as far as I was concerned. Of course, if Brock were sitting here now, I wouldn't even be saying these type of things.

Skip Baumgarten:
I wanted to go out with Patty Findlater. A lot. I have a feeling there was probably a long line. I don't know. I never talked to her. I'd get nervous, I'd sweat. Who could talk to a girl like that?

●

We met Patty several times before she agreed to an interview. She had largely cut herself off from high school and its associations, and seemed understandably reluctant to reopen that chapter in her past. Nevertheless, she kept calling us back to express her feelings about our project and to try to clear up some of the persistent rumors that had been circulating about her relationship with Brock Chester.

When she was finally ready to speak for the record, we met her for lunch in a crowded restaurant near her place of work on Hollywood's Sunset Strip. As she walked through the lobby all heads turned; she was a beautiful woman, and even dressed casually in jeans and sweater, she had the same air of mystery and inaccessibility that she had carried in high school. With our tape recorder set up on our little table, amid the clatter of plates and the noise of dining and conversation, we faced an awkward moment. Patty sat quietly in front of the microphone, looking frightened and uneasy, and as the emotion began to build in her eyes we wondered why we should be putting her through this ordeal. But it was she herself who urged us to begin, with a firm voice and a nod of the head, and we opened the interview by asking about her family background.

•

Some of my ancestors came over on the *Mayflower*. My mother's side is from England and my father's from Scotland. My mother is a housewife. My father is one of the vice presidents of Universal Studios.

When I was growing up I was very reserved. In junior high school I never thought I was pretty. In fact, I remember spending most of my time being embarrassed about my red hair. I was very conscious of dressing, and I spent a lot of time with my clothes. Then when I was voted Most Sexy in high school, I went into a state of shock. I didn't understand why, and to this day I don't understand why. I don't know. It must have been a joke.

Over the summers in high school I went to the beach. I never worked. I didn't know what work was at the time. Now I am definitely more aware of it! I also took trips during the summers to different parts of the United States and foreign countries.

The summer after we graduated I wanted to get a job for the first time, and I decided to try commercial modeling. My brother was already in the business and he encouraged me to do it. So I went out and had some pictures taken, and my brother told me to just take them to his agent. Not knowing what I was doing and thinking this whole thing was really ridiculous, I took the pictures to the agent and she said, right then and there, "I'll sign you." It was an unbelievable moment for me.

So I was signed and I had my first interview for a job the next day. It was a commercial. Here I was, this young kid, going, "Oh my God, now what do I do?" When I went to the interview all the others there were well-known models. They were all sitting there talking about the work they'd done before. I was just sitting there praying they wouldn't ask me to talk about *my* experience. But when the interview was over, it turned out that I was the one who got the job.

Eventually you just get used to the modeling business. It's a job. I did TV commercials and magazine ads. I did a commercial for New Dawn hair coloring. I was smiling on TV and the commercial said "Pat Findlater uses New Dawn." No, I didn't use it. Then I did the cover for a Clairol box and they wanted me to have brown hair. They spent four hours putting black rinse on my hair. It would not change color. They finally got an auburn tint.

I liked modeling because I had a lot of free hours. I also made a lot of money. When you're a model, you do a commercial and you just keep getting money. It bought me a car and I lived very well on it. I had no sense of money at the time, and I just spent it and enjoyed it. But it got to a point where it just wasn't worth it any more. I didn't like being treated the way models are treated. You know—getting up at five in the morning and running through the ocean freezing to death and having a photographer say, "You're turning blue! Don't turn blue! You're ruining our picture." I never liked being in front of the camera, with all the attention focused on me. I'd rather be in the background somewhere. So one day I just decided it was enough—I wasn't going to go through with it any more. I wanted to go to school. I wanted to be somebody on my own. I wanted to study psychology, to learn a little more about how people work inside. So I started school at USC, and I loved it. I just loved it. I continued studying there until the day Brock died.

Brock and I had been together for nine years. We first started going together in the eleventh grade, and he'd been in my mind even years before that. In junior high school I used to watch him, just watch him quietly day after day. He just had that kind of way about him that I was very attracted to—a shy quality that I identified with myself. He was always going with someone, but then in the beginning of the eleventh grade I heard that he wasn't seeing his girl friend any more. So I somehow signed up for a class that he was taking, and somehow managed to sit next to him. He was quite shy and I was very shy. It was really a battle to make contact between people who were both so shy. I remember we played little high school games, doing silly things to get each other's attention. Then one day we just started talking.

Oh, I do remember our first date. It was a double date. We went to a party. I remember. I was in complete ecstasy because I'd been waiting for this moment for years.

That first night when he took me home, we didn't kiss good night. We just kind of held hands and he said, "It was really nice. Thank you."

We started going together on a regular basis and we fell in love. Brock used to come over to my house to watch TV. Just relaxing together and holding hands. We were always happiest when we were alone, alone in each other's company. We never got into fights when we were alone. But when we got out in front of people, sometimes things didn't go as well. A lot of it was jealousy on both our parts. Brock knew that I would never leave him for someone else, but he did have intense jealousy.

I think he was insecure about me. He needed me and he needed me around. He needed me to be his, which I was. But as far as he was concerned, that meant *his,* period.

He always wanted his friends to look on him as just an easygoing guy. We could be having a huge fight, a major battle, and he would open the door and there would be one of his old friends, and Brock would start smiling like nothing had happened and everything was okay. But with me and his mother, and maybe one or two other people, he showed his real feelings. His emotions really came out.

Oh yes, there was a time when we dated other people. When I was twenty-one, we didn't see each other for a whole year. We had no contact at all—no phone calls, no letters, nothing. Then one day we just ran into each other. I was driving down San Vicente one way, he was driving another way. The cars came to a screeching halt and we pulled over and talked. And I saw him that night. I continued to see him from then on.

Brock and I had lots of fights when we were together, but just before he died was one of our easiest times. I know that a rumor's gotten started that things weren't going well between us, but that's just not true. The last time I saw him was when we went together to my girl friend's wedding. There was no fight, no scene, no jealousy. I don't care what other people say about it, because I know the truth. I have the pictures from that day, and you can see that everything was pretty much normal between us.

Near the end of the wedding, Brock took me outside and we held each other and hugged each other for about twenty minutes. We were both crying. What he said to me was, "I'm sorry I have to leave you." He said he loved me, and we held each other, and then he just walked off. I went back into the wedding. Looking back, it seems obvious that he knew what he was going to do. He probably knew two weeks beforehand. No one can really know exactly what was in his mind. Brock had gone through a lot of traumatic experiences in his life, but he'd never killed himself. I think the reason that he died was that he was just too sensitive for this world. Too honest. Too naïve. No self-confidence at all. It was just too much pressure for him trying to be an actor. Whenever anything went wrong he took it personally—like there was something wrong with *him*.

I remember two days after that wedding when Brock left town to drive up north. His mother called me and she was upset. She was worried that Brock might do something, and she thought it was because we had a fight. She blamed me. She had to blame me —she was his mother and I was the girl friend. But we didn't have any fight—I know how things were between us. Later on, when she could put things in perspective, I think Brock's mother could see all the sides. We're close now. I see her on all family occasions. We're much closer than we ever were when Brock was alive.

When I first heard that Brock had died, my immediate response was to kill myself. I never thought I could exist without him. Then I realized that I couldn't die because Brock would have written something for me. The letter he left was written very beautifully, very poetically. He described the natural setting around him, and said how he felt about me. Reading it, I felt very beautiful and very loved. We had this thing between us—when I kissed his nose or he kissed my nose, it meant "I love you." One of the things he said to me in the letter was "Kiss my nose and call me love." A couple of days after he died I got a postcard that he had mailed the day of his death. It showed a beautiful sunset over the Pacific Ocean, with one of those California cypress trees like a shadow in front of the waves. On the back of the postcard he'd written those same words: "Kiss my nose and call me love." There was nothing else. Not even his name.

In the two years after Brock died, all I experienced was a feeling of nothingness. Everything just seemed gray. It didn't matter if it was day or night. It just didn't matter. I would wake up and do nothing all day.

I was a burden on my friends and my family. I was unaware of people around me, and sometimes even unaware when people were talking to me. Actually, I remember very little about those two years.

During that time I had something inside of me that was very strong, almost defiant. I wanted to make it on my own—I really wanted to succeed. I think what really helped me was having done volunteer work with mental patients when I had been studying psychology in school. I remembered those people and the way their emotions had taken over their minds. It made me realize the inner strength I had, and how I must use it, to keep my own emotions in perspective. So I got a job as a hostess in a restaurant. It was just something to get me back in contact with people. It gradually worked. I took one job which led to another job, and my life just kind of developed.

Today I'm working for a movie production company. I'm an assistant production secretary. I love my work. It's fascinating for me to see a film from day one, bringing a script in and then watching it develop until the final film comes out.

I've never gotten married because I've never found anyone I wanted to spend the rest of my life with. I'd love to keep working for a while, but someday I want to have my own home and I want to have kids. I'm sure sometime someone will come along for me. But I don't think it can ever be quite the same as it was with Brock. Our relationship was very emotional and very romantic. No one ever really knew the way things were between us, or what we shared. I feel that I was very lucky that I could spend the amount of time with Brock that I did. We went together for nine years. I'm glad those years were there. I feel now that even though he's gone, I've had something that's better than most people will ever have in life. I am very grateful.

Graduation

•

Jeff Stolper:

It was exciting and yet a little bit sad. I mean, the fact that you've gone through twelve years of school and now all of a sudden you're going to be out on your own.

I got my brother tickets for graduation. He took one look at the size of the class—more than five hundred people—and he walked right out. He knew what it was all about: just calling off the names, walking across the stage, and automatic applause. All the parents applauded for their own kids. Of course, some people got louder applause. Brock Chester for one. I think Mark Holmes got the biggest applause because he was the quarterback of the football team.

Grad night was at the Beverly Hilton, and the Byrds came as the main band. I remember Wasserman was there, and carrying on quite a bit. I don't know if he was drunk or high, but he was yelling and screaming up in front. He was up there by the band, just egging them on, and so forth.

Ron Conti:

Grad night was just unreal. I loved it. I had a date that was a year behind us. She acted like she didn't know anything, but that night I found out she knew a lot. We were drinking up a storm. After the party

117

Pali Students Lacking in Honest School Pride

Every eleven seconds a baby is born in America, and every eleven minutes somebody claims Palisades High's just not on the map. Most of you have said it and very few of you have been known to stand up for your school under such an attack. Palisades is a great high school, but the students fail to back their accomplishments with honest pride.

It's time we really tried to let the other parts of the city know we exist. Both academically and athletically we have made great strides for a three-year-old school. Traditions have been started and now our pride should be nourished.

How long did it take Westchester to win a varsity football game? Everybody knows: five years. But it took Pali only two! Try bragging about that, Dolphins!

How many students drop out of Pali every year? Something like ten? If we're not at the top academically speaking, we're pretty close, and that's nothing to be ashamed of.

One object of attack is Pali spirit. It's been called everything from weak to lousy. But if everybody who criticizes the lack of spirit would try and develop it we might again win the title of "Most Spirited School in the Western League."

So how do we get our school on this great big map of the world? No problem—we're off and running already. As one step toward school recognition the journalism staff has taken a poll of the top ten records at Pali for the KRLA Teen Topper program. Listen for your school on the air and stop knocking it long enough to feel a little pride.

—The Tideline Staff

118

we got a boat—some other fellows and myself. One guy's father had this forty-five-foot cabin cruiser, and we put it on automatic pilot to Catalina. Then we all dispersed to our separate cabins, doing our own thing and staying out all night. We came back at eight the next morning. When I got back on dry land I took my date home, and that's when I went over to see Gary and Brock in their motel room. They were just getting up, and we proceeded to drink together for the rest of the day.

Sally Lobherr:
Graduation was miserable. Graduation day I sat next to a girl and she brought this little puzzle with her and we played with the puzzle. I didn't listen to any of the speeches. Grad night was boring too. We all rented a motel on the beach and drank champagne and supposedly got drunk. It was very boring and I hated it.

Lee Grossman:
Graduation is the dullest experience known to man. I remember going through the exercise and reading *Steppenwolf* at the same time. You sit there for three hours, listen to the worst corny speeches you've ever heard, given by people for whom you have no respect. In those days there were people that I considered keepers of the intellectual flame, people that should have been in charge of what was happening. None of those people were speakers.

Mark Holmes:
I remember standing in these huge lines and wearing blue gowns and feeling this foolish thing on my head —the cap. I was hoping it was really time to get going—okay, now I'm going out in the world. I remember thinking. Wow, I'm really getting out now! I was ready. I had gotten a big trophy for being Sportsman of the Year, and somebody said, "Tonight you can drink out of it." But I don't think I did.

119

Carol Shen:

I don't remember anything from graduation, except for those turquoise robes. I looked horrible in it, I'm sure.

Mike Shedlin:

We played tricks. We turned on radios. I wore tennis shoes and didn't wear a tie and my hat didn't fit and my long hair was sticking out the bottom of my hat. I had little respect for the ceremonies. I consciously scorned it.

Reilly Ridgell:

Mike Shedlin was sitting behind me, and he kept telling me he had to take a piss, but he couldn't get up and leave. I told him, "Listen, if you've got to go, you've got to go. Get up and walk out." And he said, "Well, maybe the sun will come out and the heat will expand my bladder and I'll be able to hang on for a bit." I think he was at the stage where it hurts—if you touch it or jiggle it a little bit, it's about ready to spurt out. He just kept talking about it, but nothing ever happened.

I remember walking out after graduation, through that tunnel by the field, and I remember seeing this pretty girl from the grade behind us. She was sort of standing there watching everybody file out and I think she was crying. She looked at me and said, "Hi, Reilly!" and I thought it was kind of strange because she never would have talked to me before—or since.

William Quivers:

I really didn't want to be there. I wish they'd just given you the piece of paper. That's all I wanted. No need for this marching around or anything like that.

Jamie Kelso:

I didn't attend graduation. I didn't go to grad night. I didn't pick up my diploma. It was mailed to me. At that time I was in another world. People were signing up for gowns, buying annuals, signing pictures, telling each other what college they were going to. Some of them were getting married. They were making plans to go here and there. They were all busily and gaily entering the world outside. For me, the whole thing was a complete drag. I did not put in an application to any college. I didn't buy an annual. I didn't go to graduation. I didn't even go to school the last couple of weeks.

Just coincidentally, I was long-distance running on the day of graduation and I ran by the school to spy on the ceremonies. I just saw the people lining up in columns, getting ready to march down onto the field. Marshaling the graduates. I didn't stay there to observe it further. I definitely felt alone. A stranger in a strange world.

Jon Wilson:
I had a friend, and his parents had a boat that was anchored in the Marina. After grad night, me and Jeff Stolper and maybe one other person went there with our dates. We brought some champagne and we brought hangers so our dates could hang their formals and we could get loose and have a party.

It was like two o'clock in the morning, and all we were interested in was getting into their pants. We were fooling around and getting drunk. I remember Jeff Stolper brought a hot dog with him. He was going to put the hot dog in his pants, so he unzipped his zipper and stuck the hot dog right in there. He was with this girl he hadn't gone out with that much, hadn't slept with or anything. He started kissing her and grabbed her hand and put her hand on the hot dog. All of us knew that he was going to do this, but the girl didn't know, and she screamed bloody murder. Then the hot dog came off in her hand and you could hear her screams all over the place. Later on she took it in pretty good stride. Jeff was just a great guy! Those were the kind of things he always used to do.

Jeff Stolper: The Surfer

•

Lee Grossman:
Jeff was a surfer, and he involved himself with that whole subculture. I used to see him after school, walking down Chautauqua to the beach and carrying one of those big nine-foot boards. He had surfer hair bleached the color of mustard, and its length was a matter of some controversy at the school. He even listened to surfer music: I think Jan and Dean and the Beachboys' "Surfin' Safari" were his personal favorites. He used to listen to a transistor radio in class, with the earplug in his ear, and whenever they played a song that he particularly liked, he would turn it up so everyone could enjoy it. This didn't exactly endear him to the teachers.

Jeanne Hernandez, teacher:
Jeff was a troublemaker in high school. Really, a most disagreeable young man.

Jamie Kelso:
Jeff was a friend from way back. We used to do all the little-kid stuff together, like stealing plums off a tree in somebody's yard, or playing with Erector sets, chemistry sets, touch football in the street. Then there was the surfing thing—we were on the same frequency there. Jeff got into being a really good surfer.

He had an amazing humor. He engaged in riotous

122

practical jokery. I lost touch with him when the super-intellectuals isolated themselves from the rest of the universe at Pali. In retrospect, I don't know why Jeff didn't go with the intellectuals—he had a very strong mind and on an even keel. Maybe that was the reason!

Jon Wilson:

One of the biggest things that happened in high school was the controversy over hair length. Jeff Stolper, who was a friend of mine, was one of the initiators. He was a surfer, and he wore his hair a little longer than the rest of us. It wasn't long by today's standards, maybe just an inch below his collar or something like that. But the gym teachers were telling everybody to get their hair cut, and Jeff wouldn't. He just refused. They finally had a demonstration where they actually made signs, and they marched around in front of the school that they wanted long hair. I remember that the gym coaches got the football team together to come and break this up. All the football players had short hair, and some of them had almost shaven heads. Jeff was a friend of mine, and I thought he should have hair the way he wanted. When nothing else worked, the coaches sent him to the vice principal's office and told him he couldn't graduate unless he got a haircut. But Jeff held out. He told the vice principal some story about having to keep the long hair because he played in a rock-and-roll band. Finally they decided to leave Jeff alone, and he got to graduate with his long hair and everything. Jeff had always been a lot stranger than the rest of us. Very few people knew him that well, but he was one of the funniest people in that high school class.

•

Jeff Stolper today is a tall, lean, fashionably dressed young man with a walrus mustache and a head full of soft reddish curls. He recalls his former hair style with great fondness. "I used to straighten my hair with No-Kink Hair Straightener and I'd put lemon juice on it so it would be sun-bleached kind of blond. I remember when I straightened it the first time, Jon Wilson asked, 'What happened to all the kinks?' It just looked like a lot of straw coming out of my head in all directions. It wasn't that I was so proud of my hair. But when they told me to cut it, I felt it wasn't a reasonable thing for them to ask. What business of theirs was it how long I had my hair as long as I did my job at school—which was to pass my classes? I felt I should fight it. As it turns out, most of the people who criticized me at the time now have hair that's longer than mine."

Jeff and his wife live in a neatly kept ranch house in the Palisades which they bought recently to "ride out the inflation. A house like this is a good investment." Every detail in the furnishings and decoration of their home is modest and conventional, except for one corner of the living room. Here Jeff keeps his personal record collection, including more than fifteen thousand items. Here also is his antique 1942 Wurlitzer juke box with its decorative, multi-colored plastic tubes and flowing Art Deco lines. An additional hobby involves black-and-white ceramic dogs with one ear cocked in a listening position—the old trademark of RCA Victor. Jeff collects these "Nipper Dogs," having paid $135 for the largest of them, and has twenty-five of them scattered throughout his living room. "I think I've always had a thing for nostalgia," he admits, "but I try not to wrap myself up in it to where I'm living in the past." Nevertheless, because of his present occupation, he recalls with particular relish the torments he visited on his teachers at Palisades High School.

●

I remember one time in biology class we got to use a stethoscope. When it was my turn I insisted on using

it on a girl instead of a boy. The teacher said no—
only girls could listen to girls' heartbeats, and the boys
had to listen to boys'. I kept on asking her why I
couldn't listen to a girl's heart. She eventually became
rather upset with me.

Then there were the weird stunts we used to pull in
Auto Shop. We used to teach the new people all sorts
of things. Like we taught one guy the oil filter. We
told him one part was the testes, the other part was
the condom. He believed it and went and told the
teacher, "I just learned the oil filter. This is the testes,
this is the condom, and this is something else." We
pulled that same stunt countless times. Finally the
teacher pulled me aside and told me that it was funny
and he enjoyed it, but to ease up in the future. I guess
it could make some people feel rather foolish.

All through high school I never cracked a book. I
knew I was going to go on to junior college, and then
to college, and so forth. As long as I passed, my
grades really didn't matter. So I lay back.

On the weekends I had a job. I worked at the Bay
Theatre. Once I got that job I had more friends than
I ever really knew because they all wanted to get into
the show for free. The Bay Theatre was the place to
go on Saturday nights in high school. That's where you
could really count on everyone's showing up. You could
go in alone and pick up, or you could bring a date
there. People used to do everything in that movie. I
mean everything! One night I caught some guy and a
girl really going at it. I had to get the other usher to
come and take a look. She was actually going down on
the guy. It was a good show to watch. I felt that the
people sitting around them should actually pay a higher
price because they were getting a better show than
the rest of the people in the theater.

The summer after high school I spent virtually every
day down at the beach in Santa Monica. I had started
body surfing when I was eight, and I always liked being in the ocean. I liked the challenge of the waves—

overcoming the fear of something I was scared to do. Those were the days, that summer, when there was good surf almost every day. That was also the summer that the big Vietnamese build-up first got started, and I spent a lot of time figuring out how to avoid the draft.

I went to Santa Monica City College in the fall and got a student deferment. In that first semester I used to go back to Palisades occasionally for Sports Nights, and one time in November I met Mary there. I actually met my wife at a Pali Sports Night! We started dating right away. She was a tenth grader, and I was three years older than her at the time. In fact, I'm still three years older than her at this time.

After five semesters at City College I decided to transfer to Valley State. The expenses of going out of town were so astronomical, and I liked living in the Palisades so much, that I figured I might as well finish up there. I majored in public speaking, and at graduation in 1970, they lumped the public-speaking majors together with speech therapy. The person I sat next to was telling me all the fantastic job offers he had because he was in speech therapy. That's what really prompted me to go into that field, so I went back to school to get the specialization. My parents said they would fork over the bread for it. It took me another two and a half years to get through to my credential, and then I was hired by the Board of Education in December of '72. I work with students who have any type of speech, language or hearing disorder.

When I first got the job, I never expected to be teaching at Palisades High. It's the top high school in the city system, without any doubt, and any teacher would jump at the chance to work there. I knew there was already another speech therapist for that area. But the second year I was teaching, this other therapist wanted to work with special kids and he bailed out completely, leaving Palisades a wide-open field. I became the first person in the history of the high school who graduated from Palisades and later came back to work there.

Jeanne Hernandez:
At first it came as something of a shock to be teaching alongside someone who was once a student. I gasped a little—especially with this particular one. I will admit that I was a bit prejudiced. But it turned out that he related to the kids so beautifully that now there's no barrier whatsoever. It's just fine. Jeff's a member of the Establishment, although he does wear the beads, and so forth.

When I first walked into the administration building as a teacher, one of the people in the office asked me for my hall pass. I had to explain. It felt funny going back—walking through halls, into the office as a teacher, reintroducing myself and getting on a first-name basis. I still tend to call my old teachers "mister" instead of by their first names. I'm always being corrected by them.

Unfortunately, one of the gym teachers remembered me from our big fight over hair during high school. For the first six months after I came back he refused to talk to me at all. I would sit at the same table with him in the teachers' cafeteria and say "Hi!" He would actually turn his head and look the other way. The first time he said something to me was when I dropped one of those little cream fillers on the floor. He said, "You'd better pick that up before somebody slips on it." We've still never carried on a real conversation.

The most obvious difference between Pali today and the way it was when we went there is the racial composition. Because of the voluntary busing, the school is almost twenty percent black. They are now serving fried chicken and watermelon in the cafeteria! Truthfully, I think the busing is a good idea. It enables the upper-middle-class Palisadian to get involved with people from a different income level.

There are no dress codes at school today, and about half the guys have beards or long hair. A lot of the girls tend to lay back too much and look very much like slobs. I had one girl who was coming in wearing a very low-cut sweater. Like almost down to her belly-button. And wearing no bra. Actually, she was hanging just about completely out. She'd stick around after the bell rang, and she'd be in there alone with me. I'd say, "I've got to go and meet someone now." But she'd sit there and lean forward so her sweater would open and expose her boobs. She kept doing this for a whole semester. Finally I had to talk to the administration about it. I like my job too much to chance losing it over some sort of over-night relationship with a high school girl. But any male would be tempted to look. I've spoken to a number of teachers who have had this sort of problem where they are approached by a girl student. Or get calls, as I have gotten them, at two o'clock in the morning. It's good for the ego, naturally. But everyone I've spoken to has been smart enough to avoid any involvement.

If I had to choose, I'd rather go to high school when we did than go back as a student today. In our time a lot of things were a challenge. The bit with long hair was a real challenge that I enjoyed. Even the idea of avoiding the draft was a big challenge for me. There's no draft today. Breaking down the resistance of the opposite sex so they'd do what you wanted—that was a much bigger challenge when we went to school.

It's hard to say if the kids today are having a lot of fun. I think they're maturing faster because of all the freedom that is thrown upon them. There's a lot of dope floating around. I know that they don't go to the Bay Theatre. There's no more Sports Nights. The dances that I've seen, nobody dances.

Times are tougher now. It's harder to get a job. The kids in high school feel that. I always talk with my students and ask them what their plans are. Every one of those students has some sort of plan and some sort of goal set up. I have a lot of kids whose parents have been laid off work. They know that they've got to go out and face the world, and what it's really like. I don't think we had the problem when we were seniors.

I'd say that the whole country has lost some of its innocence. When we went to school, Kennedy was probably one of the biggest heroes. We had the Beatles and the Rolling Stones. Today the big hero is Superfly. It's a very different thing.

A lot of people from our class had a very tough time. I think some of them just peaked too early. They were trying so hard to achieve that number-one status in high school. By the time they got rolling into college, they had probably burned themselves out.

I never had that problem. I graduated way down in our class, and never felt the pressure that other people felt. I could never have pictured myself going back to Palisades to teach. I never had any desire! But once I started teaching, I was happy to be back at the old school. I enjoy it very much, although I still consider myself to be somewhat rebellious and hope to continue to stand up for what I feel is right.

•

Jeff's wife and children came in from the patio, where they had been enjoying the summer sunshine, and joined us in the living room. Mary Stolper is a dark-haired beauty nearly six feet tall. Tanned and lithe in her white bikini, she was every inch a high school surfer's dream, and did not seem old enough to be the mother of two daughters. A Palisades graduate herself, Mary knew nearly as much about the class of '65 as Jeff did. We sat down together and went over several scrapbooks and boxes of old photographs. Jeff suggested a whole list of names for inclusion in our book, but he was particularly insistent that we contact Jon Wilson.

"Jon who?" we asked. "We didn't know any Jon Wilson in the class of '65."

"Jon was there," Jeff told us, "he was just the quiet type. You should go up and see him, even if no one remembers who he was. You can take my word for it, he has an amazing story."

•

Jon Wilson: Jon Who?

•

Donald Golden:
Jon Wilson? I don't think there was anybody by that name at Palisades High School.

Anita Champion:
Wasn't he a friend of Jeff Stolper's?

Lisa Menzies:
Who?

Lee Grossman:
Jon Wilson? He looked ordinary. He had an average haircut. He was average size—he was either big or

small. His hair color was either light or dark. He may have worn glasses. He was a muscular guy. I think he might have been a shot-putter.

Gary Wasserman:
He never fit in with the people I ran around with.

Jamie Kelso:
He was a Palisadian. A real Palisadian from the WASP end of town.

Reilly Ridgell:
He was big, quiet, and liked to play football. That's about it.

Mike Shedlin:
One time at Sports Night I was a little too drunk, and the teachers were going to come down on me. I was out there flailing around on the dance floor when a big guy sort of picked me up, held me against a wall and said, "You're too drunk." It was Jon Wilson. He was trying to help me. I thought it was a very decent thing for him to do.

Jeff Stolper:
Jon was one of the few guys you could count on for just anything. Extremely dependable. Extremely level-headed. But I definitely think he was very horny. He was always looking for a girl. I think he still is.

His parents were quite conservative. Typical Palisades Republicans. Mostly, Jon was interested in girls and sports. A typical kind of high school guy. He had a big, high forehead and there was usually a little curl on it, so he had a resemblance to Charlie Brown. We used to kid him about it. He was an average guy, but very likable. He wasn't plastic. He wasn't phony at all.

●

To see Jon Wilson, we drove all the way up to Santa Rosa—a dusty farming community about fifty miles north of San Francisco. He was living in a small white ticky-tacky house on the Mexican side of town. The crowd of children playing ball in the street scattered as we pulled up.

We found Jon Wilson to be a slow-moving, muscular man whose sandy hair was thinning notably. He wore purple-tinted wire-rim glasses which hid any traces of emotion in his eyes. Having recently been released from prison, he seemed to take great joy in simple pleasures, like sitting back in his easy chair in stockinged feet, and sipping can after can of chilled Coors beer. He settled himself so that the afternoon sun poured in over his face, and narrowed his eyes as he tried to bring back the past.

●

In high school, I used to walk home after school and make excuses to get my mother's car. I'd ask if she needed anything at the market, or tell her I had to go to the library or something. Then I'd take the car and race around town. I pretended I had a stick shift—it was a big Pontiac—and I'd go over and get this friend of mine who could get his parents' car—a big Chevy—and we used to race up and down the streets and drive all over the Palisades.

I also spent a lot of time in the hobby shop in the Palisades. It was a really nice hobby shop. They had models, they had train sets, they had plaques, they had all sorts of things to do. I knew the people that ran it, and they used to call me Will—which was short for Wilson. I'd spend my Friday nights in there because they were open till nine. If they needed any little thing done, I'd do it for free because I liked to hang around there, because there were always new things, there was novelty, and the people were nice.

When we lived in the Palisades my father had Wilson Realty. He's still in the real estate field but he's government-employed now. I had an uncle who was a good friend of Richard Nixon's, and worked on his campaign for several years.

I remember one semester in high school I got five D's and one F on my report card, and I was ashamed to take it home to my parents. My father was really smart. He had skipped a grade in school, and they were always pressuring me about school, so I forged their signature without ever showing it to them. I would have gotten in a lot of trouble if they had seen those grades.

When I graduated from Palisades I didn't know what I was going to do. I figured that I'd probably get drafted somewhere along the line, but I knew that if I didn't want to be drafted I had to go to college. I wasn't that good a student in high school, but I signed up for the junior college in Santa Monica and went for a year. I had no real plans. I didn't know what I wanted. I was living at home, only fifteen minutes from the school. At this point I was getting I-A notices from the Army, so I went down and talked to them and they told me that I'd be drafted very soon. So I quit college. I didn't go back in September, and then January third I got drafted.

I was nineteen at the time. I didn't look forward to the Army, but I didn't dread it. When I was growing up I used to have dreams about myself as a soldier. I would watch John Wayne and Audie Murphy movies and identify myself in that position. I identified with heroes. So I wasn't against going.

My parents thought I was doing the right thing. I was drafted and I was going, just like my father did in World War II. On the other hand, I think they hated to see their son leave home. This was the first time I had left home. My mother is very emotional. She cried. My parents took me down to the draft board that morning when I left.

That afternoon they put me on a bus that took us

all the way up to Fort Ord. Once we got there, the first thing I remember is this big sergeant getting on the bus and telling us: "From now on I'm your mother, and I'm your father, and you're going to do everything I say. If I tell you to shit, you ask me how much; if I tell you to jump, you ask me how far." And then he said, "You've got exactly five seconds to get off this fuckin' bus. Move out!"

And it was scary. I didn't know anybody there. I was young. I wasn't used to being away from home. I didn't really know what I was getting into. I was at Fort Ord for the rest of basic training. In basic they all put up the hard-ass image. They yell at you. Discipline is what you're supposed to do. Then when you're through, the next step is advanced training.

At that time the Vietnam war was at a high. It was 1967. So they sent me down to Jungle School in Louisiana. That was essentially training for Vietnam. They had mock-up Vietnamese villages, and they had a very nice swamp down there which was probably thicker than any of the swamps in Southeast Asia. After Jungle School I had thirty days' leave, and then I was to report to Oakland for shipment to Vietnam.

Jeff Stolper:
I saw Jon when he was home on leave. We got together the day before he was shipped out to Vietnam. That was over at his parents' house. It was actually very quiet. We were all sitting around in the living room and Jon was still able to joke about it. He looked as if he had accepted it. He knew what he was in for by going over to Vietnam. At least he said that he knew what he was in for.

It wasn't so much that I wanted to be a hero. But I had an image of myself as a man. I wanted to be a man. I didn't want to show that I was afraid of anything. I didn't want to be afraid to go over there. I felt like I could deal with it.

I remember the morning we flew to Vietnam. I remember seeing the water underneath me and then suddenly I saw land. At the point where the water stopped I saw green, solid green all the way up to the airstrip, which had red mud all around it. But it was just green jungle, *so* thick. From the air base they took us in a bus over to some barracks. We could see mountains off in the distance about a mile away.

After about a week they shipped us out to our units. They flew us by helicopter and dropped us right in the middle of the jungle. I was in the jungle for six months after that without a break.

The routine in the jungle was just boring most of the time. You march single file through fairly thick jungle looking for tracks, looking for old campsites— whatever you can find. If nothing happens, then at three in the afternoon you find a nice hill, go to the top of it, dig holes in the ground and make camp. The next morning you break up the camp and start all over again.

For the first six weeks nothing happened, so naturally we started getting really lax. We would make our bunkers at night, but we didn't really think we would ever use them. We were actually itching for a fight, 'cause all we did was walk around all day, and do the same thing day after day. We thought we wanted action.

I remember lying in bed about ten o'clock one night, and I was still up because I didn't feel well. All of a sudden I heard about six mortars going off about three hundred yards away, and I remember someone yelling *"Mortar!"* Then I heard some rifle fire, so immediately I ran out of my tent, grabbed my rifle and got into my bunker. About a half second later the mortar rounds started landing. Immediately a fire fight started and there were bullets flying every which way. There were chaser bullets just whizzing by us and you could hear 'em going by. The bunker next to me had a machine gun in it, so the Vietnamese

135

were shooting directly at that bunker. There were maybe a hundred machine guns and rifles all firing at that one bunker, and the people inside that bunker were yelling. We were doing whatever we could. We were shooting almost directly in front of us, a little to the left where we saw flashes from guns. They were shooting at us out there, they were throwing hand grenades. One of the men in my squad panicked. Your natural instinct from training is to fire, but if you're really scared, then you're not concentrating enough to aim your gun and you're just firing into the air. We had one man that was doing that, but we finally got him straightened out. He was in a daze like the rest of us. We were just doing whatever we could. There was a tank in back of us, and I remember people yelling for some guys to get in the tank and shoot. But the tank people were afraid, it was the first time we'd made any contact. One mortar shell hit the ammunition bunker and it blew up—with flames shooting about three hundred feet in the air. Finally our people got into their tank and started shooting out into the jungle. We kept getting return fire for a while, but after half an hour the helicopters flew in and started shooting into those bushes. Then a little while later it all stopped.

I didn't really see anything till the next morning. I was on the detail that had to go into the bushes we had been firing into and drag out the bodies. Some were dead and some weren't. We hauled about thirty North Vietnamese soldiers out of the bushes, but we knew there had been a lot more because of the amount of fire. I was assigned to following the trail and finding the others. I took about ten men, because I was a squad leader, and all along the trail we were finding blood and pieces of intestine and things like this. The blood wasn't dry yet, so we knew they had left an hour or two earlier. But we were getting fairly far from camp, so we called up on the radio and they told us to come back. We probably could have intercepted them in another two miles.

The whole time I had thought I would be ready for all this when it happened, but I didn't like seeing people blown up, particularly American soldiers. We intended to identify the Vietnamese as something less than human. We weren't really dragging humans out of the bushes. We were dragging—Vietnamese. To me what was important was the transition in my mind. I found that I wasn't a hero. When the firing started I didn't panic, but I didn't want to get up and charge like they do on TV, like John Wayne and Audie Murphy do. I was concerned about my life. I was scared, and everybody was scared. And eventually I saw a few of my good friends die. I saw that we would go into areas where there were North Vietnamese soldiers and fight them for days. They would kill twenty percent of us, or whatever, and then we left the area and they still had it. I began to wonder why the people died, what good it was doing. They still had the same piece of land. Even if we went in and overran an area, they'd come back again after we left. All these people would be dead and I couldn't see that it was getting anywhere.

After I'd been in the jungle for about four months we went into a village. As we came in, a couple of people drove up on little motor scooters and asked if we wanted to buy drugs or if we wanted to get laid. At this point we had a new captain, trained at West Point, who was very gung ho. You expected to see him with his sword at the beginning of a cavalry charge. So he told us not to fraternize with the natives —that was his order. But of course we all wanted to get laid, so about six of us went into the bushes and paid three dollars each and we got laid. Then we left that village and went back into the jungle.

About three days later I came down with the clap. I went to the medic and told him I needed treatment, and he went straight to the captain. The captain told me he wanted to make an example of me. He had ordered us not to fraternize and I guess fornicating was fraternizing. He told me I could choose either a court-martial or an Article 15. In a court-martial, they can actually pronounce a death penalty or they can send you to jail, but usually if you sign the papers for an Article 15, they just bust you and fine you. So I finally signed the paper. Then they busted me—they fined me four hundred dollars and took away my stripe. That was an expensive piece of ass!

After you've been in Vietnam for six months you get on R & R—Rest and Recuperation. They send you some place like Hong Kong or Tokyo, and you have seven days to enjoy yourself. When it came to be my time, people had already taken a lot of the other cities, so I signed up for Taipei. On the way out I went through base camp and got held up. It just happened to be Christmas time and Bob Hope was in Vietnam. So they forced a certain amount of people to go see Bob Hope. I didn't want to see Bob Hope but they told me, "You're new and you have to go. Here's a pressed and washed uniform, and you're gonna go." Raquel Welch was there that year and I was only interested in looking at her and some of the lady dancers. Hope himself wasn't funny at all.

Then finally I got to Taipei, and the first thing I did was check into my hotel. Right away a guy came up to my room with a briefcase and said, "Do you need underwear, do you need any belts, do you need a wallet?"

I said, "No."

He said, "Okay, do you need any girls?"

I said, "Yeah!"

He said, "Okay, just pick out the one you want."

So I took a shower and changed. There was a bar downstairs in the hotel. I walked down to the bar and looked at all the girls on the way down. They were sitting on the stairs—all these Chinese ladies with mini-skirts and low-cut tops and their hair down, and they looked really good. I found the one I wanted and we went down to the bar. Then I went behind the bar and signed a contract for her. Prostitution is illegal in Taipei, so officially these girls are hostesses. So I paid fifteen dollars a day for her to be hostess.

In Vietnam, of course, there are whorehouses all over the country. But they are the wham-bam-thank-you-ma'am model whorehouse, where you go in and get your rocks off and then you go out. I've been in other houses since then—in Istanbul, and one in Germany. But Taipei has it over all of them because there they treat you like a virile man and they really want to please you. They really do.

So my lady and I went out to eat, we went out to clubs, we went back to the hotel and we made love. We did just everything together, twenty-four hours a day for four days.

A lot of my friends were getting a different girl every day—that was the thing to do if you were a stud. We were in the Army and we were infantrymen and we were supposed to be studs, so I felt really guilty about being with the same girl. I really liked her, though. Still, I wanted to get some variety so I could talk about it when I got back. I told her that I couldn't be with her any more. She cried and made a big scene, but I finally took her back to her bar and went out and got another one.

After seven days they sent me back to Vietnam. I remember I felt like crying on the plane on the way back. The first girl that I'd been with had been telling me that I shouldn't go back, that her father had this farm out in the country and they would never find me. I remember thinking about it, but I was too chicken to do it. So I went back to the jungle, even though I knew I had six months before I could go home.

•

Jon excused himself to make a short trip to the bathroom; his beer consumption was taking its inevitable toll. While he was gone a freight train passed nearby with a mournful howl, rattling the thin walls of the little house. It was late afternoon of a hot, bright day. When Jon returned to his chair he sighed, folded his arms across his chest and continued his story.

•

I'll never forget the day I finally left Vietnam. I'd been in the battle zone for a year, had a gun for a year, had a knife for a year, had hand grenades for a year. Then the day you leave they take it all away from you. They took us in a big truck to the Air Force base which is about five miles away, across the city of Pleiku. We had no weapons and we were sitting in the back of this big truck. I remember thinking, This is my last day and they're going to get me today. I don't have a gun or a hand grenade. I don't even have a *knife!* I was scared and everybody else was scared in the truck. We were pretty silent, just driving along this road.

When they flew me back to the States, I still had six months in the Army left to go. They sent me to Texas and put me on riot-control training. They were training us to fight against the hippies, who were supposed to be rioting. I felt pretty disillusioned with the Army at this point, and I was beginning to have some strong feelings about the war. All the men we sent over there were wasted. All the money we put in was wasted, because we didn't have a chance to win. We shouldn't have been there at all. I realize that now.

We were trained to think of the Communists as animals. But I saw several of them—I was in on a couple of captures. And they weren't animals—they were men. They looked just like the men I saw when I went to Taipei. They were Oriental, they were soldiers like me. They were scared like me. And they didn't know what was going on—like me. That's the way I felt about it.

I came home in December of '68, getting out twelve days early because of Christmas. Back in Los Angeles I had to move in with my parents again. They thought of me as their son the hero, who had gone off and done his duty.

By the time I got home, the hippie generation was pretty much in full swing. All my friends had changed. People were turning on. People were getting loose. I came home and all my friends had long hair, they looked like hippies and they had glazed eyes. They were smoking pot, getting loaded constantly. They were tripping out. I had come home as a soldier with short hair. I still had a lot of redneck thoughts, and I looked like a redneck.

I had only smoked dope once in the Army, but I couldn't enjoy it because I was so paranoid. When I got back I started getting into it. I started thinking, Well, everyone I know is doing it. It can't be all that bad. So I started getting loaded regularly, and not letting my parents know. I was still living at home. The more I got loaded, the more I started thinking, and the more I started thinking, the more I hated the Army, hated having been over there at all.

At this point I thought I should go back to school. I didn't really know what I wanted to do, but I knew it was good to have an education, so I went back to Santa Monica City College. I enjoyed the classes, but the school was like an advanced stage of Pali High—a very social school. Then when my parents moved, I got my own place in Santa Monica and really became loose because I could do whatever I wanted. I took different drugs. I took mescaline, I took LSD. I tried jimson weed. I did cocaine.

I quit school because I still didn't know what I wanted to do, and I felt like I was wasting my time. So I started just hanging out. I got on unemployment.

I happened to know some people who told me where to get dope in bigger volume. I found out that rather than buy a lid every week, I could buy five lids and sell them and then get a lid of my own with the profit I made. It kept going and going until pretty soon I was selling a pound of weed every month. I also did a little dealing in cocaine. After getting out of the Army, I'd noticed that I was different from my friends. A year and a half later I was accepted. Not only was I accepted—people enjoyed my company. I had long hair and wire-rim glasses. I was a freak like everybody else.

Then along came this guy with a scheme for smuggling hashish out of Lebanon. He'd made the trip three times before and gotten a lot of money out of it. He was twenty-four, my age. He told me it was easy and there were hardly any risks involved. We got to be friends. He wanted me and another guy to meet him in Lebanon. He'd put up all the money and make all the arrangements—all we had to do was pick up the hashish, put it on our bodies, and leave. If everything worked out, we'd get a free trip to Lebanon plus seven thousand dollars each. The guy who set up the deal stood to make about three times that. So I went from this small-time marijuana pusher to an international hashish smuggler!

We flew into Lebanon and made the connection with our guy. We got hashish oil, because it's more concentrated and you get more money for it. The oil came in sealed plastic bags, about an inch thick. It was flat and you could bend it. So I put one bag on my stomach, a bag on each side, and then a big piece in the back. Then I put an Ace bandage around the whole thing.

We made reservations for the next morning on Pan Am flight 1. We had been with Pan Am before, and because it's an American airline, they normally don't frisk people. They just send them through the metal detector. If you have any metal on you, then they search you. Naturally, we took all the metal out of our pockets, and we didn't wear belts or anything. I was wearing a special jacket I had bought, a big jacket that was supposed to hide the extra weight I had on. I also had a big pair of pants. And we took some Valium so we wouldn't look nervous when we got on the plane; I took two Valium.

The third guy, who had set up the whole deal, drove us out to the airport. He told us not to worry, but at this point I felt bad. The packets of hash oil weren't as thin as they were supposed to be. I ended up looking really heavy with it strapped around my chest, and I could barely breathe and I could barely move with it on. But even if we got caught, our guy said he knew people in high places and he could get us out right away. He told us the only penalty was a fine and you could pay people off and it was no big thing.

We got to the airport, checked into customs, and went downstairs in the waiting area of Pan Am. Then they called our flight. Everyone got in line in front of the security booth and they started sending people through the metal detectors. I was about the tenth person in line. They were searching everyone after they went through the metal detector. I was thinking, Maybe all these people had metal in their pockets. So I went through, anyway—and they searched me. The guard put his hand right on the hash. He said, "What's this?"

I tried to tell him that it was a bandage, that I'd crashed water-skiing, but immediately he called over two other guards and they took me into a side room. They started interrogating me. They kept asking, where were my bags? I told them I didn't have any bags. We had made the mistake of going up to the check-in counter together, and putting both claim checks on my friend's airline ticket. I didn't say anything because I didn't want to bust him.

Then they started asking, "Where's your friend?" I said, "I don't have any friend."

They looked on the flight list and saw who had the seat next to me and started paging him on the plane. He knew that they had busted me, so when he heard his seat number being paged he ran into the bathroom and tried to rip the stuff off him. He had spent four hours putting it on! He couldn't get it off. He got half of it off and tried to stuff it down the disposal unit in the bathroom of the plane, but you can't get anything down there. He finally went back to his seat. They kept calling his name over the airplane intercom. They held the plane over. They sent a jeep out with flashing red lights and guys with machine guns, and they surrounded him.

After they had been interrogating me for about twenty minutes, I saw him come walking up the stairs. He had finally turned himself in. Some of it was still on his body and he told them the rest was in the bathroom.

They sent us to several different jails for processing, and then to a great big main jail. They put us in a cement cell, about sixty feet by twenty feet. There were forty people living in that room. We got two blankets per person and we all slept on the cement floor. There was one toilet for everybody, which was just a hole in the floor. There were three barred windows, twelve feet off the ground, and a solid-steel door. I stayed in that room for seven months, until I went to trial.

When I first got in there I really had a hard time. I was sick a lot and I couldn't settle down. I kept thinking that this third guy would get us out with all his influence and all his money. Actually, as soon as he saw that we were busted he flew back to the States. He went over to my apartment in LA and took out all the dope I had lying around. He sold it, and made good money off it. I guess he felt like I owed him something because I'd gotten busted carrying *his* dope.

My parents were pretty much helpless back in the

States. When we went to court there was supposed to be a public defender, but there wasn't. The trial was all in Arabic. There was one man in the audience that spoke a little English, and they called him up to be interpreter. They asked us about four questions, and the whole trial lasted maybe five minutes. We were sentenced to three years.

After I'd been in jail for a while, I decided I'd better make the most of it. So I started reading. I read anything I could get my hands on. There was a small library in the room because so many people had been given books. The first book I read in there, which was really the first book I'd read in years, was *The New Centurions*. I kept a journal and kept count of all the books I read. I read one hundred and thirty different books, most of them twice. Science fiction, novels, I even read an English textbook. It was better to read something than to sit there all day. They had nothing for us to do.

For a while they put me in a room where no one spoke English, there were no English books, and nothing to do. I was pretty spaced out. I had stomach disorders for several months. Occasionally there was a doctor that came around, and he kept trying different pills on me. I had a form of diarrhea for a long time. I had a skin disease. Bubbles would break out on my skin—I was in a cell where there was no sun at all. I had a lot of colds, and I got tonsilitis once. At this point, I remember writing in my journal that I'd rather be back at war. To me, the jail experience was much worse than the war.

I actually got out after a year and a half. After you've been in Lebanon for eighteen months, if you're a foreigner, you can apply for an amnesty. It's just a matter of routine—a matter of paying off the right people. The Lebanese government is so corrupt! It's really a screwed-up place.

When I came home, I got a lot of weird reactions

from people. I had a girl that I'd never actually slept with but that was a good friend of mine. When I was in jail she started writing me nice letters, and saying, "When are you coming home? I can't wait to see you." So she let me move in with her for a while, but I don't think she was ready for the state I was in. I hadn't been with a woman in twenty months, so I was very emotional, and she didn't understand me. She didn't expect that I'd be that different from the way I was before I left. So I moved out of there after about a week and got a job and went to work.

I worked making tables—hardwood tables and bars. That's the same job I'm doing this summer. I've always been a pretty good carpenter, and I happened to know this person who was doing that, so I started out working for him.

●

Jon showed us one of the tables that he had built: it was circular, sturdy and simple. He was proud of his handiwork.

●

At the same time that I started working, I got in an application to Sonoma State. I knew at this point that I needed some structure in my life, and that school was a good structure. When I'm in school I get the GI Bill, which comes to $270 a month. I came up here to go to school because I was too paranoid to be around a lot of people; the thought of being in the city upset me. If I go to school for another year and a half, I could probably graduate, but I'm not sure I'm going back after this summer.

I get the feeling that somewhere along the line I'm going to make money. Right now I'm not really sure what I'm going to do, but I think I have the potential to make money if I can find the right field.

I don't smoke dope nearly as much as I used to. If

I smoke, I get into a weird frame of mine where I start getting remorseful. I always wonder what would have happened to me if I hadn't gotten drafted, if I would have gone through the hippie generation at the same time my other friends did. Maybe things would have been easier and I wouldn't have had to waste a year and a half in jail. If I had it to do over again, I wouldn't go into the Army, and I wouldn't have anything to do with dope.

I enjoy things more now. Whenever I have bad times, they don't seem so bad because I have worse times I can think back on. I have the diary that I kept in jail. If I feel really bad, I go to my diary and look up where I was a year ago today. When I see that, I think, Why should I feel bad? I'm a lot better off.

I enjoy being with friends, particularly ladies. I enjoy making love. I enjoy being happy. One thing I learned from Vietnam and jail is that when things are taken away from you, you really start appreciating them. For a year and a half I didn't see the sun. Today I can go outside and be in it all day long, and I love it. I can walk out this door and do whatever I want.

When I was in jail, reminiscing was pretty much what kept me going. I'd reminisce about high school, about being with girls, sexual experiences . . . When you don't want to deal with the present, you think about the pleasant things in the past. I'd think about Sports Night, because even though I didn't score, it was always a big social activity, with a lot of energy flowing. I'd think about track, how neat it was to be in the track meets, and about the football games.

A lot of the times I felt out of it in high school. I wasn't good-looking. I wasn't a real good athlete. I wanted to be both. All the girls—Suzanne Thomas and the others—I wanted them to like me. I wanted to go out with them. I wanted to hang out with the big-shot guys. I couldn't because I was in a different social position. That's what I wanted at the time, but it's interesting now to see how people turned out. The people that were in the Saracens and all are now no different than the people that nobody liked. Everybody turns out different and everybody is into his own trip.

•

In the conversation after the interview we were able to satisfy Jon's curiosity about a large number of his high school classmates. He seemed surprised to learn that so many members of the class of '65 had been arrested at one time or another on narcotics charges. We had begun to compile a partial list, and that list already contained more than forty names. One of the people on that list was Candy McCoy, and her experience had been very different from Jon Wilson's.

•

Candy McCoy: The Flirt

•

Time *magazine, January 29, 1965:*

"You can't marry anyone important without going to college," says Candace McCoy, a Pali senior whose looks suggest the Mona Lisa melded with Gidget. "But there is more to it than that. I don't want to go through life uneducated." Her father, an aerospace engineer, "is always on my back about grades," but "mother just gave up on me about six years ago and

148

decided I was destined to enjoy life, nothing more."
Twice a week Candy dates basketball players, her
way of steering between tribal obligations to the social elite and a "guilty" attraction for intellectuals
("They are so worthwhile"). The specific attraction
is Jamie Kelso, 16, a skinny near genius who studies
only those subjects that interest him, mostly political
science and history.

Jamie Kelso:

I never knew Candy at all except in class, and was
mortified when *Time* magazine informed the world that
there was a romance between us. Candy was beautiful.
Every teacher's pet. She was so far beyond my range
that I never even entertained the thought. Girls like
that were the special preserve of the Romeos. She was
the number-one choice of all the eager-beaver, go-
getter boys, with whom I couldn't possibly compete.

Lynn Marble:

I remember that I was quite jealous of Candy McCoy.
She seemed to represent everything which perhaps I
should strive for but really didn't want to. I thought she
was pretty. I remember her complexion and her coloring particularly. Yet there was an aggressiveness about
Candy which I didn't like.

Reilly Ridgell:

What comes to mind is that old going-steady, switching-
around, "dating game" type thing—that's my memory
of her.

Lee Grossman:

She was the most notorious flirt in the class, but my
main recollections of Candy all go back to the *Time*
magazine article about our high school. She was so excited by the fact that *Time* was doing the story that she
went out of her way to be cooperative with the reporters, to set up interviews and to make contacts for them.

She, probably more than anybody else, was involved in doing that. When the article came out, it was quite a blow to her. She took it very badly, as well she should have.

Judy Tomash:
To me, she was a social climber. She did this surveillance job on all the groups in school, chose the ones she wanted to belong to, and then worked to become part of them. I think she was very intelligent, and somewhat embarrassed by the fact that she was that smart. I just remember her being sort of a snob, and I could never quite trust her. She would be my friend one day, and then the next day everything would change. I can remember her dancing at that party we had before I went away to Brazil. She was really liking the boys and being very flirtatious, but not at all honest with them.

Jeff Stolper:
We had an old joke, some of the boys that knew her: "You want a piece of Candy?" Reddish hair, kind of short. Kind of cute. She'd dig going out with a lot of guys. She seemed like she enjoyed life and living. I would tend to think that she's probably married now and maybe has a family.

•

After a few miles of winding mountain roads we found our way to the secluded home in Beverly Glen Canyon where Candy McCoy lives alone. We arrived for our interview precisely on time, but when we knocked on the front door there was no answer. Meanwhile Candy's big Labrador proved notably ineffective as a watchdog: he came bounding up from behind the house, licked our hands thoroughly, then lay down to wait with us until Candy arrived. As the sun went down behind the hills, we walked over to a large window and looked into Candy's living room. The house was fashionably furnished, with a brick fireplace and a huge tropical-fish tank. Adjoining the living room was a sun porch, crowded with a jungle of thriving house plants. Our view of Candy's living space offered evidence of a hectic and high-pressure existence:

After we had been waiting for about forty minutes, Candy roared up the driveway in her blue Citroën, muttering her apologies. She told us she had been delayed at the office and emerged from the car with a briefcase and an armload of papers. She wore pink-tinted glasses and an elegantly tailored green pants suit. Though she seemed exhausted from her day at work, Candy found the energy to feed her dog and to prepare gin and tonics as a token of hospitality. She told us she had become semiprofessional in preparing this particular refreshment during "one long hot summer in Boston." She carefully wiped a lime slice along the rim of each glass before dropping it into the drink. We asked Candy if she had been an experienced drinker while still in high school; she laughed and recalled her own innocence.

•

Whatever other people's recollections are, I remember myself as being really straight. The only time I ever got drunk on a date was the time I had cramps and my dad gave me a Bloody Mary before I went out. That got me totally drunk.

My state of consciousness when I was in high school was so incredibly low that I didn't have any aspirations. I was pretty happy with my life. I never thought about the future. I didn't fantasize about it at all. I can remember distinctly in the seventh grade looking at myself in the mirror for a long time one day and wondering what I was going to look like. That was the extent of my thinking about the future. It was always assumed that I would get married as my mother had.

I had a lot of nice clothes, and I used to love hanging around with my two best girl friends. We used to go to Jack-In-The-Box for hamburgers all the time. It was always important for me to have a date, but I don't remember any relationships that had any meaning at all. No depth whatsoever. Because I flirted all the time, I'm sure I promised things that I didn't deliver.

I had cars. My dad started acquiring cars for me through various means when I was sixteen. I had a Jaguar XK 150, a beat up old red beautiful sports car. For a while I had a TR-4. I had a red MGB for a while. My dad had a Porsche and an Avanti, so he used to give me those for extended periods of time.

I remember I got a D in chemistry my junior year. My father got real angry with me because I wasn't going to get into a good college. That was sort of the first time we came to grips on that issue. I sort of said, "Well, I could go to City College or UCLA or something." My father used to call them "Pali High with Ashtrays." He wanted me to go to a big school back East.

When the time came, I got into Mount Holyoke because of my college boards. I test abnormally well. I had an 800 on the English—which is the highest score possible—so it didn't matter that I graduated far down in our high school class.

So I went off to college in Massachusetts, not having any idea what to expect. As it turned out, Mount Holyoke was the most deadening academic experience that I have ever had in my life. If I went into it knowing nothing, I came out of it even stupider. That school was such a fraud, it's hard to believe. My subsequent experience at UCLA and Harvard made that abundantly clear to me.

Socially I was just a total smash from the beginning. I found myself to be the fulfillment of every East Coast man's fantasy—the classic fantasy of the California Girl. I was hot property, and even as a freshman I could go out with seniors with fancy cars and stuff.

But after a few months of dating fraternity men, I decided I had enough. At that point I got into being as degenerate as I possibly could with my limited understanding of how to do that. I wanted to smoke dope, but I didn't know anyone who smoked dope. So at first I drank a lot of cough syrup—that kind of thing. The Beatles had been my first introduction to an attraction to hippies, and once I was in college I really got into that. Back in '65 and '66, smoking dope and having long hair were real badges of friendship.

About this time I got very hung up on my roommate. Very, very involved with her. Physical attraction was part of it, but the relationship was never consummated in any way. We had a lot of trouble because we would be jealous of each other and we didn't understand what we were doing. We certainly didn't have any assistance from the outside world in telling us what we were feeling for each other. Then I started going out fairly seriously with a guy from Amherst. As far as my roommate was concerned, I had left her, and that was that.

During Christmas vacation of junior year I was driving to New York with one of my best friends. On the way down we were smoking dope in a water pipe with sherry in it. We were just so excited and completely pleased with ourselves. We were going to have a week in New York and then fly home to California. My friend was driving down Interstate 91 and it was like three o'clock in the afternoon and kind of drizzly. We were coming into Hartford, Connecticut, over a railroad bridge when the car in front of us jammed on his brakes and we jammed on our brakes. We were driving a '56 Oldsmobile named Babe the Blue Ox, and the car started to spin. We started to careen back and forth from railing to railing, which totaled the car without smashing into anything. Just battering. We came to rest. I rubbed my head and looked around me and all there was anywhere I could see was dope things: water pipes, papers, dope, sherry. We were even underage to have the sherry! I had bumped my head and was bleeding so I wasn't in too great shape. I started saying, "We've got to get rid of the dope." I was a little spaced out.

Anyway, I grabbed the paper bag that was lying on the seat and started throwing in everything that I could see that looked incriminating. I got about a quarter of it. I had the dope and I had the sherry—that was the main thing. Then I got out of the car. By this time there were people everywhere. I walked to the other end of this bridge, I was maybe a hundred feet from everybody else, and I leaned over and let this bag drop off the edge of the bridge onto the snow and all the garbage. I went back and everything was fine. The cops came, and they were going to take us down to the station and have us fill out an accident report, and then they were going to take us to the airport. That was going to be that. As we were riding back to the station a call came over the radio about how someone had seen someone drop a bag off the bridge and there was a suspicious substance in it, and so on and so forth. The officer driving us turned around and said, "Hey, you know anything about a bag?" I said, "Who, me?" But it turned out that when I put the dope inside the bag I hadn't looked to see what was already there. One of the things was a Christmas card with my friend's name and address on it, just in case anyone had any doubt who the dope belonged to.

We paid fifteen hundred dollars to get a lawyer who was a former DA and was supposed to have wonderful court relations. We were charged with a felony, but our lawyer copped the plea to a misdemeanor. We got off with a fifty-dollar fine.

But we still got thrown out of Mount Holyoke. We were told to leave campus even before our trial. The president of Mount Holyoke made it very clear that he wanted nothing to do with us, and he also wanted to fix it so we could never get in anywhere else. He wanted to make us an example.

That winter when I came back to California was

one of the low points of my life. I couldn't get a job anywhere. The post office wouldn't even grade my civil-service exam because of my record. I finally got a job at the phone company as an information operator. I was an information operator for most of the next year.

Basically, I felt freaked out and totally abandoned. I had no idea that my own life was in any way in my control. I couldn't handle it and I felt that I was a complete failure. I decided that I was going to put my life in someone else's hands. I went East to my brother's wedding, and I took up with one of the ushers. He was on his way to St. Johnsbury in northern Vermont, where he had a teaching job. I went up there to live with him. We had to pretend we were married because it was a very straight town. The whole thing was obviously a mistake from the moment I got there. Then when the snows came, I got freaked out that I was going to get trapped there, so I got into my car and came back to California.

It was shortly after that that my father died. He and my mother had separated while I was at Mount Holyoke, and he was living in an apartment by himself. When he didn't show up at work for about a week, his best buddy in the office went out to look for him. He found him in the apartment—he had been bleeding for a week. He was obviously unconscious some of the time because there was blood in a lot of places in the apartment. He had a sliding glass door in his bedroom with a curtain by it. Blood was soaked up into the curtain for about eighteen inches. The phone was off the hook. I can't really imagine what condition he was in if he was able to get around the apartment like that but not in any way get help for himself. He spent a week like that. By the time they found him he was still alive, but his brain was totally full of blood. Even if he lived, he would never have been able to think again. He was in the hospital another week before he died. All the evidence in his case indicated a murder, but the police don't even have a clue. It's still a totally unsolved crime.

Mostly, his death was a numbing experience for me. I've still never been able to cry about it. It's just one of those things I can't really comprehend. It was only two years ago that I stopped thinking that I saw my father on the street.

After he died, I wanted to go back to school. I got into UCLA, and my life started to pick up again. I got seriously interested in English history and I wanted to go to grad school. I studied a lot and had a really good time with my friends.

Before I finished at UCLA, I became really interested in the concept of the Free City that was floating around. It was a new idea to me that everybody could just trade services—instead of using money. We were just going to give what we could and take what we needed, and everything was going to be wonderful. I realized that they didn't really need English-history professors in this free society. So I tried to figure out what I could do that would be useful enough to be exchanged. I just decided that I might as well go to law school. I took the law boards and did pretty well. I applied to Harvard, Yale and UCLA.

When I graduated, I still hadn't heard from the law schools, so I just took off and went to Europe. I traveled around and got into some down-and-out things in a not very serious way. I lived for a while with a fellow with a club foot, and I lived with some Portuguese draft evaders. It was fun. Then I met this really wonderful woman in Paris who had been smuggling dope into England from Morocco. I went with her to Morocco, and then went on to Istanbul.

When we got to Istanbul, there was a letter for me from my mother saying that I had just gotten into Harvard Law School, and what did I want to do about it? I apparently had missed the letter saying I had gotten into UCLA, and never did get the letter saying I was rejected by Yale. I remember standing there in the lobby of the Hilton kind of going, "Well!" I knew I had applied to law schools, but I had forgotten about it. It wasn't part of my plans any more.

But I went back, anyway, and started law school. It was difficult, and I really hadn't thought about it very well before I got there. In the middle I quit. I didn't know what I wanted to do. This fellow that I had met in Istanbul was living in western Massachusetts on a farm, and I lived on that farm for about eight or nine months. During this same period I went through a very unhappy love affair that left me completely devastated. At that point I took up with a woman who nursed me back to health to the point where I could function again. Why she decided to take me on, I'll never know. I was really a basket case when she met me.

There have been several men and several women who have taught me really important things and have given me a lot of love. I've never had a sexual relationship with a woman, but I've certainly had love affairs with women. I always assume that I will have that kind of sexual relationship some day, but it never seems to happen. That's fine. If it's going to happen, it will happen, and that will be fine too. I will say I've heard from a lot of people that I have a reputation for being gay.

Finally I realized that I might as well go back and get it over with. And do it right. The thing that made the rest of law school a great experience was the women's movement, really. It was very exciting and I started working on women's issues and understanding what the women's movement was all about.

I graduated from law school—not without a few other hitches, but yes I finally made it in June of '74. I was working for a while for Legal Aid in Manchester, New Hampshire. I really liked that. If Sam Yorty hadn't been thrown out of office as mayor of Los Angeles, I would probably have stayed there for quite a while. But when the new city government took over in LA, I wanted to come back and be part of it.

I got a good offer from the city attorney's office to work on the policy level, and that's where I am today. My formal title is Director of Personnel. I do the recruiting and certain administrative functions. I'm also a trial deputy. I'm prosecuting. For the last couple of months I've been working in the traffic court as a prosecutor. I handle drunk driving and hit-and-run cases almost exclusively. Within the criminal-justice system, it's the prosecutors who can really do justice. They're the people who can make it work or not.

This is not a happy time for the world at all. The Buddhists say we've got several thousand bad years ahead of us, and it looks that way to me. I would describe myself as a person with Buddhist aspirations. I've always been interested in different religions, and I've been studying Buddhism for the past four years. It's something I'm hoping to understand and integrate, but I feel my own imperfections very heavily.

More and more as I get older my privacy becomes important to me. I don't mind living alone, but the only problem is that I would like to have children. I'm coming to think that I might have to do that on my own. I figure I'd have to do it within the next five years while I'm still young enough.

My basic problem, as is obvious, is that my relationships don't last very long. I've watched a lot of children that I really like go through this whole rip-off syndrome when their parents split up. I sort of feel that if I get married, it's inevitable that my child is going to go through that. Since the chances are so high that there's going to be a separation anyway, I wonder if it isn't better for the child never to have a father to lose.

But when you start talking about a child without a father, all the options are bad. One is to just get randomly pregnant and not ever know who it was. Another is to pick a person and not tell him, because

I should think that for a man it would be a very difficult thing to have a child in the world and not get hung up with it. My problem is that when I think about doing it that way, what I really want to do is just clone myself. I don't want to get a man involved at all.

•

As we listened to this, we had to remind ourselves that this was the same Candy who told *Time* magazine ten years ago that "you can't marry anyone important without going to college." There was no question that she had changed. In fact even her name had undergone a transformation. Candace was now making use of the second half of her first name and was known as "*Dace* McCoy." The new name had a tough, competent ring to it.

•

It's obviously perfect for you to be writing a book about our class, because the changes in the country started just when we started. I came out of high school with no politics at all and I went into college and became more and more aware. The period when the left was more active, when SDS was really active, affected all of us, I think, in the way we lived and what we thought we wanted. Today I've come to the point where I can have nice things and be comfortable without feeling like I'm a traitor. I feel like I am honestly working to make things better. I really do like my life right now. I go through ups and downs and all that, but my feelings about myself are pretty positive.

I think I'm a tremendously lucky person. I really am. Without having any direction or drive to get me some place, I've just kind of gone along and not made any serious mistakes and not committed myself to any of the stupid ideas I've had. My self-destructive instincts are strong on the surface, but very shallow. I've somehow managed to stumble along and get myself to a place where I'm able to make a life that I think is purposeful. I feel now that I'm in control of my life and I'm beginning to have an overview of it. I'm finally beginning to feel that I'm conscious.

Bob Searight: Most Reserved

•

Lee Grossman:
He had a crew cut, braces, and chewed gum. Most of the time he wore his class sweater, which was too big for him. He was a skinny fellow who walked in a slouch. He was good in sports. He turned in all his homework on time. He got good grades. He had a reputation as a nice guy. Actually, he was one of the dullest people in the entire school.

Carol Shen:
He was just sort of one of *that* group of guys. There was a group of ten or fifteen who were very good friends all through high school, and they all seemed to be nothing very outstanding. He was just one of the group. Sort of a passive personality, really.

Debbie Gordon:
He was my boyfriend for a while. I don't really understand it. He was nice, skinny, simple, not too bright, and his kindness wasn't very deep.

160

Sally Lobherr:
I think he was shy. I remember that I used to copy off his papers. He didn't seem very comfortable with himself. Like I'd talk to him and his ears would turn red. He had large ears that kind of stuck out. Below-average looks. He was kind of skinny and maybe a little immature-looking compared to some of the other guys around school. I never understood why everybody thought he was such a nice guy. Maybe it was because they couldn't think of anything else to say about him.

Lynn Marble:
Everybody thought that Bob was a really fine chap; a very presentable example of the Youth of America. I would assume that he's a businessman of some kind, with family.

•

When we talked with Bob, we noticed that he had gained weight since high school. He had also shaved his head completely except for a ponytail on top, and dressed himself in simple white robes. Having chosen a spiritual path, he was reluctant to talk about the past, but we persuaded him that he had to describe his starting point for people to appreciate how far he had traveled.

•

When I was growing up I was a good kid. I didn't get into any trouble and I always got along good with my parents. But sometimes they bugged me because I watched too much TV. *Leave It to Beaver* and *Ozzie and Harriet* were my favorite shows.

I remember when we graduated from high school, I was voted Most Reserved. I was somewhat surprised, but it was nice to see my name in print. I didn't really consider myself reserved, but I guess I was pretty self-conscious. I didn't like to speak in class. I remember in government class we had political parties and somehow they ran me on the Republican nomination for President and I won. I had to give a State of the Union address and I didn't know what to write. So a friend of mine wrote it. It was very wordy and everybody knew I didn't write it. I couldn't even read it because I couldn't pronounce all his words.

I was always looking for some identity, like having a girl friend or something like that. I dated but I didn't date that much. It was more or less whoever would have me. I remember when people were talking about french-kissing. I didn't know what it was and I was afraid to ask. Then one time it came out. I found out what it was and it seemed kind of vulgar until I started doing it, and then it seemed all right.

Looking back on high school, it doesn't seem like much was significant. You know, just day by day—this girl smiled at me, passing this test, or getting through this course.

I went on to college because I wanted to get a good job so I could make money and live comfortably. I decided that I'd go into engineering because I thought that was a pretty pragmatic field. And I was good in math and I liked to mechanical draw. But the big thing at UCLA was joining a fraternity. A friend of mine joined Sigma Pi, and so I decided to join that one too. It was kind of mediocre. It wasn't one with such a high social esteem.

With school it was just a matter of getting through. When I went through school I always wondered, "Well, what does an engineer do?" I never found out. I still don't know.

In the summer of 1968 I went to Europe. I grew a beard and let my hair grow and I smoked marijuana for the first time. We bought some stuff in Amsterdam and I got off on it, and we did it as much as we could. At the time it was intoxicating, euphoric. The trouble is that you come down. That's what's nice about Krishna consciousness—you get higher and higher.

On July 4, 1969, I dropped some LSD for the first time to celebrate Independence Day. It was real nice. It was illuminating. It gave me a vision of the hypocrisy of material society. That summer I was by myself for the first time. I went up to Berkeley and stayed at the People's Pad, which was some deserted wartime barracks. Each night there would be a big bonfire and we would try to get some food together. Everyone would drink wine by the fire at night. I met this girl at People's Pad and she had an edition of *Bhagavad-Gita As-It-Is,* by His Divine Grace A. C. Bhaktivedanta Swami. She and I would go to Telegraph Avenue and watch the Krishna devotees who would come out and chant there. She said she was thinking of joining, and I said, "You mean those crazy people with the shaved heads?" She would chant with them, but I couldn't get into it. Still, their ideas started going through my mind.

When I came back from Berkeley, I stayed with some people in Topanga Canyon who were growing marijuana and were into yoga. I read *The Teachings of Don Juan.* Then we got kicked out of the house, so I got an apartment near the beach. This was my last quarter at UCLA. I went to a class taught by the devotees on the Bhagavad-Gita. They explained who we were—that we're spirit soul—that we're not this body. This body is just a covering. So I started to understand this, and it was just like a light bulb turning on.

I finished college in December of '69. There's a class that all engineering seniors have to take the last quarter—Engineering Occupations or something like that. I did my term paper on Krishna Consciousness, about how the cosmos was created and the different time spans and why we're here. I had to give an oral report in front of the engineering class. My teacher said I should have been a philosopher instead of an engineer.

So I graduated, and I stayed on one more quarter working as an audio-visual person, setting up films and things like that. I was preparing to go off to the woods and chant and read and decide what I wanted to do with my life. I finally quit work, but I didn't have sufficient purity to go off by myself, so I stayed with a girl in Topanga Canyon. I didn't have anything to do all day except read and chant, so I decided I would try to stay at the Krishna temple in Culver City for a week. When I went there I saw that these people were actually cultivating a spiritual life and devoting their whole lives. That's what *I* wanted to do, so I decided to stay.

Just before I joined, I had one last fling. I tried to engage in some of the material enjoyments like sex and getting intoxicated, but it wasn't satisfying. Even while I was doing these things, I just kept thinking about Krishna, because I understood that there was something higher than physical pleasure.

•

During a break in the interview Bob took us on a tour of the Hare Krishna Temple, in which he has spent most of his life for the last five years. We reached the kitchen just as lunch was being served, and devotees were arriving from all the surrounding apartment buildings. We soon learned that the Krishna movement owns virtually this entire block in Culver City. Each of the devotees gathered a large plateful of food, prostrated himself, chanted a prayer and began eating with great fervor. Everywhere he walked, Bob was greeted with a hearty "Hare Krishna!"; he was clearly a person of some importance within the movement. He explained to us that he was the treasurer of his temple, and that his movement name was Madhukantha Das, which, in Sanskrit, means "bodily luster like honey." Near the end of the tour, Bob showed us the main deities: two brightly colored life-size dolls named Rukmini and Dwarkadisha. These idols were fully and elaborately clothed; Bob explained that they each have more than fifty different outfits. In fact, Bob himself is personally responsible for supervising their wardrobe.

•

We generally arise early in the morning before four o'clock, and shower. At four-thirty each day there's an Aratrika ceremony, where we chant and worship the Lord. I'm in charge of the worship of the Deities and we clothe them and put their jewels on them. From seven to eight-thirty we chant and we have class on the Srimad Bhagavatam, which is the Beautiful Pastimes of the Personality of Godhead, which describes the different activities of the Lord when he was on this planet and on different planets. At eight-thirty we have breakfast, which consists of hot milk, cereal and fruit. I'm the treasurer, so from nine to eleven I work on the books. Starting at eleven, I chant. We have to chant on our beads the Hare Krishna mantra—"Hare Krishna, Hare Krishna, Krishna, Krishna, Hare, Hare, Hare Rama, Hare Rama, Rama, Rama, Hare, Hare"—we have to chant once for each bead. There are one hundred and eight beads on a strand. We have to do that sixteen rounds each day. It takes about two hours.

After lunch I usually engage in working with the Deities, trying to organize things, fixing up their quarters or rearranging schedules. Then at six P.M. we shower again, and at a quarter to seven there's a Tulasi worship—the tulasi is a plant dear to Krishna. At seven-thirty we have a class in the Nectar of Devotion. During the classes I have a duty where I cook *puris,* which are special breads for the Deities. Usually from eight-thirty to ten is cleaning, and sometimes individual study. At ten o'clock we take rest. Simple—and sublime!

Harvey Bookstein:
I hadn't seen Bob for about eight years, and then I ran into him once in Century City. He was a Hare Krishna. He had no hair and he had this little thing hanging down. I don't think they talk. I don't understand what they mumble. I was actually afraid to go up and ask him, "Are you the guy I think you are?" To each his own. It's his right. But I could never do a thing like that.

I got married in December 1972. The marriage has to be approved by our Spiritual Master or by the Board of Directors. We can only have a physical relationship if we want to have children. We've tried to have a child, but we haven't had any success. You can only try once a month, on the most optimal day for conception. Before you do it, you have to chant extra.

•

We were joined by Bob's wife, Karlapati Devidasi, who was very friendly and quite interested in the interview. But Bob was clearly uncomfortable talking about his life in her presence. After two or three minutes Bob turned to her and said, "Don't you have to do your services?" She left immediately.

•

Every once in a while I go to talk to my parents. My father's a real nice person, but he's kind of materialistic, and he's not too philosophically inclined. So usually he gets hung up on some point like, "Don't try to convert me, don't try to convert me." My mother gets upset easy. She has a strong attachment to me, and she wants me to do what she wants me to do, so it kind of upsets her me being in this. We all get along and they like me, but I only want to talk about Krishna. I'm not so interested in talking about family things, and this and that. I think they kind of resent it. It really shows you how temporary the material relationships are. As soon as I'm not doing what they think I should be doing, then there's no common ground.

One aspect of spiritual life is simplicity, or not keeping so many possessions, and renouncing things that aren't needed. This is what we do here now. It's very simple, we just sleep on the floor and eat on the floor, and like that, and it's so simple, really. I want to minimize all my possessions. I've got my possessions down to two sets of clothes. This set of clothes consists of just two pieces of cotton cloth—a long piece and a short piece and I wrap it around.

I also have a set of all the books of our spiritual master. And then I have a razor and my shaving equipment. And because I'm the treasurer at the temple, I also have a briefcase. Other than that, that's about all.

I can only hope that how I used my last five years can be an example, a model for others to follow. Ten years from now I'll be doing the same thing, except with more devotion, hopefully. But who knows?

•

Remembering Bob Searight as he had been in high school, it was hard for us to isolate the traits that led him to the path of a Krishna devotee. The one point that seemed most clear was that his had always been a thoroughly passive personality. He had told us of his arguments with his parents regarding the number of hours he spent in front of the TV. *Ozzie and Harriet* had left him poorly equipped to handle the freedom and confusion of the late sixties. After graduation from college, he had nothing but free time and open possibilities; unable to deal with that, he sought refuge in the regimentation of the Krishna temple. For the last five years he seems to have returned to a passive sort of TV trance. He is no longer watching *Ozzie and Harriet*, but for Bob it was simply a matter of switching channels.

●

Sexual Revolutions

●

For the generation of the 1960's, no aspect of life has received so much publicity as our sexuality. Countless books and articles have hailed us as the proponents of a sexual revolution, the pioneers of a new style in human relationships. It was commonly supposed that among the most privileged children in American society, this new freedom would be particularly pronounced. Yet for the members of the Palisades class of '65, the process of sexual initiation remained a torturous and confusing experience. We may have come to our experiences earlier than members of previous generations, but the basic range of emotions and responses seems to have remained surprisingly consistent.

●

Bob Searight:
Until the time I was twenty-two, sex was a major preoccupation. Now I look back and wish I'd never gotten into it. I was always wanting to go further, to have as much sex as I could. It was a whole distraction from

the spiritual life. Sex life is the main grip of our attachment to the material world.

David Wallace:

I couldn't stand the fact that I was eighteen years old and still a virgin. I was obsessed by it. Then I met a girl in my Spanish class at Santa Monica City College who I could deal with because she was very shy, and not so experienced. A friend of mine was having a party, so I really screwed up my courage and asked her out and she accepted. I was overjoyed and petrified. I picked her up at the drugstore where she worked, and we went to this party where we proceeded to get drunk and make-out on the floor. This was the first time I had ever full-out made-out with somebody. We were under the pool table at somebody's house. I reached up under her sweater and felt her soft, lovely breasts. That was wonderful. So I started dating her right away. We used to go further and further as our relationship progressed.

At this time a group of friends, about five of us, got together to rent a garage for about twenty-five dollars a month. We pooled our resources and decorated it, and put a bed in there. We used this place to bring girls to. It meant a lot to us. We each had a key and we had little signals so that you would know if you weren't supposed to come in because somebody else was in there with a girl. With my girl friend, things were building up to the point where we knew that we were going to do it. We were going to go all the way. So I acquired some rubbers from a friend. One night we went to this garage and we petted for about an hour, and got very hot and moist. Then we moved onto the bed. She removed all her clothing. I didn't know what to do and felt very uncomfortable about this. I said to her, "Well, do you want me to take off all my clothes?"

She said, "I don't care. Whatever you want."

I left my shirt on. So then I went over and un-wrapped the prophylactic and rolled it onto my erect penis and mounted her. As soon as I got above her, as soon as I got my erect penis next to her vagina, it was almost as if it were a collapsing slinky toy. It wouldn't go in. My penis just contracted completely, and the rubber fell off. It was a horrible, devastating experience. I felt terrible and I didn't know what to do. We sat and talked. I might add that I've never used a rubber since then. I've always associated it with that night.

My girl friend was very nice about the whole thing. So we continued to heavy-pet for a couple of weeks. Then vacation came and we went to Las Vegas together, and stayed in a hotel. There we did have intercourse. That was a delightful experience. It was all that I would have wished the first time to be. She had an orgasm, which was really exciting. Then I had my orgasm, which was wonderful, and we both went to separate rooms and thought about it. We came back together again and both felt very good and made love a couple of times after that.

Sally Lobherr:
Sex has never played a really big part in my life. Except for a few times, my experiences haven't been that fantastic. One night I guess it just happened. It wasn't with anyone special. It wasn't "Wow, this is it. Here's my virginity on a silver platter. Now you owe me your life." I don't even remember that much about it, so the guy must have been really terrific, right?

I went on the pill when I was twenty-one. Needless to say, I didn't tell Mother, even though I was still living at home. One day I was asleep on the couch in my room when my mother came in and told me that Heinrich, who is our Doberman, had taken my purse out to the living room. My mother took these things that she had in her hand and said, "This is what the dog was chewing on. What are these?"

I said, "They are birth-control pills."

My mother just looked at me with this face and said, "Whatever are they for?"

I looked up at her and said, "What do you think?"

She was crushed. She had to go to bed for two days and cry.

Jeff Stolper:

I lost my virginity while I was still in high school. I'd been going with this girl for quite a while, and we planned the whole thing out. The hardest part was finding a place. It came down to a choice between the back seat of my '56 Chevy or the garage. We compromised, and so I drove the car into the garage. But I couldn't get the car in there because my dad had hung up all sorts of punching bags and stuff which I couldn't move. So we decided to do it on a bench in the garage and shut the garage door. We had like three dogs that witnessed it. It was a new experience. The whole thing must have lasted, if we were lucky, maybe two minutes. I was completely sober. I didn't want to miss anything. We were actually scared. I was afraid my brother would open the garage, and there we'd be. He was home, in the back room, and all he had to do was to walk out the door and into the garage.

The next day at school all my friends knew it. I didn't have to tell them. I think KFWB must have had it as one of their local news events. It was a big triumph for me.

Lisa Menzies:

In junior high school, I found out that I was always pressured for sex. So before I stopped being a virgin, I learned how to give head. I became quite good at that. That way I could keep my virginity as long as I did. Otherwise I wouldn't have been able to. I didn't feel at all guilty. I was very free, very free. I satisfied everybody I went to bed with.

The first time I reached orgasm was when I was in the seventh grade. That was actually just playing with myself. Sexually, in interaction with a fellow, I think I was about twenty. I was on LSD at the time. It was very intense and very relaxed. There was nothing spectacular, really. Since then, love-making has become a very different thing for me. More intimate. Spiritually, it's intensified greatly.

Skip Baumgarten:
It's different in Chicago. If you're Jewish and you've gone through puberty, right away you get involved. I had an older brother. He was at the University of Illinois while I was in ninth grade. The whole family went down to visit him for Parents' Weekend and my father gave my brother twenty dollars to take me to a whorehouse and get me laid. I was really scared. I hadn't read enough to know anything. The whole way there, I was very worried. We were going to Danville, which was about a forty-five-minute ride. We got there, and fortunately the place had been closed down. Although I never let anybody know, I was very relieved.

But after that I knew that it was expected that I start *doing it.* One day I stayed home from school. The story was that I was sick, but actually there was an exam that I didn't want to take. At the time we had a housekeeper, a black woman about forty-eight. Martha. And Martha and I did it. I'm pretty sure that Martha mostly did it *to* me. As it turned out, I stayed home the whole week. It was a very brief affair, because when Martha realized that she was in bed with a guy who was thirty-four years younger than she was, she quit. After that there was a succession of housekeepers over the next two years. I'd say we went through more than twenty of them. I was sleeping with a good percentage.

My parents were convinced that the reason all the maids were leaving was because I kept my room dirty. That was fine. I could never afford to clean up my room, or they might find out the truth.

Mike Shedlin:

In high school, I had a library of erotic books and marriage manuals. My parents told me that masturbation was okay, that everybody masturbates. It got pretty intense. This artificial adolescence where you're not supposed to fuck until a certain age—that weighed very heavily on me and distorted my whole personality. One of the things we used to do for enjoyment was run around in cars and yell out the car windows at girls. We would yell, "Oh, you sweet thing!" or make lewd noises.

The furthest I ever got in high school was getting my index finger *nearly* into this woman's vagina. However, she always kept her legs closed. One woman tried to give me a blow job in the basement of a Malibu flat. I don't even think I got an erection. It amazed me that she was doing this. I didn't know how to respond.

After high school, I went to the University of Hawaii. I was obsessed with sex and I was reading books and magazines about sex. I was masturbating heavily, perhaps four or five times a day, taking showers all the time after lunch. I had made out with people and done heavy petting, but I had never achieved any penetration. Then I met a girl who was older and more experienced. She had had lovers. So in Hawaii, in my apartment, right there in my bed, we had a fairly smooth union. I was in a sort of delirium. I came really fast. I was just too amazed to do anything else. Right after the first time or two I got hip to what to do, and from then on it was very nice.

Candy McCoy:

Good God, no—I didn't make love in high school! I don't know if anyone even had his hand in my shirt. I reached puberty very, very late, so for most of that time I wasn't fighting anything, I didn't have heavy instincts to overcome. I didn't masturbate at the time. I didn't get that together till I was twenty-five or twenty-six—a long time after I'd started making love with men.

Jamie Kelso:
I would say I am a sexual novice, simply because it isn't that important to me. In a decade I have been romantically in love with only four girls. Sex divorced from romantic love struck me as absurd, a cherry without a stone. Sex is the titillation of robot nerve endings, utterly by-passing the mind. What a debased sport!

Reilly Ridgell:
In my sophomore year of college I went back to a Pali Sports Night and picked up this girl. We went out a couple of times, and over Thanksgiving I took her back to the frat house. The house was pretty much empty because of the vacation. We started making-out, and she was actually one of the first girls I ever made-out with. She was very strong—a swimmer or an athlete or something—but a little goofy up here. She was wearing one of those girdles that was about three inches thick, and she had a hole cut out right *there*. A little opening right in the business end of her girdle! So I guess I was getting a stinky finger, but I didn't want to screw her because I didn't have any rubbers. It was really a surprise to me that she wanted to go that far. She kept fainting on me—she'd pass out, or pretend to pass out. I don't know if it was a guilt reaction, or if she'd try to pretend like she was unconscious, so she couldn't be held responsible for what she was doing.

Then I took her out again Christmas vacation, and this time I was ready. At first she acted like she didn't want to, but I finally got her into this little room in the frat house and closed it up. She just sort of collapsed on the bed and wouldn't respond to anything, so I undressed her, and oh God, it was the first time, and I was so fucking nervous I didn't know what the hell was going off, and it did go off—really quickly. And she just

174

sort of lay there, and then put herself back together and walked out the door and fell down. She collapsed right in the hall, fainted dead out, and all I'm thinking is, What the hell is going on here?

Judy Tomash:
The first time it was awful, just awful. I was twenty years old and I didn't know a thing. I had no idea what was expected of me or what the possibilities were, and the fellow I was with didn't know anything either. All he could do was get inside and bump around. It was terrible. All I could do was be afraid and say, "This is what I've been holding out for? They say you have to wait for this? Blech!"

Mike Medved:
The summer after my freshman year at Yale, I came home to LA to earn some money but found it impossible to get a job. In desperation I devised a scheme to cash in on my academic abilities. I went over to UCLA summer session and sold mimeographed class notes, text outlines, study guides, and tutoring. By the end of the summer, with finals coming up, my business was really booming.

In the big American-history class that I was doing, there was one short, buxom girl who'd been staring at me for most of the summer. At the end of the term she hired me as a tutor for six dollars an hour, so one Sunday I went over to her dorm to try and tutor her. We sat down on the lawn in front and I tried to talk about Henry Clay and the Compromise of 1850, but she started to talk about Vivaldi. It turned out that we liked some of the same music. She had very intense brown eyes behind thick glasses and kept staring at me while I fiddled with my books and papers. This girl had a remarkable figure. She was wearing sandals, jeans and a tight-fitting black tank top. I had the sense that she was attracted to me, but I couldn't quite believe it.

After a while I closed my book and said, "You know, I don't feel like doing this any more." She said, "Oh, really? What do you feel like doing?" I said, "Kissing you." So then she put out her cigarette and kissed me and we started making-out, rolling around on the grass in front of afternoon crowds at UCLA. At one point she came up breathless and whispered in my ear, "I want to make love to you tonight." We agreed to meet that night at eight o'clock.

In the hours in between I was frightened and nervous. I walked three miles from my parents' home to a drugstore where I could buy rubbers. I circled the store four times before I made up my mind to go in. The guy behind the counter ended up selling me this huge box, about a year's supply of Trojans, which was obviously absurd.

That night we met as planned and went down to the beach. The girl was wearing a loose-fitting brown flannel shirt with nothing on underneath. She announced this to me before we even arrived at the ocean, and by the standards of 1966 this was quite exotic. We proceeded to roll around on the dark sand, but after a few minutes I was so excited that I came in my pants. I tried to keep this a secret, and sort of pulled away and started talking about my moral objections to sex. These objections were real enough: I didn't want to compromise my sensitivity, and give in to the cheapness and degradation I saw all around me. I was special. I was saving myself for true romantic love, and for the woman I would marry. The girl I was with listened to all this with a good deal of patience. She was a very experienced young lady. She had slept with everybody, including her own younger brother, and she let me know about that. After I was finished with my tirade, she patted me on the head and said, "I'll wait for you. Whenever you're ready."

This was the worst thing she could have done, because I was plunged into four days of indecision. At the end of that time I was flying back to school, so I had to make up my mind. I proceeded to talk to everyone I knew about what I should do, whether I should ball her or not. I talked to my mom, I talked to my father, I talked to all my friends. The consensus was, "Of course you should do it! What's wrong with you?"

In spite of this—or perhaps because of it—I resolved to preserve my virginity at all costs. I considered myself some sort of hero. I called the girl on the phone and told her my decision, but she persuaded me that the least I could do was explain to her in person. We agreed to meet one last time at UCLA. A friend drove me up to a deserted part of campus the night before I flew back to New Haven. I remember sitting in his car, waiting for the girl to show up, and listening to the radio. They were playing Aaron Copland's "Appalachian Spring." That was a very important piece of music to me, so sweet, pure, nostalgic. I didn't know what was happening. I felt like a lamb going to slaughter. I was afraid I would never be the same again after seeing this girl—and I didn't want to change.

So finally we met, and within half an hour we were walking to the house of one of her friends where there was an extra bed in a private room. By the time we got there I was so nervous and so hot that I could barely control myself. She took off all her clothes, very dramatically and with a lot of flair, and it was the first time I'd seen a lady with all her clothes off. She lay down on the bed and beckoned to me, and I sort of did my best to enter her right away, but I only got as far as her thigh before I exploded, much to my chagrin and horrible embarrassment.

At this point I wanted to walk down the hall and flush myself down the toilet. But she said, "Don't worry. It will be good. Don't worry."

So we lay down next to each other, and I was shaking. She said, "Just take it easy. Be calm." And she started touching me and stroking me and then we tried

again. And we did it this time. I entered her and we
actually had sex. She was a wonderful lady. We were
very sexually compatible. In the next few hours w
stayed in that room and did it about a half-doze
times. She actually complimented me on my prowess,
which I'm sure she did to be kind, because my prowess
wasn't anything. It was just nature. I had a lot of semen
stored up after all those years.

Donald Golden:
Up until the time I was twenty-three, my experience
with sex was basically unpleasant and frustrating. There
were a lot of impotent experiences. In fact, my first
time was halfway impotent and not at all enjoyable. I
think I just felt that women would have expectation
of me that I couldn't fulfill and that freaked me out so
terribly much that it made me impotent. It actually too
several years before I realized that sleeping with
woman wasn't like a contest where I had to demonstra
something.

Debbie Gordon:
My first year at Berkeley I lived in the dorm, and t
big difference was being in charge of myself. I me
wow, I was looking around and there was nob
standing behind me. It wasn't very wild living, re
but I was more adventuresome then. I remember sor
going downstairs for a blind date, and hanging aro
talking to the boys in the dorm after dinner, and
having a lot more access to boys.

The first boy I slept with was a musician—a g
player musician—as were most of my loves and
friends at the time. The setup with this boy was
we'd go out, ostensibly to drink a beer, and find s
hidden place, not in the dorm, but out of doors, to m
love. An hour or so later I'd go back to the dorm. It
December or January—pretty cold in the open
had one older friend who was, like, a junior or ser
a history student. He used to take me for long v

ʳk Holmes and Lany Tyler "reunited"
.he ten-year class reunion.

(ABOVE) *Mark Holmes in 1965:*
"Most Likely to Succeed."

(LEFT) *Rev. Mark Holmes at the*
class reunion.

Lisa Menzies in high school.

Reily Ridgell in the high school yearbook.

Lisa Menzies in her element at the class reunion.

Reilly Ridgell poised in his outrigger canoe on Puluwat Island.

(ABOVE) *Lee Grossman: medical school application photo, 1975.*

(LEFT) *Lee Grossman on his way to a high school debate tournament: 1964.*

(ABOVE) *Suzanne Thomas in high school.*

(ABOVE RIGHT) *Suzanne Thomas at the class reunion.*

(RIGHT) *Sally Lobherr in the high school year book.*

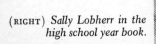

(LEFT) *Gary and Suzy Wasserman at the opening of a new store of Gary's and Company.*

(BELOW) *Gary Wasserman: "Best Dressed" in the high school class poll.*

Sally Lobherr Simpfenderfer: seven months pregnant, in front of her home in Glendale, California.

(ABOVE) *The last photograph of Brock Chester—with Patty Findlater at a friend's wedding—April, 1971.*

(BELOW) *A group of Saracens wearing their official club jackets. Gary Wasserman is at the extreme right and Brock Chester is second from right.*

Beautiful Sunset on
Central California Coastline

Kiss me on the
nose — and call
me love.

to
Patty Findlater
LA 49 Cali
90049

Brock Chester's last postcard.

(ABOVE) *Patty Findlater in the high school year book.*

(LEFT) *Patty Findlater: a recent photo from her modeling portfolio.*

(ABOVE) *Jeff Stolper and his family today.*

(LEFT) *Jeff Stolper surfing at Malibu, age fifteen.*

Jeff Stolper at graduation.

(LEFT) *Jon Wilson: official high school photo.*

(BELOW) *Jon Wilson on patrol in Vietnam, 1967.*

(LEFT) *Jon Wilson at the class reunion, flanked by old friends Mike Shedlin (left) and Jeff Stolper (right).*

M. WM. KATZ/KATZFILM

(RIGHT) *Candy McCoy: in a pensive mood, posing for* Time *magazine, 1965.*

(BELOW) *Dace McCoy today.*

**Bob Searight
S.M.C.C.
Engineer**

(LEFT) *Bob Searight in high school: "Most Reserved."*

(BELOW) *Madhukantha Das (Bob Searight) in front of his Temple today.*

Carol Shen Glass today.

PALISADES
HIGH SCHOOL
Pacific Palisades, California
1963–64

STUDENT'S SIGNATURE

PRINCIPAL

Carol Shen: eleventh-grade high school ID card.

(ABOVE LEFT) *Debbie Gordon: graduation photo.*

(ABOVE RIGHT) *Deborah Gordon on her ranch in Northern California, 1971.*

(ABOVE) *Mike Shedlin in high school: "Agent 006.9."*

(LEFT) *Michael Shedlin: going over his interview in his Berkeley home.*

Ron Conti at the wheel of his '63 Falcon, circa 1965.

Anita Champion: high school yearbook photo.

Ron Conti: high school yearbook photo.

Ron and Anita Conti celebrating
Christmas at home.

Lynn Marble Erler today.

Lynn Marble: high school
yearbook photo.

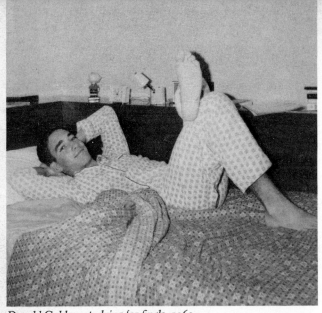

Donald Golden: studying for finals, 1963.

Donald Golden: "Down on the Farm," 1976.

(ABOVE) *Harvey Bookstein: advising David Wallechinsky on his tax return at the class reunion.*

(RIGHT) *Harvey Bookstein: high school aspirations.*

**Harvey Alan
Bookstein
U.S.C.
Accountant**

(RIGHT) *Skip Baum-garten in 1975, enjoying his interview.*

(BELOW) *Skip Baum-garten, 1964: the new kid from Chicago.*

Margie Williams in the high school yearbook.

Margie Williams Sandorf at home in 1976, with her youngest son.

William Quivers: a face in the crowd, 1965 (second row, third from right). Also visible: Harvey Bookstein (second row, second from right); Donald Golden (second row, sixth from right); David Wallace (second row, seventh from right).

William Quivers: outside his Cambridge apartment, summer 1975.

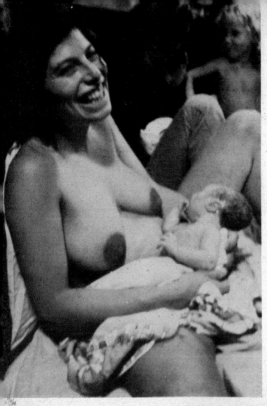

(ABOVE) *Judy Tomash: with her son, Suresh, twenty minutes after giving birth.*

(RIGHT) *Judy Tomash: newly selected foreign exchange student to Brazil, 1965.*

BRAZIL
OR
BUST

Lany Tyler, Head Cheerleader: "Push 'em back, push 'em back, way back!"—1964.

(ABOVE) *Professor Elaine Tyler May.*

(LEFT) *Lany Tyler: Homecoming Queen, 1965.*

(ABOVE LEFT) *Jamie Kelso: reading Sartre's Nausea, 1965.*

(ABOVE RIGHT) *Jamie Kelso, leading Scientology Executive Training Session, 1969.*

Jamie Kelso (front row, center): chanting "Nam-myoho-renge-kyo," 1968.

Jamie Kelso, visiting Los Angeles, summer 1975.

(ABOVE) *David Walle-chinsky: doing kitchen duty at home.*

(LEFT) *David Wallace: high school graduation photo.*

(ABOVE) *Michael Medved: enjoying the ten-year class reunion.*

(RIGHT) *Michael Medved: a sour expression for his college application photo, 1965.*

and introduce me to Berkeley, and he spent one whole evening describing how my first sexual experience should be—you know, candles, a night to ourselves in a room, and music, and wine. But as it turned out, mine was under a tree somewhere.

Debbie Gordon: Golden Girl

•

Candy McCoy:
I remember Debbie as athletic and outgoing. She was also incredibly bright. I know she graduated near the top of our class, and she seemed to have everything going for her. She was capable and competitive in all the classes, and did especially well in science. She must be a doctor now or something.

Jamie Kelso:
She was always smiling. A real hunk of woman, nearly six feet tall. Venus-like. She exuded health and physical strength.

Lee Grossman:
I think she was the first girl I ever French-kissed. I thought she was pretty, in a special way. It wasn't cheerleader-pretty. She had a glow about her. Debbie was tall. I think she was romantic. She had an overly saccharine vision of things. I used to think she would be good in bed, but of course I never had a chance to find out.

Her father was the biggest person I had ever seen in

my whole life. When I walked into their living room for the first time I had difficulty keeping a straight face. Here was this hulking giant of a man staring at the television. As we came in, he didn't turn his head. He said, "De-bo-*rah*." I don't recall much conversation after that. He kept his eyes riveted to the television. That was his style. A remarkable man.

Bob Searight:

I guess it was the summer after ninth grade, when we went to the beach a lot. There was sort of a set group. Debbie was part of that. She was real intelligent, and we got along okay. Then we were going together for a little while. She was pretty chaste. She liked French-kissing, but that was about it. Her parents were really strict. We broke up after just a couple of months. I don't really remember why. Probably she found someone else she liked.

Carol Shen:

Debbie is probably the brightest woman I've ever known. Just an incredible person who could do anything she wanted to, and also had that great facility for putting people at ease and being very warm and friendly. I guess throughout the three years of high school there were times on and off when I considered her my best friend.

She certainly was someone with an extremely high energy level. Life was always an adventure to her. I really did suspect that someday she would be highly involved with something. But I also would have predicted that she'd drop out at some point and go off to a beach somewhere. You know, I wouldn't be surprised to hear someday that she's farming out on the island of Maui, or something like that. She definitely had that adventurous streak.

●

When we visited her Berkeley apartment, Debbie was dressed in the traditional uniform of the Bay Area bohemian: loose-fitting striped jeans, turquoise turtleneck with no bra, and a black-and-white Mexican serape. She wore her light-brown hair cut short and wavy, and her enormous blue eyes were astonishing in their purity. It was strange how little one paid attention to such things in high school! But now, sitting at her table and sipping tea from a set of chipped mugs, we noticed how those eyes burned with the blue intensity of gas jets. When she became excited or amused in the course of her recollections, her eyes grew larger and the color deepened, as if someone were turning up the gas behind the flame.

•

I remember in high school we had to wear stockings—that was part of the dress code. I'd wear nice shoes, and probably a plaid skirt, a blouse and a sweater. Usually mohair. I went home the other weekend and I found my mother still has all my old mohair sweaters. One whole drawer full of ugly, fluffy sweaters!

I'm very competitive, and I would have loved being valedictorian of our high school class. As it was, I graduated fifteenth out of five hundred. I guess I've always had more intelligence than I've ever really used. The image I have of myself is that other people think about things more than I do. In high school, I wrote poetry just because everybody else wrote poetry. I remember the summer before senior year, my father somehow brought e. e. cummings into a conversation and said, "That idiot!" And I said, "Nonsense. He's a very good poet." At that point I had read nothing, I knew nothing about cummings, but I insisted to my father that I loved every poem he had ever written. So for my birthday my father gave me a collection of e. e. cummings' poetry and I pored over that book thoroughly.

My father is very conservative, but basically soft-hearted. He and I would sort of watch late movies and root for the good guys together. He's a self-employed businessman, a corporate broker. There were rules when I was growing up, and we always had to have dinner together every night. My father would honk as he drove up coming home from work, and we always had to run out and say hello. If I was in my room studying, he'd come in and say, "What's the matter? Why didn't you come out?"

After high school I really wanted to go to college back East, but my father wouldn't let me apply outside of California. So I ended up at Berkeley, and when I first came up here I was really glad. I made new friends, and I went out with boys that I'd just met, and went to parties. For the first time I was in charge of my own life. There were two other girls who lived near me in the dorm, and the three of us became very good friends. We walked in the rain together, and sat after dinner with the boys we liked, talking very late, and one of them pierced my ears for me. We were all kind of experiencing new things. That's when I had my first sexual experience, and that's also when I smoked dope for the first time. I guess I sort of enjoyed getting stoned, but I just did it socially. I never bought dope.

After I'd lived in the dorm two years, I moved into a house full of girls I knew from the dorm. It was wonderful. My father was horrified—he thought it was a barn we'd moved into. We painted the whole house from top to bottom. It was a big, open house. People slept over all the time, we all cooked, we ate ice cream every day.

I got kind of a regular boyfriend for a while—as usual, a guitar player. I thought I was being very discreet about sex, but my parents just seemed to know. One day they just confronted me. They said, "You're sleeping with your boyfriend, aren't you?" I must have been glad to tell them yes, because I said, "How did you find out?" I didn't try to conceal it. It was a very ugly fight, and all summer my father would sort of shake his head and look down when I walked into the room.

I dropped out of school in my junior year. What I said to everybody was that I hadn't even been trying, and I still got all A's—so what a hypocritical thing to be doing! I didn't see any reason to stay in. I went to the dean's office, full of fear and trembling, but they thought it was a wonderful idea. They encouraged me to drop out, and said that it was just too bad that boys couldn't do it, because of the draft. I didn't have any idea what I wanted to do. I guess I wanted to travel for a while, or work, and then maybe go somewhere, or something like that.

But I stayed here in Berkeley and got a couple of nothing jobs. Then I quit, and for a while I did nothing. I made bread, and stuff like that. Then I got a job on campus in the economics department. I suppose, being on campus anyway, I wanted the life of a student again, so I went back to school. I didn't acquire any direction in that year I was out, but I don't feel ashamed about it, either. Sometimes I have a tendency to romanticize it, and think of it as a wonderful adventure.

After I went back, school was pretty uneventful, except for the political activity. Gradually in Berkeley I had begun to learn things about the war, and I participated in a lot of antiwar demonstrations. Then I got involved in People's Park, and the big strike of 1970 at the time of Kent State and the Cambodia invasion. When Berkeley closed down, I went to special classes in Vietnamese history and the legal implications of the war.

About this time I was applying to law school. I got into Harvard, but then in the middle of the summer I was working on my bicycle and I hurt my back. The doctors told me to spend a week in bed, and I got all these Fritz Perls gestalt psychology books on one side of my bed and all the law books on the other—which I didn't touch. At the end of the week I wrote Harvard a letter—I just really didn't want to go. I wanted to do something with education, I thought.

So I went to Europe for four months. I had an inheritance from a great-uncle. That was a fine adventure—a fine four months of being on my own, and every morning I could decide what I wanted to do. I treasured that time, and it was beautiful.

When I got back I got a job at an alternative school in Marin County. I taught a class on backpacking and a class on Bob Dylan. But after about a year I was bored, so along with this fellow I was living with, I decided to go skiing for the winter. We moved up to Lake Tahoe. I remember getting down to our last pennies and putting them in the slot machines. Then I got a job making salads at a French restaurant. I was a vegetarian—I'd been a vegetarian for a couple of years —but I used to bring home Rock Cornish game hens for my boyfriend. Of course, right after I left the restaurant I decided not to be a vegetarian any more, but I'd already lost the chance to enjoy all that food!

When spring rolled around we moved up to Hurd's Gulch in northern California. Along with twenty other people from Berkeley, we'd bought a share of a big ranch up there. We slept in a tepee, and we had the door of the tepee facing the Marble Mountains. Or else we slept on the water bed which we had set up in an open field with no cover at all. It was filled from an underground spring, with a hose that we borrowed from a neighbor. It was just lovely. When you woke up in the morning the sky was blue and it was hot, but there was still snow on the mountains across the valley. The Scott River runs down the middle of the valley, and there's farming there, and then the Marble Mountains are on the west. The country is beautiful.

We were there for six months. One night, watering the garden after sunset, we decided, very romantically, to have a baby. I had also decided that I was interested in medicine. I'd already applied to graduate school in psychology and been turned down. I wasn't sure that I wanted to be a doctor, but I thought about being a nurse practitioner. It seemed like a more down-to-earth job—a way to be more myself.

So I got a job as a nurse's aide. I was working at this hospital which was a half-hour from the ranch. At the same time I was pregnant. I was just beginning to get morning sickness, and I was having it terribly. The term "morning sickness" must have been invented by a man—it's really *all-day* sickness. I just decided it was too much—I had to go back to the city.

When I came back I was going to decide whether or not I really wanted to have this baby. I just didn't feel like my boyfriend and I had the proper commitment to each other. I think we both sort of wanted the baby, but we weren't sure we really wanted each other.

And so I had an abortion. This is very hard for me to talk about. An abortion isn't a nice thing. But I feel strongly that it should be okay for women to do that. I don't want to feel ashamed of it.

After I left the ranch and had the abortion, I felt like I needed some distance from what I'd been doing. I didn't want to get another job in a hospital. So I worked as a legal secretary for two young hip lawyers in Berkeley. You might say this sounds like I was going backwards. I was. But I still knew that I was primarily attracted to medicine.

In June I started pre-med courses at the university. At first I didn't know if I could really do it. Then I met Ken, who was also a pre-med. He had spent a year in Africa, and seeing all those crippled, diseased, poor people inspired him to do something with his life. Medicine was something good that he could do. That just won my heart! The week before finals I got evicted from the house I was living in, so I had to move into Ken's house. I was going to take Ken's room while he was away on vacation and when he came back he was going to move down the hall. But when he came back from vacation, for some unknown reason I kissed him as he walked in the door. We began spending time together. We found ourselves getting involved, and ended up living in the same room. That was fun. The room was so tiny, it was absurd. We had a very romantic first month or so. The first three days especially, over vacation, before school started. That was when it snowed in Berkeley. We went up to the hills and played in the snow and threw snowballs at my dog Esa. We went to the movies, and we stayed up all night talking and, oh, it was just a wonderful three days!

When we were finishing pre-med, just before we applied to medical schools, we started talking about getting married. Ken doesn't feel very romantic about marriage, but we knew if we wanted to get into the same medical school it would be a lot easier if we were married. So we made the decision on a practical basis. One weekend we just drove to Gardnerville, Nevada, and got married by a justice of the peace. Then we went gambling and won a lot of money, and found a lovely nude beach on the corner of Lake Tahoe and went swimming. It was a nice weekend.

We actually got into a number of med schools, but we decided to go to UC Medical Center, right here in San Francisco. That's what we'll be doing in the fall. For the last couple of months I've been working in the pathology department of Kaiser Hospital while waiting for med school to begin. It's basically a dreary job, and the highlights of my life are the few hours when I'm not at work. I'm in a Woman's Group, and that's a very important part of my life. We meet for three or four hours every week. I've been in the group for two and a half years, and we're struggling along, learning a lot of important things.

Reilly Ridgell:
It really blew my mind when I ran into Debbie about two years ago. I was visiting back in the States, looking up this Peace Corps volunteer who'd been on Puluwat Island back in 1966. Then I found him, and it turned out he was going with Debbie Gordon! It

was mind-boggling! When I saw her, she told me her name was Deborah—not Debbie—Deborah. And okay, that's her name, so it's her business. A person's name, there's nothing more personal, so that's fine, I'll call her Deborah. But she's also very strongly into women's liberation, and she got down on me because of it. I was traveling with one of the guys from the island, and I said something about trying to get him laid, and she got down on me for being a male chauvinist. She said my friend wouldn't have any trouble, anyway. You know, I backed off, naturally, because I guess it was a chauvinistic remark, but you do make chauvinist remarks now and then.

I want to have a baby someday, and I hope I have the time for two. I think maybe in the middle of medical school I'll take a year out and have one. It's very hard to fit a baby into a career. But I imagine my future working either in Africa or out in the country somewhere, and my family life and work don't have to be that separate.

There isn't a week that goes by when I don't have some reservations about being a doctor. One of the fears I have is what a sobering influence, what a chilling influence it will have on me. I think doctors get immune, somehow, to feeling other people's pain. They also get a little muted in their response to life. That's something that scares me about it.

Sure, I want to stay young. Who doesn't? Recently I've been thinking about that a lot. When I was younger, it seemed that I was very pure about everything. I was very ardently political, for instance, and very outspoken about my politics. Everything was wonderful—or it was awful. Now I've begun to see things as grays, and I'm losing the real extremes. But I don't imagine that's going to be permanent. I don't know why. I wouldn't go back to the past, but I miss the extremes. I'm real confident they're going to come back some day.

Thinking seriously about my life, sometimes even today I'd sort of like to drop out. I'd feel so liberated. You know, free time, doing what I want, going to the country, being a waitress, being this and that. But I know that after six months I'd be destroyed. I want to do something that keeps me more than just active. I need something that will keep me involved—and give me some satisfaction on my own, apart from what other people bring into my life.

•

Sitting cross-legged on her chair, Deborah talked with shining eyes of the new career she had chosen. As we listened, we wondered if she would really survive the five years of medical training without another change of plan, or whether her current interest in medicine was simply the latest in an endless series of "adventures." Deborah was obviously blessed with an abundance of talent and energy, but she seemed to suffer from a chronic inability to make lasting decisions. We saw in her dilemma a key to many of the stories we had heard from the members of the class of '65. Our group had been offered a range of opportunities unparalleled in human history; for this favored generation nothing was impossible. We were free to explore new alternatives in love, careers, living arrangements and basic values. With so many options to consider, was it any wonder that we had such a difficult time making up our minds?

Yet it seemed that Deborah Gordon had at long last found her way; after all, her parents and teachers and peers were all impressed by her new resolve. She even talked of trying to revive a friendship that had been lying dormant for several years.

"You remember Carol Shen, don't you? She lives right here in Berkeley but I haven't seen her for years! But now that I'm married, and going to med school, maybe we can get together . . . I don't know. Were you planning to see her while you were here?"

We told Deborah that we were, and she asked us to give Carol her regards.

●

Carol Shen: She Tried Harder

●

Debbie Gordon:
In high school, we were really good friends. She went to my church for a while, Brentwood Presbyterian. Every Thanksgiving, Carol would come over to my house, and she'd bring little Chinese candies wrapped in rice paper.

I remember her as being very active in everything. Very smart and good in school. She seemed quite ambitious. I think she had some conflicts because her parents were very affirmatively Chinese, and resented however much she was able to merge into the Palisades culture.

Judy Tomash:
She expressed to me that she felt uncomfortable being the only Oriental girl—she was very conscious that she wasn't white like the rest of us. She talked about having an operation on her eyes to make them look more western, and I remember telling her not to, for God's sake not to straighten out her eyes.

Socially, I think she did very well under the circumstances. She was always directed. She knew what she wanted and she set out to do it, and she got it done. She watched who was popular in school, and who she would relate to was governed somewhat by where she thought they were in the social sphere.

I remember having an argument with her about Communist China. We were on a camping trip together and I was spouting off about how great Communism was and she said that all her relatives had lost possessions and money. I was very unsympathetic.

Jamie Kelso:
She seemed to be very much intent on succeeding academically, and willing to play by the rules of homework to get her A.

Bob Searight:
She was in the more studious section of our group, and sort of more chaste and prudish than most. I never considered dating her.

Reilly Ridgell:
I looked her picture up in the annual the other day—she looks pretty, really pretty. But for some reason she was not considered desirable in high school. I don't know whether it was because she was Oriental, because I certainly don't have anything against Orientals. But she was strange—or not strange, just undesirable as a date for some reason. I remember her being in the social sphere, but never having a boyfriend or dating that much. Like I say, I can't figure it out. Where is she now? I'll call her up right now . . .

•

Carol Shen lives today in the steep wooded hills behind the University of California at Berkeley. She and her husband recently purchased a three-bedroom house, which they have remodeled together. They are proud of the new interiors: bare white walls, hardwood floors, low-slung modern furniture. Sitting down with Carol in the dining room, we found it hard to believe that this sleek, tall, strikingly beautiful woman had found it so difficult to lead a normal social life at Palisades High School.

•

In terms of my appearance, I know I really tried. I felt terribly self-conscious all the time—sort of the struggling adolescent. The perfect example of the struggling adolescent. My parents at home reassured me: "It's really your personality that counts, and if you're a good person, it doesn't matter what you look like, or if you wear glasses or not." This went on and on. We sort of made this pact that when I was sixteen I could get contact lenses. I recall my first day going back to school with them on—and no one noticed anything. I finally got up my nerve in my phys. ed. class with the girls standing next to me at the locker, and said, "Do you notice anything different?" They didn't know what it was. When I said "contact lenses" they said, "Oh, I guess I do remember you wearing glasses." You know, I was pretty much convinced at the end of the day that maybe my parents were right, that I had blown it all out of proportion.

I was always raised with this basic drive from my parents to compete hard, to do the very best I could, and to achieve the most that I could. I guess I did study hard, but for me it was really enjoyable. I would easily put in three or four hours a night on homework. I very rarely watched television.

My father's family was a banking family in Shanghai and my mother's family was a landholding family in central China. My parents were betrothed to one another when they were five and six years old. In the thirties my father came to this country for his college education. My dad is an aeronautical engineer. My parents were planning all the time to go back to China, but as events unfolded in the forties they were forced to stay here. I don't even know if my mother's family survived to the point of the Revolution. My father's family got out—my grandfather is living now in Taiwan. My parents still speak Mandarin to me, but I only understand enough to get around in our house.

I don't think I ever went through a period of real rebellion against my parents. They never forced me to be Oriental—I just was. Socially, it was . . . I don't know. Instead of being Chinese, I could have had a broken nose, or a gimp leg, it could have been anything. I mean, in high school I might as well have been crippled—I just felt *so* different.

The year after graduation I went to Berkeley and I finally got my Asian identity crisis over with. It was not resolved in the way that you might think. I had to prove that I could be just as good as any American, despite the fact that I was Asian. I accomplished this by going through sorority rush the spring of my freshman year. I went through the whole routine of going from house to house, sitting down and chatting with people, and being accepted, and rejected, and selecting certain ones to go back to— just going through the whole process. Finally I managed to get into a house that had never had Asians in it up to that time. In fact, a San Francisco newspaper ran a little teeny clip that said: "The first Oriental has gotten into this sorority." For me, it was a way I could test myself and prove to the world that I could do all the things that a blond and blue-eyed girl could do. Of course, I had to really be a sort of superperson in order to do this—you know, super nice and super bright and super everything. But as it turns out, there's nothing wrong with being super nice or working super hard.

I think the sorority thing was really a prescribed

cure for all the ills I was feeling up to that point. I started going out with no apparent problem. I went our fairly often, almost every weekend. I never went out with someone who was Chinese. Subconsciously, that may have been my choice, but you know, I never really had an opportunity to interact with Chinese people very much.

I never went back to LA. I spent all my summers up here at Berkeley working. I had gotten interested in architecture because I used to study over at the architecture building. The spirit of the architecture students really hit me as a neat thing to try and get involved in. They always worked all hours of the night, and the classes and the studio life seemed a lot more energetic than the normal sort of program I was seeing.

I wasn't involved in drugs at all at Berkeley. With freaky friends I was considered so straight that I could be irritating. Then in the sorority I was also a little strange—really into my architecture and getting straight A's at it.

In senior year I got together with Bill. He happened to see a picture of me in the school darkroom, and then he got in touch and asked if I'd be a subject for his photography. I said of course I didn't mind. So we went out and spent a day on campus and he photographed me.

When we started going out, I thought I had met my match—someone who had gone beyond me in terms of involvement with work and demanding perfection of himself. He was the kind of architecture student who got so much reinforcement from his work that he didn't need anything else. There was really no weakness that I could see. It was his strength that I found amazing. I still do.

Bill went off to architecture school at Harvard, and I eventually got into MIT, and the winter after graduation from Berkeley we were married. Bill is Jewish, but there's no racial or religious problem at all. Sometimes I sense that my parents accept him more than they accept me. They're really sure he's good, but they're not sure that I am.

The two years we were in architecture school was just an incredibly busy time. Both of us worked in architect's offices while we were going to school, and then after we graduated we got jobs in Honolulu helping to design a new rapid-transit system. That was the first time we worked together in the same office, so in Honolulu I had to face the whole women's-lib thing of establishing separate credibility. I remember the first time we had a conference with some people from a shopping center that our transit line was going to go by. I was designing the station for that particular site. I was the one doing the thing, and we called together a conference and these people arrived in the conference room and the project manager introduced us: "I'd like you to meet Bill Glass and his wife Carol." Immediately they sort of looked at me quizzically, like "What's his wife doing at the meeting? Did she just come in on her way from shopping?" Then finally: "Oh, she's an architect!" But before that was even cleared up, they told me that they took cream and sugar in their coffee.

Today we work in the same office in San Francisco, one of the biggest engineering firms in the world. When I think about it, it's just phenomenal that two individuals have been created that work together as well as we do! If I ever want to depress myself, I just think what if some horrible disaster happened . . . We have gotten very close. So close, after five years, that I know it could never be replaced. I'd have to say that I think our marriage is pretty special.

I definitely would like to have children someday, but I don't think I would ever take time off from working. Well, maybe a few hours! But really, that's one advantage that architecture has—it's something I can do any hour of the day. Ten years from today I just hope the recession will be over, and Bill and

I will be busier than we can even imagine, putting more and more new buildings together.

Debbie Gordon:

Carol used to be one of my closest friends, but we've only talked about a half-dozen times since high school. She seems very happy, very successful in her architecture, and with her husband. And I don't feel very close to her. I don't think I could ever be really close with Carol again. We are really in different worlds. Perhaps I'm entering her world now—I'm going to be a professional too. She's very much into that professional world and she travels all over for her work. That's no reason, really, why we can't be friends, but just in talking to her, our speed seems very different.

When I look back, it's very easy to think that I would not have needed so much reinforcement from the work I do had I been socially accepted when I was younger—had I been blond and blue-eyed. Had I not needed acceptance from work, had I gotten it from friends and from boys as a teenager, it's perfectly conceivable that I could have gotten married in the middle of college and had two kids and lived happily ever after.

Well, I don't know about "happily."

•

There were so few complications in Carol's story that we finished our interview unexpectedly early. Carol got up to fetch her husband from the study in which he'd been working, and we spent the balance of a pleasant evening telling Bill Glass what his wife had been like in high school. Darkness had settled completely on the hills, and the lights had gone up all around San Francisco Bay. It was a clear night and the view from the bay window was magnificent. As we sat back sipping

Carol's freshly ground coffee and enjoying that view, we decided we would stay an extra day in the Bay Area. There was another member of our high school class who. deserved a visit. He lived only a few miles away from Carol, but it was definitely another part of town.

•

Mike Shedlin: The Goof-Off

•

Jamie Kelso:
Mike seemed to be a rebel, a malcontent. He really didn't know what he wanted to do, but he had a great dissatisfaction with the school and with the rather nebulous world we all existed in. It was standard operating procedure for him to go to the limit of what you could do wrong. But he wasn't a hoodlum; he was more of a practical joker—though there was often a mean streak to his humor.

Jeff Stolper:
Shedlin was a weird person, to put it bluntly. He came off as being obnoxious to a lot of people. He was totally sarcastic. I enjoyed his sense of humor, but a lot of people didn't. I know this because people used to ask me how I could stand to go around with him. I think I actually lost a lot of friends because I used to hang around with Shedlin.

Mike Shedlin: The Goof-Off

I remember the senior prom, when Shedlin told me they were having an unannounced dance contest and the top prize was fifty dollars. It was going to be at such-and-such a time for a half-hour. So my date and I danced for a full half-hour, me in my tuxedo and her in her formal. Just sweating and the whole bit. Afterward I was sure we'd won because we danced the whole time. There was Shedlin in the corner cracking up.

Mike Medved:
In high school, I probably had only three or four conversations with Shedlin, but I remember them well. I always thought of him as a racy character, someone who was doing things that I associated with an older group of people. He had a tough, slick demeanor and there was an association in my mind between Shedlin and the James Dean image, the sort of 1950's Rebels Without a Cause.

Candy McCoy:
He had lots of blond hair, and I remember him being very pretty. I'm quite sure I had a crush on him, but there was some reason I wasn't supposed to.

Jean O'Brien, teacher:
Shedlin had the great need to feel totally and completely comfortable. He had shoes that were made like moccasins, but the inside was like sheepswool. We talked about the shoes, and he had this special feeling with his feet. And did you ever notice how Shedlin's clothes stayed on, but there was nothing binding? I guess it was a womblike need to be suspended without touching. Remember the long blond hair—and those blue eyes? He was a marvelous kid. He really was. I remember when he got onto the yearbook staff, and did all those awful things. It was off-color, but my God, it was hysterical.

●

Along with five other people, Mike Shedlin shares a run-down two-story house on one of Berkeley's most heavily trafficked streets. His housemates include his former girl friend, his current girl friend, and the new girl friend's six-year-old son. The residents of the house seemed engaged in a losing struggle against faulty plumbing. The kitchen faucet suffers from a constant, heavy drip, and the house is blessed with only one functioning bathroom. The front lawn is untended except for a small patch which has been given over to a homeless hippie, who uses this space to grow wheatgrass, the staple of his diet. Throughout the house, on the walls and the doors, are numerous 3″ × 5″ cards with neatly typed quotations from famous anarchists, evidence of one of Michael's most recent projects.

Michael's household manages to support itself with the help of federal food stamps and a monthly general-assistance grant from the County Welfare Agency. He is satisfied with his current living situation because the rent is low and there is lots of space, but he wouldn't mind moving to a safer neighborhood. More than once he has been awakened by the screams of a rape victim.

During our visit a soft drizzle tapping against the windows of Michael's bedroom seemed to make it easier to evoke memories of the past. A smirk of satisfaction lined his face as he recalled some of his school exploits.

●

I was on the Annual staff senior year; I maliciously fucked up one of the pages in the annual. I made obscenities out of people's names. I changed "Finkelstein" to "Fucklestein" and "Rapf" to "Rape." It was my idea of a practical joke. I had no consciousness of how brought-down these people would be if their names came out that way in two thousand copies of the annual. I finally got busted at a late stage. It cost the school fifteen hundred dollars. I was called down to the Boys' Vice Principal's office and he threatened to give me an F. My father was there and he was upset. He didn't come down on me, but when we got home he told me I should be more considerate of other people.

Once I stole the Boys' Vice Principal's office stamp so that I could insert phony messages into the daily announcements on the public address system. I also used the stamp to get my friends out of class. One time Miss O'Brien found out and cornered me and said, "I know you did this, so you might as well confess." I denied it, but I think she knew that I was lying. I respected her for confronting me like that.

Another time I wore a "Pussy Galore" sweat shirt to graduation practice. I was a James Bond fan—I'd seen the movies and read all the books—and I thought it was funny. The Boys' Vice Principal called me into his office, and then sent me home. My mother called him up and chewed him out, which I thought was great. My parents' support of me against the school had a tremendous effect on me in terms of not submitting to arbitrary authority.

My parents are extremely wonderful, super well-educated, nonauthoritarian people. I've never been able to hate my parents. I've never been able to reject them. We understand each other real well. We get along and I can be totally open with them. My mother went to college and got a master's. She was a social worker and worked for the Army. She is a strong woman. My father is a humanist psychologist, a teacher and a consultant. They were always left-liberal sympathizers with revolution. Very wise, compassionate, radically oriented people.

In high school, I had a room of my own, separated from my parents' house. I could come or go at will. They let me take the car out. They never grounded me.

I remember dating a couple of prestigious, sexy

girls, out of my social class. I was always amazed and upset and titillated that these women, who I figured had actually fucked college guys, would go out with me. I always considered myself . . . funny-looking? I was obsessed by how unclassical my profile was. It was good for my ego that these fancy women would go out with me. But I would only go out with them once or twice because I had nothing to offer them. We would go to a movie and then go home to my little room back there. Once I was trying to seduce a girl as far as I could and she looked at me and said, "You have the saddest eyes I've ever seen." Boy, that stopped me.

My parents knew that I was not a gung-ho student, so they suggested that I apply to a "C" college like University of Hawaii or University of Colorado. I chose Hawaii because I thought it would be easy and fun and I would be really away from home.

In biology class of my first year I met the first great love of my life. We hit it off real strong and spent all of our time together, literally. It was a whole new world, and it was exactly what I wanted. I paid no attention to school. My parents had given me fourteen hundred dollars so I would learn to take care of money. During the six months I was supposed to be going to school, mostly what I did was fuck or spend money. It was the most lovely and free and learningful time of my life. Consequently, I did not achieve too much scholastically. As a matter of fact, all of my teachers gave me F's.

So, in scholastic disgrace, but in a great erotic maelstrom, I called my parents collect many, many times and said, "I'm out of money, and I don't know what to do and we want to get married." My girl friend was eighteen, and I was seventeen. So I came back to Los Angeles with my girl friend. This was okayed by my parents, and we got a small apartment on the edge of Beverly Hills. My parents were always giving me a little money, and they gave us the car on weekends.

Meanwhile I got a job as a lineman for General Telephone Company, and I brought home a hundred and thirty-five dollars every two weeks. I was risking my life up these fucking poles and crawling down in sewers and shit. I felt that I was not cut out to be a telephone lineman. I went back to school because I learned quickly that the world of jobs was more horrible than the world of school. Going to school had its advantages: I could get support from home and I could stay out of the draft for a while. Because I could rely on my parents to give me concrete financial support, I early on developed an aversion to working in a structured situation where I had to be some place at a certain time. I didn't like being asked to sell my life in order to buy back my life from the patriarchs who have turned the economy into a munitions plant.

But of course I own no capital, so I work or I hustle. I have worked as a shipper of books. I have worked as a furniture mover. I have worked as a guard on a movie set. I worked in a candy factory for one day. I've worked for the Registrar of Voters. I've worked as a free-lance editor and as a writer of film criticism.

About this time, I started to smoke pot. The release was tremendous. Pot was an easy and pleasant consciousness alteration. It was easily available and much more fun than liquor. We were obsessive about it. We would smoke all the time. We would go home from school, smoke ten joints and go back to school. I've taken the basic cycle of drugs that people try: acid twenty-five or thirty times, laughing gas, speeds of various kinds, cocaine. I sniffed heroin once. I've only injected drugs once. It was supposed to be THC —cannabis concentrate. It turned out to be bear tranquilizer, otherwise known as PCP or Angel Dust. It was an extremely intense experience. I was blind for about an hour and a half, but not unpleasantly so. They tell me that I just held on to a counter and said things like "Wow, this is God" or "Ego is nothing." You know, standard drug revelations.

I became a barbiturate addict in 1968–69. It was about a year-long process. As I got deeper into it I became more and more alienated from everyone. My lover couldn't deal with me any more. My parents were freaked. Finally I crashed their car, got busted, and had the d.t.'s for four days. It was a lame experience. I recommend nonaddictive drugs.

Anyway, for a couple of years I lived in Berkeley and Venice. Basically, I put most of my energy into the disintegration of my love affair, which took two years. Adjusting to the disillusionment of a dissolving love affair was the most excruciating thing I've ever experienced. We were together for eight years.

I also got involved in radical politics. I had read Lenin and Mao and thought of myself as a Marxist. Then, in a used-book store in Berkeley, I came across Irving Louis Horowitz's anthology *The Anarchists,* and right away I gravitated toward that. My basic instincts and training and beliefs and actions are still certainly anarchist.

I am an independent, not a party man. I believe that America needs a free, democratic socialism. Individuals are not going to liberate themselves by turning their minds over to yet another state-power ideology such as Leninism.

Culture, history, philosophy represent everything that is *past.* There is no return. We are fated to plunge alone into the future, surrounded by forces and dimensions we may never see, leastwise understand or socialize. Freedom is a practice, a personal existential revelation, not a new bureaucracy. My own activism takes the personal form of living in ways which are consciously opposed to the values and attitudes of the dominant culture and the public forms of sharing my consciousness with others through writing and other media. In lieu of indulging in any extended exhortations, let me quote from Emma Goldman: "Revolution is in vain unless inspired by its ultimate ideal."

Like almost everyone I know, I aspire to be an

ecstatic lover, a famous artist, an effective revolutionary. Should I give up my dreams because the American Establishment tells me that to be a drone is to be a responsible citizen? Who benefits from my surrender to wage slavery but the masters, anyway? Of what possible assistance to the oppressed masses can I be by working for the capitalists? I say none. I say fuck the masters and their "realities." I work for myself, for my affinity groups, for love and beauty and freedom.

It says on my voter registration that I am a journalist. However, when people ask me what I do, I usually give an evasive answer, like "I try to make ends meet." We're legitimately poor. I have very few material possessions. I sold most of my books. I sold my drug-book collection so I could buy weed.

I just went through an arduous experience. I tried to get unemployment, but I was classified as self-employed, which is basically true.

In the eyes of the ruling classes and their bureaus, I am insane. So be it. I may have an hallucination now and then, but I do not commit genocide, I do not starve and exploit whole continents, I do not sell bombs and war planes to corrupt dictatorships, I do not make killing and oppression "legal," I do not rule anybody, I do not "represent" anybody, I do not imprison anybody, and I do not seek to be judged sane by a secret government of liberal fascists.

●

Michael sighed with relief as he concluded his speech, and asked us to run the tape back for a few minutes so he could review his own words. Satisfied with what he heard, he invited us to join him for a walk in the rain to celebrate the completion of his interview. We declined the offer, and made reservations on the midnight plane back to Los Angeles.

●

Getting Stoned

•

Lee Grossman:
During senior year of high school, a guy a year younger than us pulled me aside and said, "Do you want to blow some pot?" I didn't know what he meant. When he explained what it meant I was horrified. I figured, God, it's like shooting up! He then gave me a lecture about getting my emotional self as mature as my intellectual self. I thought that was far out. He was pretty weird.

Then, during Christmas vacation of my freshman year in college, I was exposed to dope again—this time by an evil person named David Wallace. He took me into his bedroom in his parents' house and he went over to the bookshelf and very conspiratorially removed a small ebony box, very ornate, like a cuff-link box. He opened it and showed it to me without a word. It was filled with this green, immaculately manicured weed. I didn't know what the hell it was. When he told me I kind of went, "Oh yeah. Right." We went over to my parents' house because they were away at the time. We put "The Mothers of Invention" on my sister's stereo and turned it up very loud. Then we smoked the dope. It was the most hilarious experience I ever had. David was sitting on the floor cross-legged with his head between the speakers, chuckling. He looked to me like some sort of turtle,

204

with a perfectly round shell. So I walked up to him, picked him up by the knee and rolled him across the room. That was my first grass experience. It's been downhill ever since.

Debbie Gordon:
The first time I smoked dope was first semester freshman year. There were some boys in the dorm next door who turned on, and they wanted the girls they were friendly with to try it. My one friend tried it first, and she really liked it. I didn't drink or do anything and it was sort of hard to bring myself to do it. The most interesting fellow in that crowd—we all sort of liked him—was flirting with me one time and he took me out and suggested, "Oh, come on. You can try it." And I decided to do it—we smoked a joint. I remember that night very clearly, sort of laughing and carrying on. I kept saying, "I don't feel it." And he kept saying, "But you're acting so stoned!" It was a pretty typical first experience.

Mark Holmes:
My first acid trip was during a full lunar eclipse. I was taking astronomy at the time, so I was the authority on lunar eclipses. So here I am on my first acid trip explaining to my friends, who were just as ripped out of their heads as I was, what was taking place up in the sky. Having not had an acid experience before, I didn't know what I was hallucinating and what was real. I was explaining the sun and the earth, and it was very cosmic.

Lany Tyler:
When I was in my first year of college, drugs were just beginning to get started. Marijuana was getting popular and LSD was coming in. I had never so much as smoked a cigarette. I wasn't even aesthetically attracted to smoking dope. It seemed to ruin every good

gathering that I was in. I began to resent it intensely. The whole ritual. All of a sudden the curtains would go down, the Indian music would come on, the incense would start. Someone would roll a joint. Then everybody in the room would start to space out. Nobody was talking to anybody any more. It infuriated me. It became my own personal quest to avoid it and to be outspokenly antagonistic to the whole cult. That was a position that left me pretty much isolated at the time.

Lisa Menzies:
When I ran away from home in high school, the situation got extremely violent with my parents I felt that there had to be some sort of authoritative medium to help us talk. So I got in touch with a psychologist and we all got together. I called my folks and told them that I wanted to meet in neutral territory with this person.

I went to the psychologist for a year. I guess I was seventeen when I started, because when I was eighteen I was already getting stoned on pot. I walked into her office one day and I was very happy. She was smiling. I was beaming and she just beamed back at me. She said, "Oh, you're so happy today! Why are you so happy?"

I said, "I'm stoned. I've just smoked a joint and I'm stoned."

Her face dropped to the floor and she got very uptight. I looked at her and knew that I wouldn't go back to her again. This was no one I could talk to. She was just as appalled as anyone else.

Mike Shedlin:
In 1968 I came across some red pills in my parents' medicine cabinet. I called up a friend on the phone who knew about these things and asked him what they were. They were in fact "reds"—Seconal. I took three

of them. I had a real heavy experience—crying, joy of being released from my linear reality and guilt orientation. So before I came up to Berkeley we started taking barbiturates as a group. We ran around and we had barbiturate parties. We took barbiturates and went to movies. It's like liquor, only easier.

For six months it was cool. There was no thievery or crashing cars or falling down stairs. But after that I was really hooked. I finally crashed my parents' Peugeot. A nice car. No one was hurt in the accident. I remember bouncing around inside the car as it rolled over. I also remember finding myself out on the street before the police came and remembering that I had a marijuana joint in my pocket and not wanting to get busted for possession. I threw the joint away and did not get busted, but I could not walk a straight line at the police station. They put me in a tank overnight. My father came down and was so exasperated and horrified at what I had become that he said through the jail grille that I could just stay there. This was quite a blow to me, because they had always rescued me in the past.

So my friends got me out that afternoon. I lost thousands of dollars on lawyers, et cetera. After two busts and the d.t.'s, I finally stopped taking barbiturates.

My best drug experiences have been with marijuana and laughing gas, and the first few times I took acid. But today, all I do is smoke pot, if that. Sometimes I make resolutions to stop because I'll ascribe all my negative, escapist, undisciplined tendencies to the drug rather than to my own brain. However, since I know that's not the case, the next day, if pot's there, I'll smoke.

Jamie Kelso:

Drugs are exceedingly simple. They are a potent escape from reality. Someone who finds reality as it is to be perfect and pleasurable beyond words to describe it—as I do—has not the slightest desire to cut off, blank out or mix up his ability to perceive that reality. To such a person, drugs of any kind can only be an impediment. I verified this for myself by using LSD once and marijuana once in 1967. On both occasions I had what the drug aficionados would deem "ultimate trips" with such highlights as ego loss, visual inversion, cognitive blackouts, hallucinations, the whole bit. I feel sorry for poor Alan Watts and Timothy Leary. What a crumbum cheapskate nirvana they settled for!

Donald Golden:
The best experience I ever had on LSD was right here in northern California in the middle of nowhere. It was the most stoned that I have ever been. I mean, I was almost relating to things on a molecular level. I was just really disassociated from my physical body, and floating through trees—these big fir trees that threw shadows on the road. I was walking along with a dog to visit these people who had a place up the road, and I was getting really scared because I was so far removed from my normal perceptions of reality. It wasn't me at all, and I was just dissolving completely into the environment. It was real scary. I'd never been that far out. Then we got to this place and all the dogs started barking and getting real upset, and the next thing I knew I was crouched down on the ground defending myself from this invisible force that was trying to kill me. The dog I was with was real freaked out and I held on to it. It felt like if I let him go he'd just get gobbled up by this force, and so I held him and held him and just stayed there and faced this thing. I could sense it moving around, and I would move around on the ground and keep facing it. Finally it went away, and I felt I'd won.

It was a real breakthrough in my personal development. Right in that confrontation, I felt like I had dealt with a whole big bundle of fear that I had inside me.

Skip Baumgarten:

I got some inkling of what a bad trip was like while I was in Miami Beach for the Republican convention in '72.

I took the acid at the home of some jet-setters near Indian Creek. This place was almost a mansion. My trip started out quite lovely. I was sitting out by the swimming pool watching cloud formations and watching jets land. It was very heavy acid. Then people started to arrive and I became uncomfortable. Everybody was kind of wondering who everybody else was. People had flown in from all over the country to attend the convention. Jerry Rubin showed up and other assorted notables. Because of the acid, I think I became aware of the great amount of phoniness that was going around. The thing to understand about Miami Beach was that everyone was jockeying to move himself up. Not just the politicians. But celebrities, newspapermen —everybody.

I decided I had to get out of there, but all I had on was a pair of swim trunks. I went out to my car but the car wouldn't start. So I decided to walk back to my hotel, which was about eighty-five blocks away.

I had lived in Miami Beach for a few years as a child. Once, when crossing the street, I had gone out of the way to step on a bug and was told not to, that it was a scorpion. Now, on my acid trip, walking along a little after dusk, somehow everything on the street looked like a scorpion, and that freaked me out. I was very scared.

I went down to the ocean, which had always seemed like a very good friend and a good place to be. I spent several hours playing in the waves and felt much better, at which point I continued to walk home.

Ron Conti:
I've smoked pot and all that. I've never gotten into any psychedelics. But always in the back of my mind I've thought, What would it be like? But I never had the guts to do it. I felt it wasn't worth it. Let's put it this way: the experience might be great, but there's just too many people that go up and never come down. I thought maybe I'd be one of them.

Ron Conti: Big Bad Ron

•

Lee Grossman:
He was an enormous, frightening character. I don't think I ever exchanged any words with him. I picture him in the car-club class of people—maybe carrying a tire chain. His distinguishing characteristic was that he had no neck.

Donald Golden:
He seemed like a bully. Sort of a brutish, insensitive guy that I felt threatened by.

Jamie Kelso:
He was an intimidating tough guy. An enormous, hulking individual. Overdeveloped. Enormous hands and arms and legs. If you had him in your gym class, that was the ultimate horror—to have to run up against this guy or have him hit you or throw you on the

ground. You really wanted to be on his team every time.

There were some guys for whom fighting was a pastime. He would be one of those people. Real slugfests. He could definitely hold his own. He was a nonintellectual guy that wanted to get as much Driver Education and Study Hall as possible. He would have been the type to walk behind you, flip your books, and it was just too bad. Or to spit at you out the window of the bus, and it was just too bad. There was nothing you could do about it.

Anita Champion:
My impression of him was that he was one of the loudest, slobbiest, heaviest goof-offs in the whole school. Every day he used to wear the same thing. He wore black loafers, white socks, blue jeans that were straight-legged and about three sizes too big in the rear, slung down on his hips, with a white T-shirt and a blue nylon windbreaker jacket. Every single day, the exact same thing! He would wear his hair parted on the side, slicked back with all the grease on it. Personally, I dug clean-cut guys like Brock and Mark Holmes. I wouldn't have gone out with someone like Ron Conti.

Margie Williams:
I remember him as drinking a lot of beer. He drove a big black station wagon with the wheels raised way up in back. He was always crashing a lot of parties. Always a lot of fun. I recall a few fights involving Ron in high school, and he could really push his weight around.

Bob Searight:
He was one of the stalwarts of the Saracens. He was tough, but he was also a nice guy. He wouldn't beat up on people unless they deserved it.

Gary Wasserman:

In the Saracens, we used to rely on Ron as the muscle and strength in the organization. He had to really be coerced into fighting, but if he fought, he'd break up somebody pretty good. With Ron, you never knew whether he was going to laugh or he was going to break you in half, because it was really the same action.

•

When we visited his tidy apartment in the Pacific Palisades, we were astonished at the way Ron Conti had changed in ten years. The frightening monster that our classmates recalled had disappeared entirely, and in its place was a laughing, sandy-haired young man with bright-blue eyes and a trim athletic build. When we registered our surprise, Ron confessed that he had lost forty pounds since high school. "My neck used to be two inches larger than it is now, and my biceps were two inches larger." Nonetheless, he still has massive arms and shoulders, and we noticed an imposing set of barbells resting in front of the fireplace. "I run a lot, and I work out in a gym," Ron told us. "I'm smoking, but I'm in better shape now than I've ever been." As we sat down in the dining room with his wife, Ron looked back at his one-time tough-guy image with considerable amusement.

•

I had a nickname in high school that was put on me by Gary Wasserman. He called me "Hoss." How many guys were walking around that school that weighed two hundred and forty pounds, anyway? It was as if I had to portray the image of a "Hoss" all the time. I did my share of fighting, pushing around, shoving. But the big bad guy didn't exist under all this camouflage. I guess my reputation was an ego thing for me. You know, I had the world by the tail. I could walk through campus with my head held high and not worry about anybody saying anything to me. I thought that was the image for a man, to be bad. Big and bad. But I was really a big, gentle guy. It was only if someone would push me the wrong way that I went a little berserk.

One time I was at this party at Santa Monica. This guy tried to crash the party, and he had such a bad reputation around town that nobody wanted to mess with him. I'd had a few drinks, so I was feeling pretty brave. He was out in the middle of the backyard yelling and screaming that he was going to beat up everybody in the place, so I went over and challenged him. The fight took about two minutes. After we were finished he went to the emergency hospital and had a series of stitches in his eye, because I had almost knocked it out. We became good friends after that.

In high school, every one of the fights I was in was over in two minutes. To tell you the truth, I never lost.

After I graduated I thought I'd get out in the world and start earning some money. I'd never had a job before. I started living away from home off and on. I got a job at Douglas Aircraft, building giant crates for things like missiles. From there, three other guys and myself went down to the Bahamas for five months and did some carpentry work. When I came back I went to City College for a while and did odd carpentry jobs until about 1969.

For a while I was living near Topanga Beach and going through a rowdy stage. I was going around with a different group of people at this time, older, rowdy. Really fun. We were just more or less bumming around. It was like a twenty-four hour party all the time.

Then one of the guys I was bumming around with started dating Anita Champion, and I was exposed to her quite a bit. I had sat next to her for a couple of years in high school, but never really taken notice of her before. Then one day our eyes just kind of met.

We went away to the mountains for the weekend, and I was with another girl and Anita was with this guy she was dating. And everything just jelled. It was sort of a mystery to me. I'd sat next to this girl for so many years in school, and now all of a sudden she was turning me on. I wanted to find out why. She had a fantastic body. She had a fantastic personality. I could tell that she respected me. And I knew if I was gonna be her man, she was gonna do everything for me. At the end of this camping trip, I ended up with Anita. I lost a friend in the process, but that was it, man. That was it. It's been beautiful ever since . . .

Anita Champion:
Good Wife and Mother

Ron Conti:
Alphabetically, Champion is right near Conti, so we always had the same registration room in high school. I sat next to her, but she was the type of girl I was afraid to talk to. I was really shy in my own way. I never even dated until I got out of high school. All I remember about Anita is her hair piled up on her head and sticking straight up in the air, with about three cans of hair spray to keep it there.

Jeff Stolper:
She used to ride the bus with me in junior high school. That's probably how I first got to know her. She was always friendly. She never had that egotistical sense about her. I remember in the senior annual, where we all put down what our career plans were, Anita put down *"Good wife and mother."* A lot of people laughed

at her for that, but I always thought she was an all-around great girl.

Jamie Kelso:

Anita was one of the first girls to bloom in junior high school, and she attracted an enormous amount of male attention because of her early blossoming. She was stacked. It was a rather exciting development for all these pubescent boys! Breast development was one of the biggest things happening in junior high. It was so obvious. Going from A to B to C cups was just something that you couldn't miss. Falsies were very popular back then. Anita definitely didn't have that problem!

Later on, the rest of the girls caught up with her, so she was no longer such a dominant attention-getter once we got to high school.

Mark Holmes:

I remember Anita in the ninth grade and her problem with bad grades. She was the vice president of our class, and I was the president. And Anita was very upset that she had gotten some D's on her report card. The administration asked her to step down, and they put some other girl in her place. It was a very big scandal at the time.

Sally Lobherr:

She seemed very quiet. Kind of like the domestic type. I had the feeling that she wouldn't be going off to school, and if she did, it would only be a semester or two. She never impressed me as being too bright.

Jon Wilson:

Didn't she go with Brock Chester for a while? I remember that she had blond hair, and I would have really liked to go out with her. She had a really good figure. She was always tanned, always had her hair done really nice, always looked good.

Lee Grossman:

She was very popular and was considered attractive, but I could never see why. She always seemed kind of pudgy to me. She probably had big breasts. You looked at her and you knew in ten years she was going to be fat. She's undoubtedly married and settled down and has lots of kids.

•

Contrary to Lee Grossman's gloomy prediction, Anita Champion Conti has maintained her much-admired high school figure; in fact, the only change in her appearance is her hair style. In place of the elaborate teased-and-ratted arrangement she favored in high school, she now wore her tawny hair long and natural, parted to one side. "If she ever tried to come home with it the way she had it in high school, she wouldn't get into the house," Ron told us. Both he and Anita were in a laughing, expansive mood as we sat down over tea; just three days before our interview they had learned that Anita was pregnant with their first child.

•

Ron:

It better be a boy! I've already got the mitt and the bat. Nita's already made the first pair of blue booties.

Anita:

As long as it's healthy, that's my main concern. I'm sure I would love a boy or a girl. I've always been more or less a homebody and a nest builder. I really enjoy life just being a wife—taking care of my husband and my home.

In high school, my trouble with grades was because I didn't apply myself. My mind was always other places. I was thinking more of what I was going to wear to the party on Friday night than about the homework I was supposed to be doing. I just couldn't get into studying.

My father's a doctor, and I always had dreams of being a nurse. But I knew because of my inability to study I could never get through college. Just a week out of high school I got a job doing clerical work in a clinic. Then I moved on to a doctor's office and worked there for two and a half years. I learned a lot of medical terminology and I really enjoyed it. I moved out of the house and got my own apartment, and I found out what the big bad world was all about. It wasn't very much fun just trying to support myself, but I think it makes you grow up a lot faster.

I was going with a guy fairly seriously for a while, but he got drafted into Vietnam. I started seeing this friend of Ron's, and then I got together with Ron. He was very gentle and he always smelled good. He always wore Aqua Velva or Old Spice or something. He was sincere. He didn't push me into anything. I was always attracted to men with large physiques. And his blue eyes! I ended up writing a "Dear John" to the poor guy in Vietnam.

Ron:
I told her what to say!

Anita:
We were engaged for a year, and then we got married.

Ron:
For a while I was selling coffee machines. Then I went back into carpentry and did a little speculation building with other guys in Malibu. I was exposed to the real estate business, and I decided to get my realtor's license. Now I'm working for Fred Sands Realty. Great company. I love it. Very dynamic, aggressive. The company's only five years old, and already it's the largest on the West Side.

We hope to buy a home within the next six months. It will be in the Palisades, but we have no intention of staying there any length of time. The annual appreciation rate in the Palisades is higher than any other neighborhood in the United States, believe it or not. So it's a fantastic investment.

Our intentions are to move out of the city of Los Angeles. The only reason we're here now is to get a little chunk before we move on. My goal is to try and open my own office somewhere in a resort area where we can be turned on to the mountains and things like that. Some place like Durango, Colorado, or Jackson, Wyoming. I want to raise my children in a more natural environment. The bullshit around here is driving me crazy.

Anita:

Palisades High is only a couple of blocks from here, so we see what it's like over there. The students today don't seem to have any sense of responsibility or respect for the teachers. They come and go as they please, they dress the way they want, and school's just more or less something to keep them busy between eight and two-thirty. I don't think I could take it today. I would probably have more of a tendency to get involved in drugs, or whatever they're doing.

Ron:

That school just doesn't appear to be any fun any more. There's no spirit, there's no real social happenings at school. You remember Sports Night, the Friday night dances, the football games? Nobody shows up any more. There's just nothing. What are they doing there, really? I mean, we all know these kids are smart and everything else, but I don't think they're applying themselves in the right direction.

Then there's the busing that they've got going now. I don't think it's bad. I think it's good, from talking to people. It doesn't seem to be affecting the school because the blacks are staying with the blacks. Any trouble at the school seems to be the blacks against the blacks. There's no real racial problem there, so to speak, with black against whites. I'm not bigoted, don't get me wrong. But I don't know . . . I don't particularly like the idea of having the Palisades overrun by blacks. If they were living next door to me, I wouldn't be offended. There's what you call blacks, and there's what you call niggers, okay? I think everybody knows the difference.

Anita:
It's just hard to get used to. Ten years ago you could see a couple of colored maids on Friday afternoon waiting to get the bus to go home. Now you drive down Sunset Boulevard and every single bus stop has at least twenty-five or thirty black kids standing on the corner. They're not, from what I've seen, causing any trouble. They're not throwing things at cars or yelling anything. It's hard to get used to, that's all.

Ron:
'Sixty-five was for me. 'Seventy-five is a bummer. I don't envy these kids at all. They're better students than we were on a whole, but they're a little mixed up. They don't have the leadership qualities that I think the people in our class did. I was talking to a guy that just got out and he felt the same way. He was looking back on us as the last generation of real leaders. We had that boldness, to decide what to do, then go ahead and do it. It was more of a down-to-earth gutsiness. Gary Wasserman was a leader. Mark Holmes was another one—a real smart guy. These people were out to put their mark on the world. I don't think there's ever going to be another class like ours. Probably just for the variety of people in it.

●

In view of the settled and conventional existence he appeared to be enjoying, we asked Ron if he still had a reputation as "big bad Ron." We were surprised when he answered, "Yeah."

•

I proved that again the other night, as a matter of fact. We manage this apartment building. There's not much responsibility and we save a lot of money on our rent. There was a dispute here—something in the building. I carry a certain amount of authority that has to be exerted every once in a while. There was a certain individual that was giving me some trouble. He came up to me and threatened me. I told him if he took one step closer he was going to be on the ground, and he wasn't going to be able to get up. He definitely believed me. I was definitely telling the truth. He backed off, apologized and walked off.

Anita:
I don't think the sixties had such a big impact on us. We didn't change. I was uninformed then, and I never went out of my way to be informed. We weren't even registered in the last election, but we both would have voted for Nixon. The music we like now is mostly country music. Also Burt Bacharach, Frank Sinatra.

Ron:
My brother-in-law is getting me into jazz. Stan Kenton, Don Ellis, a few others.

When I think back on it, there was one movie that had a big impact on me, and I think on a lot of other people in the country. That was *Easy Rider*. It was unreal! You know, these guys were just bebopping around the country, something I've always wanted to do. We went on a camping trip for two months and did a little bit, but not enough. I envy those guys in the movie. Not so much their motorcycles, but just being free, and doing it.

Anita:

I think we feel trapped, and yet there's an invisible force that kind of keeps us in the Palisades. We could actually go if we wanted to, pack up and leave tomorrow. But there is something that just keeps us here and keeps us here. Whether it's a rut we've fallen into, or whatever . . .

Ron:

I think it's the security myself. I'm doing well in business at this point in time. If I picked up and left, you know, I'd be starting over. I want to be a little more established when I do it. I've always had most of the things I wanted, and to give that up now would be hard for both of us.

Anita:

Wherever we are ten years from now, I don't think we'll be so different from the way we are today. Hopefully, we'll have a home of our own, and I would say at least two children.

Ron:

When Nita said "Good wife and mother" senior year, she hit the nail right on the head. She's beautiful. We're very compatible, rarely argue. We know a lot of couples who got married when we did who are already divorced and things like that. They're just dumfounded by the fact that we're still together after six years. They're jealous of it, and people are always commenting that we're a beautiful couple.

Until you came over tonight, I thought we'd been leading a dull life. Not dull per se, but like I had missed a lot. But hearing about all the other people in our class—the suicides, the spun-out people—I think we've been having a damn good life.

●

After we packed up our tape recorder and loaded it into the trunk of the Datsun, we decided to leave the car where it was and walk three blocks to the campus of Palisades High School. It was midnight and the moon was nearly full. We took a familiar shortcut, scrambling down a steep canyon wall and through the parking lot to the open area at the center of campus. The squat brick buildings and patchy lawns seemed haunted in the darkness, and we laughed as we ran across the central quad. This unplanned return to empty and indifferent buildings suddenly struck us as hilarious. As we went past the apple machine, the barricaded window of the student store, the sheltered pavilion with the picnic tables where we used to eat lunch, our unhappy memories faded into the background. We could understand why the Palisades worked such a powerful magic on people like Ron and Anita, keeping them on familiar ground. Yet for others, it was not difficult to escape. We caught our breath by the flagpole, and decided to contact Lynn Marble in New York.

●

ANALECTA

PALISADES HIGH SCHOOL
1965

published by
The Palisades High School Literary Board

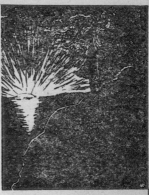

WANDERER   Lynn Marble '65

Wandering free from the sights of man,
Free! that, my life must be:
Free to roam and journey far
With dust on my heels of Lands I mar,
Glorying in the clouds, wrapped in the sun,
Free with the flying winds to run
To the ends of the earth, my arms flung free
To catch the raindrops, the roses, the sea.

Lynn Marble: The Lady with a Rose

•

Jeanne Hernandez, teacher:
Lynn was very beautiful. Always crying, and in some kind of emotional upset. Romantic. That girl was so romantic! I think I consoled her once by saying, "Oh, of course you won't find a high school boy who will satisfy you. What you need is an older man, Lynn."

Jamie Kelso:
She was a dreamer, and very few of the others were. Very mature, well-developed, a big girl. I believe she was a loner. She used to carry a rose to school. She'd bring it to class and keep it on her desk, then picked it up and take it to the next class. She did all kinds of little things like that to say, "Hey, I've got a head and I'm thinking. There's more to me than just this bland conformity."

Sally Lobherr:
She always wore matronly clothes, and she seemed like a stylish matron. I couldn't see her having much fun. I could never see her laughing or saying dirty words or getting drunk or anything like that. She was very intense. With that special intensity of an actress or a dancer.

Lynn Marble: The Lady with a Rose

David Wallace:

She always seemed to be several years older than anybody else. She was in all the school plays, and came across as very dignified on stage. At graduation she won the award for Best Actress. I remember in Play Production class there were a lot of different males who doted on her. At one point I happened to be sitting there and overheard this very serious young man telling Lynn, quite respectfully, that she reminded him of his mother. Lynn was quite taken aback. It was the first time I'd ever seen her lose control of her feelings, her expression, her façade. She said, "Oh my God! What a thing to say!" I know she was very upset by it.

Mike Medved:

I had a furious crush on Lynn Marble throughout the last two years of high school. I wrote her poetic love notes in junior year and dropped them into her locker. They were anonymous, of course. I never did go out with her—I never went out in high school because I didn't know how to drive. But by the end of senior year we were friends. She met me several times at five in the morning to drive up to the hills and watch the sun rise. From the top of Kenter Ridge you could see the whole LA basin. We watched the sky change from black to gray, and then we drove to school. One morning we went so far as to hold hands while we were sitting there on top of the mountain. Because it was Lynn, that put me in total ecstasy.

•

Lynn Marble Erler lives in a venerable brick apartment building on East Forty-third Street in Manhattan, not far from the United Nations. Her small rooms are crowded to overflowing with books, records, house plants and various mementos of world travel. She wore a conservative blue pants suit with a red-and-white scarf tied at the neck. Though excited by this re-union, we tried to keep our voices down so as not to disturb the baby, who was enjoying his afternoon nap behind closed doors. The sounds of traffic drifted up to us from the street below.

•

In high school, I used to come home after school and write and listen to music. We didn't have very classical music, but I listened mostly to that. I used to enjoy *Carmen,* for instance. I would sit and write about my perceptions of life, of my problems and desires and dreams. I called them scratches, and they were just pieces of paper that I wrote on.

Yes, I would say I was romantic. For example, I was interested only in people I thought were sensitive. The ocean was very important to me. It was right down the canyon from the high school, and any time I needed to feel consoled, I would go to the ocean and walk. Even during class I could look out the window and reassure myself that the ocean was not too far away.

I had a weight problem in high school. I never did before, but with the tensions of high school, and so many insecurities, that's when I started eating com-pulsively. I don't think I ever looked really fat, but I certainly didn't look slim and trim. I always had to wear something that hid the fact that I didn't have a waistline. I would wear tunics, or over-blouses, or jackets.

My father, for years and years, had been in con-struction as a carpenter. Neither of my parents had ever been to college. While I was in high school my mother was working in a modeling and advertising agency. She was teaching grooming, personal im-provement and also modeling. My mother being in a business that laid emphasis on physical image and appearance made me feel tremendously guilty that I wasn't a perfect representative of charm and modeling. In order to get out of this feeling of guilt, I went to the other extreme and wanted to reject physical appearance. I wanted to become accepted and appreciated for my intelligence.

After high school I went to UCLA as an anthropology major. I worked hard and did very well. I had no boyfriend. I didn't date. I knew hardly anyone at UCLA.

Then in the summer of '66 I was invited by a friend of my parents', who is an opera singer, to be governess with his children when he and his family went to Germany for the Bayreuth Wagner Festival. For the first time I became really immersed in the world of classical music. When the summer was over, I decided to stay in Europe on my own. I went to Salzburg, Austria. I had met an old German actress who said she would accept me as an auditing student at the acting academy in the Salzburg Mozarteum. I went there and I lived in a Catholic girls' home. I learned a lot. I became very involved in different groups of young Austrians—an artistic group, a sturdy Catholic group, a farmer group, a highly political group.

After six months I was ready to come home. But when I returned to California in January of '67, I found that almost everyone I knew had gotten involved in drugs to a certain extent. I hadn't. My interest was completely out of that. Completely! I just wanted to pursue my interest in music and German culture. I returned to UCLA as a German major. I felt quite isolated and quite out of it. The people from high school that I met again had more or less cracked up, and seemed unhealthy to be around. So I became involved in an intense love affair with one individual who seemed excruciatingly healthy. We shared a passion for music and literature. For a year and a half that relationship was the reason for my existence, and when we broke up it was a traumatic experience. I spent one very turbulent summer and went on to my last year of college. I enjoyed very much flirting with my professors for a while.

At this point I resumed contact with a German whom I had met in Europe nearly three years before. He was fifteen years older than I was—a lawyer, with a degree from Heidelberg. He was working for the United Nations Development Program as a legal officer. We had spent only a few hours together and didn't know each other at all, but he had become very convinced that he wanted to marry me. I was intrigued by this. In the middle of my senior year he began writing love letters to me, and I decided to fly to New York during Easter break to visit him.

I arrived in New York Friday evening, and this man took me to a cocktail party. I had never been to a cocktail party. I felt very intimidated by New York society. He was much older and well-established. He kind of dumped me at this cocktail party and sat across the room and observed me. I felt tremendously challenged, like he was testing me all the way. So that sparked my interest because I love being challenged in this way. I suppose that I passed the test because that Sunday we went to two other parties.

The first one had something to do with the Finnish embassy. It was very elegant with several wines being served first and crystal and silver and countless forks and spoons and knives. I just didn't know what to do with them, but I kind of followed along and thought, Gee, this is very impressive. After that, we went on to a party at his friend's, the Cuban's, in Greenwich Village. We had hardly walked into this crowded smoke-filled room than this crazy Cuban started stripping off his clothes, dancing in the middle of the room completely naked. I thought, Wow, anybody who has this variety of contacts and friends is someone who is interesting to me. I wanted to see the world, and I felt that anyone who could appreciate both extremes like that was someone I would like to spend my days with.

We were married in July '69, and that fall I began

work on my master's degree in German at City College of New York.

Jochen and I are very happy. We consider ourselves sort of wandering gypsies or vagabonds. It's a realization of one of the dreams I've had since grammar school—since before that. It's a realization of a dream that my father always had. Where I am, what I'm doing and the life I'm leading is exactly what I wanted. Exactly. There may have been some side-stepping along the road and following different paths now and again, but everything is as I had planned it.

I've been to Europe six times since high school. Part of that is because the United Nations gives us home leave, and Jochen's home is Germany. So every three years or so we go home for two or three months.

In 1971 we moved with the UN Development Program to Port-au-Prince, Haiti. We bought a very small house there and made it our home. When we arrived there, I made a lot of trips with Jochen by jeep into the back country. There are very few paved roads. It's a very primitive country. We liked the Haitians. I went to work teaching English as a second language at a Catholic school. Our son, Steffen, was born in Haiti, by Caesarean section.

When he was four weeks old, we started on a camping trip through the United States and Canada which lasted several months. Then we joined World Campus afloat—going on a four-month sail around the Straits of Magellan and into Africa and the Mediterranean. Jochen taught political science and I taught one private German class and worked in the ship's library.

Now we're back in New York because Jochen is working again for the United Nations. As long as he stays with the UN, we will be transferring from one country to the next every two or four years. I like that. We've lived in different places and we're constantly changing, so we build our lives around where we are.

I think everything that happened in the late sixties

made me kind of an escapist as far as America is concerned. I care about this country, but I'm glad that I don't necessarily have to stay here. I'm glad that I'm free to live wherever I want to in the world. I realize that it's kind of copping out, but I don't want to become involved in America's problems.

When I was younger I never envisioned myself as a mother. Not that I was against children, the thing in high school had been to absolutely reject the idea of becoming a homemaker, a wife and middle-class lady. Now I glory in the whole business, and I'd like to have at least one more child. For the next five years I'm going to be a mother, and I'm going to be home and have plants and play with the children, which is homemaking. I want to experiment in things like breadmaking and needlework and crocheting and sewing. At the same time I want to be very sensitive to every possibility for later work, involvement. I might very well go back to education because I enjoy teaching. When I resume working again, I'm sure I'll do it very seriously.

I feel that if men in America were secure in themselves and strong, then this women's lib would be stupid. Woman's strength is in supporting her husband. What she can get from that is far beyond what she could win through any tirades or demands for equal rights. It's a very subtle thing. You can't explain it to someone. I think that to some extent the women's movement is increasing bitterness and dissatisfaction in the United States, which is not helpful.

I think Jochen is the dominant member of our family. First of all, because he is a very dominant man. I fought against that. Very much. And I realized that I am just as strong a personality. I don't have to prove myself any longer, so I've learned the grace and the advantages of submitting.

I would say that my romantic sense is such an inate part of me that it will never be completely gone. I'd like to rediscover it, and this time in a more mature, giving, sharing sense. I still carry flowers around with me, though it's rare that I can get a rose.

●

Listening to this elegant lady talk about her busy life, we sensed the enormous gap that had opened up between us and our one-time friend. It made us sad, and we wanted to close that gap, if only for a moment. We asked Lynn if she remembered our early-morning meetings in senior year of high school, when we drove to the hills to watch the dawn.

●

Of course I remember! I can remember leaving my house in the pitch-black darkness and with all the windows open and the sun roof open on my little Volkswagen, smelling the trees in the night and the coolness, and knowing that I was going to meet a friend. Sitting in the hills with Mike, waiting for the sunrise, I felt a very intense tenderness for him and for our friendship. There was such an exquisite sense of nature and the unfolding of dawn with the mists! When we got out and walked, the whole experience seemed to be concentrated in the little droplets of water that formed on Mike's sweater.

I felt that this somehow made me—and it made Mike—extremely special. Extremely outstanding in some way. Much better than any of the groping and playing around that was going on in school.

I remember standing around on campus, waiting for the first bell to ring, as people arrived and the school buses pulled up in front. The fog was always very heavy because we were so close to the ocean. In a way that was a good metaphor: these children standing there and waiting, walking around in a cloud, a fog, and not really being able to see each other or to see anything else. High school was such an unconscious experience! I don't think any of us knew what we were doing. Of course there were some people, like Donald Golden, who seemed so well-organized and determined, but who knows what happened to them. Have you been in touch with him in the last couple of years?

Donald Golden: The Debater*

•

Jeanne Hernandez, teacher:
He was squeaky clean. He always looked like a patent-leather kid. His hair was always plastered down. His head seemed too big for his body. He spoke a good game, but he wrote at an average level. One semester he fought with me to get an A. It was something about him being accepted at some school. I said, "All right, here's a gift and I hope this gets you what you want." He didn't deserve the A.

Jamie Kelso:
Golden was my debate partner in high school and I got to know him fairly well. What struck me most about him was his incredible neatness, his attention to detail. The formality of everything he did. Going into debates, he would have boxes full of neatly typed cards. I would come in with scraps of paper with pencil

---

* In order to preserve his hard-won privacy, "Donald Golden" has requested that we withhold his real name. All other details are accurate as recorded here.

scrawlings. He would have a nice suit purchased by his banker father. I would have crummy clothes from the lower-income background.

I thought the atmosphere at Donald's home was pretty uptight. His mother was always very nice to me but it was sort of a museum atmosphere in that house. Going over to his house, I felt like I had to get an appointment. You would call up and say, "Hi, Mrs. Golden, this is Jamie. I'm coming over. Is Donald there? Is it OK?" She would clear it and then give you a scheduled time to show up. You'd show up, and go into Donald's room and do the prescribed activities. When it was time to take a break, you'd walk through that living room with the inch-thick gold carpet protected by this little plastic walkway. Then you would go into the kitchen, where there were some refreshments that Mrs. Golden was waiting to serve you. When you concluded those and after a few polite civilities with Mrs. Golden, you'd go back to Donald's room and continue your program of what you were going to do that day. Are we going to type up our debate cards? Are we going to program our strategy for the coming term?

Donald was very serious about getting grades and performing in the school world. He was very much a conformist. He played by the rules. He was very concerned about winning and losing, and so on. I could never visualize him going surfing or just goofing around. Everything had to be right. No loose ends. I don't know what he did for enjoyment.

Lynn Marble:
When we graduated, Donald wrote in my yearbook: *"Remember, Lynn, it is always better to give than to receive."* I was never really close to Donald because I don't think he really approved of me or liked me very much. I felt so very uncomfortable around him, like I didn't know what to say. I felt extremely awkward.

Lee Grossman:
Donald Golden was a very bright fellow who had no personality of his own at all. Donald would get on whatever bandwagon he thought would take him somewhere. I would describe him as an intellectual in high school only in the sense that he saw it as a vanguard movement that he could get in on. He did so very successfully.

Bob Searight:
He seemed like he had an air about him. I think he liked to drop big words. He kind of wanted you to know that he was more intelligent. He was on the debate team, and he was really into it. He seemed to get into things. I don't know what he's doing now, but I'll bet whatever he's doing, he's into it.

•

As we drove along the quiet country road near the border between Oregon and California, we found it hard to believe that we were headed toward the home of a former city slicker like Donald Golden. The nearest town, Yreka, had only 5,000 residents. For some twenty miles our route had followed the course of a rushing mountain river rimmed with fragrant meadows and evergreen forests. At last we came to a small row of mailboxes and turned onto a rutted dirt road. It took all our concentration to avoid the rocks and potholes that would have kept out all but the most determined visitors. At the end of the road we pulled up to a wooden gate and proceeded to walk the rest of the way.

When we arrived at a homemade A-frame we were greeted by a young woman who was naked above the waist. She told us that to find Donald, we would have to go "past the outhouse, through the field and across the creek." We followed her instructions, and after ten hours in the car we were glad to stretch our legs and enjoy the summer sunshine. Emerging from a clump of trees we finally spotted Donald's house: a two-room cabin which was not quite completed. Inside, Donald was discussing construction plans with Julie, a slight, dark-haired girl who wore no clothes at all, but seemed entirely comfortable with our presence. Donald's appearance had changed radically since high school. His slicked-down "squeaky-clean" image had given way to an unwashed beard and uncombed, shoulder-length hair. His well-toned muscles told us that he had traded in his studious ways for a life of physical labor. He was ready to begin talking immediately, but we were too tired from our long drive. Donald took us for a brief tour of the tomato patch, where he and Julie slept amid the thousand plants in order to discourage deer from destroying their crop, then prepared a sleeping area for us by the creek. After he made sure we were comfortable, he charged into the cabin to prepare dinner.

The following day, when the sun rose too high to allow work to be done, Donald took off all his clothes, fell back into a hammock in the shade, and told us to turn on our tape recorder.

•

I felt a lot of competitive pressure about grades because most of the people I hung out with were a little smarter than me. Although I was able to be in the more academically advanced classes, I was sort of at the lower end of all that stuff. I worked hard. On a typical day, after school I went home and studied and ate dinner and studied some more and watched some television.

In high school, I was really hung up on my hair. I combed it carefully a couple of times a day. It's so weird, because today I comb my hair about once a week. When I look in the mirror, my hair is the last thing I look at.

After graduation I chose to attend UC Berkeley, mainly because my brother went there and he encouraged me and it seemed like it had a good reputation. My first year at Berkeley was the heaviest academic trip I've ever been into. I did an incredible amount of reading and studying and I got excellent grades. I was proud of myself. I really wanted to train myself as a true intellectual and I wanted to get a Ph.D. someday in some field like history. My second year was much easier. I was taking honors classes mostly, which meant there were no tests and usually just one paper per class. So it was easy to get good grades, and I only attended class once or twice a week.

I was introduced to drugs by hanging around with hippies. In fact, all the people I was friends with in Berkeley had started smoking marijuana. So I tried it and liked it. The only other drug I ever took was LSD. My first LSD trip was a pretty wild dose. I listened to a lot of good music on stereo headphones and went outside and looked at flowers and trees. Then someone took me for a drive in the back of a pickup truck and I felt the wind blowing through my hair. It was all real nice.

I started dealing drugs very shortly after I started taking them—maybe one month. The reason I started is a little muddled in my head—it just seemed like a good thing to do. Everybody was into smoking dope. I thought it would be nice to help them get it and make a little money on the side. It also gave me a feeling of importance—I was still only nineteen. I thought I was a good dealer. I sold good stuff at good prices. At my height, I was selling many kilos at a time. I was serious about it, and I got to be fairly big-time.

Then one of my customers introduced me to a friend of his who wanted to buy thirty pounds of marijuana. This guy looked like a cop, but my stoned reasoning at the time was that if he looked like a cop, he couldn't possibly be one. So I made the sale, but when he handed me the money he pulled out a badge and arrested me. He was a state narcotics agent. I said to him, "This must be some sort of a joke." But it was obviously real because the next thing I knew, I was being driven off to jail. That was the end of my drug-dealing career, and the end of my academic career at Berkeley.

My bail was set at five thousand dollars. I called my father and he sprung me the next morning. The case made the front page of the Berkeley *Gazette*. My parents were aghast and outraged. They thought my mind was blown from LSD. Of course, this was partially correct. My case was stalled in the courts a year. My parents got me expensive lawyers and I guess they did their job. I ended up getting convicted, but I didn't go to jail. I was put on three years' probation, and I was paranoid and real careful all that time.

Judy Tomash:
While I was going to school at Santa Cruz, Donald drove up one day to visit Lee Grossman and some of his other friends from high school. We happened to bump into each other in the library, and then sat outside and talked for a long time. He had just been busted for selling dope, having made a lot of money. He told me about his folks and their reaction. I just felt very close to him. He was very troubled because all this had come down and he didn't know quite what he was going to do.

I started to reassess where I was going. I realized that I had no real interest in getting a Ph.D. and being a professor like my brother. I went to work for the first time in my life, and through the rest of my college career I supported myself. I had been expelled from Berkeley because of the drug bust, but I then enrolled at UCLA. I wanted to do something creative, and I heard that UCLA had a good film department. I decided to give it a try and right away got really immersed in it. I used to work sixteen hours a day, teaching myself about still photography and film making. I graduated with a degree in film in 1969—right on schedule. I went on to graduate school and spent many months working on my master's-thesis project: a really grand futuristic film about ecological holocaust. Today that project is sitting in a steamer trunk somewhere in Los Angeles. Before I had finished it, I got a job producing a low-budget feature film. Suddenly I came up against the whole Hollywood business syndrome, and as a result of that experience I decided to drop out of the film scene for good. As a producer, I was in charge of hiring and firing people and telling people what to do and when they fucked up. It was magnifying all the negative aspects of my personality and showed me the worst traits that exist in myself. I saw myself, and I saw my friends' responses, and I didn't want to be that person. I finished the job and had a sum of money saved, so I decided to take some time to put the pieces together in my head.

I went backpacking for three months. I liked getting out into the mountains, and being footloose and self-sufficient. Then I decided to make a trip to the Middle East: Turkey, Syria, Lebanon and Israel.

When I got back to the United States I moved to Berkeley because friends of mine were living there. The next thing I knew, I was living together with seven other people and we were looking for land in the country. I think I was attracted to the heavy emotionality of the group because there was a big emotional vacuum in my life. I was also hoping for a quiet, settled existence where I could get more in touch with the elements and the food I was eating. But when we finally moved to the country, the group of eight people was so unsettled that there were constant arguments and outbursts. We all had real high moral and political ideals and we weren't at all prepared to fulfill them. For instance, we wanted to do away with the division of labor based upon sex. But in the country that's very difficult because it's much easier for a man to get employment than for a woman. So the men ended up doing most of the working for money. When we got home each day, we expected dinner to be cooked and everything to be real nice. But the women said, "Well, wait a minute. We're not here just to do the dirty work."

Living communally did have its advantages. It made it much easier to build a house. We put together that big A-frame you saw and it's large enough to accommodate eight people. None of us had ever built a house before. We were really happy to be able to move indoors, and that was sort of a high moment. But that first winter in the house there were such close quarters and there were lots of emotional traumas. Our monthly mortgage payments were a terrific burden. By the time fall rolled around again, the people were just not getting along well enough to live together another winter. So ultimately everyone moved away—except me.

I got a job cutting down trees, milling them on a portable sawmill, stacking the boards and loading them on trucks. In the meantime I was living alone on the land and constantly on the lookout for new people to come up here and live. By this time I figured the original people weren't ever going to come back. Then I met Julie, and we became friends. She decided to move up to the land, but we weren't lovers. Until I met Julie, the longest relationship I had ever had with any woman was a couple of weeks. My image of women was based on my family experience and on watching TV. I thought of a woman as someone who was very dependent on a man—someone irrational and sort of insane. Later I realized that what it really was, was a dimension of emotionality and inner awareness that I wasn't in touch with.

When Julie first moved up here, I was freaked out

and sort of pushed her away. But she was here, and I was here, and within three or four months we became a couple. Now we're just two babies living together with each other. We both love the land a lot. We built this little house last year and now we are trying to support ourselves growing plants, being farmers.

I usually wake up every morning around dawn and then lie around in bed for another hour, playing with Julie until she gets ornery, because she doesn't want to be awakened. Then I get up and walk around and look at the plants to see if any have been eaten by deer. Then I get it together to make breakfast, which means cutting wood. These days Julie and I have been doing carpentry until noon, trying to get the inside of the house done. In the afternoon I do some other sort of work, like weeding, planting or chicken-coop building. About a half-hour before the sun goes behind the mountains, we gather dinner in the garden. After dark I cook, eat, drink some tea, read in the Sears catalog a little bit, yawn, feel very fatigued, go to bed, look at the stars, fall asleep and dream. And some days, if we can squeeze it into our schedule, we make love. Sometimes, in the morning, it's spontaneous, but usually we make an appointment.

•

Hearing this, we thought of high school days—of Jamie Kelso's recollection of calling in advance for formal appointments before he could visit Donald at his parents' home. It was reassuring to know that in addition to all the changes, there were some consistent elements in Donald's personality.

•

The only power that we have here is kerosene for light. We use wood for everything else. In terms of health, I'm a vegetarian and I've gotten really interested in herbal medicine and psychic healing. Most of my contact is with plants—not with people. On Sundays we have a local potluck and volleyball game, and our neighbors on the river come and visit. Our main contact with the outside world is going to Ashland, Oregon, once a week and taking a class in t'ai chi—which is a very relaxing kind of Oriental exercise.

I'm sure my parents are still a little skeptical about who I am, but they accept that I've made my choice of life style, just like my brother chose his. And I'm stable—that seems to be the most important thing. I'm in the same place, and I'm supporting myself, and it's a nice place. Of course, I have no idea what I'll be doing ten years from now. I'm open to suggestions.

Harvey Bookstein: The Cashier

•

Donald Golden:
When I think of Harvey Bookstein, I see a very short, pudgy guy with dark hair and a very Jewish-looking face, standing somewhere in the back of gym class having trouble doing calisthenics. He was always dealing with money somehow. We used to call him "Booky." I would think that today he would be a certified public accountant.

Judy Tomash:
He was very much a little businessman who enjoyed working in the student store every day at lunch, selling

PALISADES TIDELINE

Friday, December 14, 1962

Nut-Selling Laurels Won By Bookstein

"I really enjoy selling," says Pali's champion nutseller, B10 Harvey Bookstein, a student in Mr. Keech's homeroom, F213.

The fact that Harvey enjoys selling is shown by the fact that he sold a grand and illustrious total of ONE HUNDRED TWENTY-ONE cans of nuts, thus raising $121 in Pali's recent "Nuts to the Debt" fund-raising drive.

When asked where and how he sold 121 cans of nuts, Harvey replied, "I went all around the Pacific Palisades area, from the ocean to 'the center'. I only sold about six cans to people I knew—teachers and family. I took home several cases each day, sold them that night, and brought back the money the next day."

Belongs to Service Group

Harvey is a member of the Tritons, the boys' tenth grade service group. He also works in the student store selling school supplies before first period, operating the change booth during nutrition and lunch, and then selling candy after school.

candy and U.S. Savings Stamps. I guess the reason he wasn't popular was that he was so short, and because he would never break the rules for you. He wouldn't sell you a candy bar after the bell had rung.

Jean O'Brien, teacher:
Harvey was seventeen, going on forty. He had this tremendous need for order. In the student store, he knew where everything was and usually what the closing balance was. I imagine that today he's an accountant. He should be.

Bob Searight:
I got a job at the Bay Pharmacy, and Harvey worked there too. The boss really liked him because he was real gung ho. He was kind of the typical accountant.

Reilly Ridgell:
I remember Harvey always walking around trying to balance everything with that huge briefcase on one side of him.

Lee Grossman:
My memory of him in a black suit is so strong that I can't remember him taking it off to shower or to sleep. Always with a black suit and several pencils. When the senior class was measured for their sweaters, Harvey had the job of writing down all the vital statistics. He had somewhere—and I'm sure he still has—a record of the breast measurements of all the girls in our high school class. Harvey Bookstein was a born accountant. Everything that you say about an accountant could have been based on Harvey Bookstein. I would imagine that by now he is the superaccountant of all time. I think he will ultimately be handling all the accounts for the planet.

Lynn Marble:
He was the brunt of a lot of jokes, a lot of adolescent

cruelty. Yet even though he didn't fit in and everybody made fun of him, I felt that he was a person with some concept of himself. He felt himself to have a place within the scheme of things.

•

We had no idea where to find Harvey Bookstein but decided to play a hunch: we picked up the West LA telephone directory and looked in the Yellow Pages under Accountants. Sure enough, there he was—

> Bookstein, Harvey   1801 Avenue of the Stars
> Century City

On the telephone Harvey seemed amazed that anyone would want to interview him and warned us that his life held few surprises. But we persisted and he invited us up to his large, sparsely furnished office overlooking Beverly Hills. As we shook hands at the door he stretched himself to his full five feet four inches, then scurried off to settle himself behind his enormous desk. He spoke with great candor, and spat out his words with such unnatural speed that at times it was difficult to understand what he was saying.

•

My father is an accountant, so I never really had a father: he was a business associate. From very early childhood I always wanted to do what he did. He took me under his wing very early and I enjoyed it. Other kids wanted to be policemen or firemen, but I always wanted to be an accountant. I was put on this earth for that purpose.

In high school, I stuck around with the crowd that always got picked on. I remember I used to come home very depressed. Sometimes I used to go home and cry. It bothered me a hell of a lot. I could have understood not being liked if I had been a nasty mean person. But I wasn't like that, so it just didn't make sense. My world didn't stop, though. I had my own little world to escape to, where people's reactions didn't make any difference. I had what I considered my happiness.

I used to always work. Before classes it was in the student store, during Nutrition it was the change booth, and at lunchtime it was the food line. I signed up for a program that allowed you to work one period instead of going to class, so I worked in the student store again. After school I worked selling candy and supplies. As soon as I finished working at school, I went to the Bay Pharmacy and worked a four-hour shift there. In the evenings and on weekends I sold Fuller brushes. I used to love selling. During Christmas time I would sell Christmas cards. When I was in the eleventh grade I had saved up enough so I could start investing in the stock market. I bought this stock for thirteen hundred dollars, and the next year, when I was a senior, I sold it for eleven thousand. I was very happy with that, but I don't think anyone in the whole high school knew about it.

What they did know about was my part in the school nut drive. The high school needed money to buy a football scoreboard, so the students sold canned nuts to raise the money. Most people had trouble selling six cans, but I sold one hundred and twenty. There was a prize for the homeroom that sold the most cans, and because of me, we won. The homeroom threw a really neat party for me and they gave me little gifts. They were stupid little things, like an old tennis shoe and a ceramic rat with a penny attached to its stomach and my name on it: HARVEY. I still have those gifts. They meant a lot to me. I wasn't recognized much by the students or the instructors—and that was kind of the nicest thing that happened to me at school.

The worst thing that happened had nothing to do with kids picking on me. I was working in the student store and one time my change bag was short ten dollars! I had worked there for a year and a half and I'd earned everyone's trust. I was accused of taking the ten dollars. As it turned out, in the following day's deposit the bank found an extra ten dollars that had not been counted properly. I was vindicated. I'm sure it must seem insignificant to other people, but to me it meant an awful lot.

I didn't want to go to college after graduation. I went for one reason only: to get that piece of paper that said I was a CPA. It meant I had to sacrifice four years of my life. I went to Santa Monica City College for two years. Then I got accepted to UCLA, but they had just dropped the undergraduate business program. They said I could go to Berkeley, but being the meek little person I was, I thought that was too radical for me. So I went to Valley State because it had a fine accounting department. I continued working for my father, and during tax season I worked up to a hundred hours a week. I didn't care about my grades. I never studied. I just wanted that piece of paper.

My father has a very small firm. He does personal tax returns. I enjoyed it for all the years I did it with him, but I wanted to be a *real* accountant, an *all-around* accountant. I wanted to help small clients make something of themselves. You just feel good. You pat yourself on the back when you see a small company that has bad records and has nowhere to turn, and they call you up and you make a few right decisions and they really make a go of it. You feel kind of proud. You feel like a piece of them.

So when I graduated from college, I interviewed with fifteen or sixteen companies. I liked the free lunches, so I interviewed with almost every company there was. After a lot of thought, and narrowing it down, drawing graphs of the pluses and minuses of every firm, I chose Kenneth Leventhal and Co., which is a national firm that specializes in real estate. I worked for them right here in Century City for four and a half years.

I met my future wife at Valley State in the dormitory. We dated for about four years before we got married. Kathy was in favor of us living together first, but I didn't believe in that. It's not that I don't love sex. If I had a choice to do anything other than accounting, I'd choose to have sex. But sometimes I don't know what I'd put first. That's the problem.

My wife is an artist. I'm really proud of her. After we got married, because of the fights we had, she got out of the mood to paint. But all of a sudden she's gotten back into it quite a bit. I'm very much a male chauvinist. I don't believe in women working. At least not my wife. But Kathy doesn't believe that way. She works as assistant manager in the art-supply department at the May Company.

By the time I got married, I had already saved forty-five thousand dollars. My mom used to ask me, "Why don't you spend it?" I'd say, "I'm saving it for the woman I marry." I didn't tell Kathy about the money. I told her I had been in the stock market and lost everything. Then the second year we were married, I gave my wife the passbook as a gift. She was shocked! It was really neat to watch her reaction. I've got the wife I want; I've got the house I'm going to live in for the rest of my life. Hopefully, someday I'll have the children that I want.

I was making twenty-eight thousand a year working for Leventhal, but another fellow and I decided to take a chance and start our own business. We put together our little financial packet and we did a projection. What we expected to do in twelve months we've already surpassed in the first four months. I'm very proud of our new firm. There is no question of the fact that any person we do work for is going to get the best service available.

•

When Harvey had finished we glanced at the clock and were surprised at the time that had elapsed. We had never expected we could have such a good time talking for two hours about accounting. As we got up,

Harvey validated our parking ticket and walked us to the elevator. We stepped in, and he slapped us on the back. "I really wish you luck on your book," he said. "In fact, I hope you make a million dollars. Because if you do, believe me, then you'll need an accountant . . ."

●

The Draft

●

Since 1965, nothing has disrupted the lives of so many young American males as the U.S. government's attempts to field an army in Southeast Asia. The youth of most strata of society responded with either obedient resignation or patriotic fervor. Palisades graduates, however, knew that they had options. More often than not, their parents gave them financial support so they could go to school and enjoy II-S deferments. When they finally finished college, more money was available to pay one of the many draft lawyers who specialized in protecting young men from the not very selective Selective Service. With the help of legal counsel it was possible to win I-Y medical deferments, which were temporary, or the coveted IV-F deferments, which were permanent.

There were exceptions, and some men, like Jon Wilson, did in fact fight in Vietnam. But the number of Pali graduates who actually entered the armed services is disproportionately small. Not one member of the Palisades class of '65 lost his life in Indochina.

•

Harvey Bookstein:
Being nonpolitical, I just couldn't understand why anybody had to lose their life over something as unimportant as a war outside our mainland. I could never kill anyway. I don't like guns. If they put a group of people like me in the Army, it would be a disaster.

My father was a gung-ho Navy man. He was in World War II. Pure Navy. But he completely understood the way the times were and that World War II had nothing to do with the Vietnam situation. Also, from a selfish standpoint, he was afraid to lose someone to help him during tax season. So he was in favor of me trying to follow up what I could do to stay home.

As soon as I graduated from college and lost my student deferment there was no question that I was going to be called. I had a very high priority number, and they were all ready to draft me, so I decided to join the Army Reserves to stall for time. I searched like heck and found the only reserve unit that took nothing but accountants. So I joined the group reluctantly.

Meanwhile I had wasted five or six hundred dollars of my own money on an attorney who didn't do a thing for me. So when I finished the five months of reserves and got closer to active duty, I went to another attorney. This one got me out on a medical discharge. High blood pressure, which was pretty true. I'm a very nervous type person.

Skip Baumgarten:
I found out that I could get out of the draft if I was obese. To be obese enough, I had to weigh two hundred and fifty-six pounds. At the time, I weighed two hundred and thirty-three, and I had forty-eight days

to put on the twenty-three pounds. I took the situation in hand and began eating fervently, and for the first time in my life, with purpose. It was really kind of an ideal situation for a fat person to be forced to put on weight. I enjoyed it to the utmost. I've dreamt of it since. I could eat anything—particularly if it was greasy or thick. Fried was good and chocolate was excellent. Every meal included a course of chocolate something. But as the deadline got close, I was still six pounds too light.

At this point I found a rather shady doctor who agreed to shoot me full of cortisone so that I could retain water and swell up. So, armed with my cortisone and several sandwiches, I took off for the Induction Center in downtown Los Angeles. It was a terrible day. I followed this yellow line through a large warehouse type of building and it was totally absurd. The first test was to judge whether or not you were color-blind. There was an inspector standing at the front of the line with a book of patterns—numbers hidden inside the patterns. A guy would walk up and the inspector would flip through the pages and say, "What do you see?"

"Number thirteen, seven and nine."

Then the next guy: "Thirteen, seven and nine," and the next guy: "Thirteen, seven, nine."

When he got to the guy in front of me, he said, "What do you see?"

"Nothing."

So the inspector says, "Nothing! What do you mean? Didn't you hear the guy in front of you?"

The day was spent like that. When I was through, I hadn't been kicked out anywhere along the line. They didn't pull me out when they weighed me and I was kind of frightened that the scale didn't work or something. I got through and I was terrified. I asked one of the inspectors what my chances were. He looked at me and said, "Are you kidding? A tub like you?" (Much laughter.)

As soon as I received my I-Y classification in the mail I went on a five-hundred-calories-a-day diet and lost about eighty-five pounds in ten weeks. I came down to a very shapely hundred and seventy-five or hundred and eighty. Unfortunately, I also ended up in the hospital with mononucleosis. I'm not exactly sure how that works but there was a definite relationship.

Mike Shedlin:

I started receiving induction papers informing me that it was time to report for my physical. By then I knew that I was not going to go into the service, so there was no reason to go through such a horrible experience as the physical. At one point I was sitting in my apartment on the ocean in Venice, California. I was having a bad time in my relationship with my woman and I didn't have any money. I got my induction papers and I smoked some opium and I decided to flee. So, illogically, I went down to my parents in Cuernavaca. By doing so, I violated not only my federal induction notice, but my state and county probation. I was on probation and trying to pay off a fine for my earlier drug busts. So I fled. I wasn't really fleeing the country in a hard-core way. They probably didn't even know I was gone, because I only stayed away a little under a month.

When I was down in Mexico I met a stoned lawyer, a guy named Seymour. He suggested that to get out of the draft, I should go to this commune in Arizona where they could certify that I was getting psychological rehabilitation from the swami at the commune and all the people there. So I tried it. I sneaked back into the U.S. with my tail between my legs. I was very paranoid and I got crabs or some bullshit. I stayed at this ashram for three weeks and they took care of me, but I didn't see that as a viable way to get out of the draft. So I came back to California and got a public defender to help me with my probation violation. I went back to my draft lawyer and he got me out on technicalities.

I later got more draft notices. I would report in the wrong town and get a postponement. I finally got out because I had a high lottery number.

Reilly Ridgell:
I was a hawk. I felt that way almost all the way through college. I was very much against the demonstrators. I thought they were unpatriotic, and ungrateful for the rights they had living in America—like being able to come out and demonstrate. I was in Air Force ROTC for four years. I wanted to graduate from the program and go in as an officer, but they disqualified me because of some allergy trouble. I went all the way out to Maxwell Air Force Base before they decided I wasn't physically qualified to sit at a desk for the Air Force. They wouldn't give me permission to serve. Then one day I got a letter in the mail that said I was I-A. So I was physically qualified to carry a rifle in Vietnam, but not to be an officer and sit at a desk for the Air Force. But I went through the physical and was classified I-Y. The last time I looked they had changed it to IV-F.

Bob Searight:
I was pretty confident all along of becoming IV-F because I had asthma. Somehow or other I became IV-F. I didn't even apply to get tested or anything like that. It was Krishna's mercy.

Mike Medved:
After four years at Yale my student deferment ran out and I had to look for something else. That same year they stopped giving graduate school deferments, so the fact that I was going on to law school didn't help. In my confusion, a friend of mine gave me the name of an ultra-Orthodox Jewish sect that ran a day school for about a hundred kids in New Haven. I went to

them, and it turned out they needed teachers for secular subjects. In return for teaching grammar to seventh graders, the rabbi who ran the school would write a letter to my draft board saying I was indispensable. The letter went out, full of hand-wringing and pleading, and the draft board graciously granted me an occupational deferment. They were convinced that my teaching was essential to our national security. The only problem was that I got stuck teaching two classes of pre-teens every day—at the same time that I was doing my first term in law school. For all my teaching efforts I got paid not a penny—the only salary for nine months was that single letter to my draft board. It was a lousy deal, but it was still better than the employment opportunities that the Army was offering at that time.

There was a good deal of hypocrisy involved in this whole arrangement. At that point in my life I had no serious commitment to Judaism, and this was my first real exposure to the Hasidic world. Suddenly I was surrounded by bearded rabbis in black coats who ran a strict Dickensian school that seemed entirely alien to me. While I reported dutifully every day to this pious environment, I was sharing an apartment with a Catholic girl. Our place was only a block and a half from the school, and I lived in constant dread that the rabbis would discover my secret and call down the wrath of the Selective Service System on my guilty head.

After nearly a year of this sort of tension, Nixon instituted the draft lottery and the lucky number 232 delivered me from bondage.

Lee Grossman:

I guess I dropped out of school officially in December '67, and I wrote my draft board a letter asking permission to leave for Europe: such a thing apparently was required. They wrote me a nice letter back saying permission was denied. The fate of that letter is another story. I put it in my wallet and forgot about it until six months later. I knew that I had injured myself just enough in my motorcycle accident to get my IV-F. If I had to do it all over again to get a IV-F, I certainly would.

Anyway, I then went down to my draft board and said, "Look, you won't let me leave the country because I'm II-S, and its silly to call me II-S. I haven't been in school for months. Reclassify me I-A, and give me a physical, and then I'll flunk the physical and get out of here." So, naturally, when I let them know what was happening, the wheels started turning—nothing happened. Finally I got my physical, which I failed, of course, and left the country in April.

I spent six or seven months in Europe. I guess the highlight of the whole trip, at least from my current perspective, came when I found myself in a john in a train station in Barcelona—one of those great toilets that consist of a little hole in the ground that you squat over. I discovered, much too late, that they didn't have anything resembling toilet paper, and that kind of bothered me. So I was looking around for pieces of paper and I couldn't really move around much, but I managed to reach my wallet and I opened it and found my letter from the draft board. I put it to good use. I even considered saving it and mailing it back to them.

Mark Holmes:

About a week before I was supposed to take my physical, I was in the sauna and I touched the edge of the hot sauna with my knee and pulled it away—a muscle reflex—and my cartilage gave way and I fell to the ground. So then, after a while, I failed a couple of physicals and got a IV-F. I celebrated the IV-F by going to the beach with my dog and running eight miles.

Jamie Kelso:

I am not a pacifist. I consider it my duty to defend,

with force if necessary, my ideals and values against attempts to destroy them by violence. But it was very clear in Vietnam that the rulers of the United States were not defending freedom and they were not upholding values. Vietnam was clearly butchery and betrayal with the victims being guys my age. Of course the North Vietnamese are beasts. The Communists are butchers and beasts. I would gladly fight them to *win*. But I won't fight to die—which is what these guys were doing.

Nineteen years old, and I had determined not to go. The question now was, How do you prevent yourself from being classified I-A? I had no student deferment because I had not gone to college.

I attempted to get out by flunking the first physical. I tried to flunk the color-blind test. I did flunk it. The guy passed me. I went into the hearing test, and in a very studied manner, flunked the hearing test. In a foolproof manner. They took me out of the hearing booth with the other guys and put me in a special soundproof locker and individually the two technicians in white robes observed me as I took a second test. They gently studied my graphs and readings. They passed me on that. Next, I tried to flunk the vision test. I said I couldn't read the four-foot-high E. They passed me on that.

Then I came to the blood station. They wanted to take some of my blood. I said, "I'm sorry. You're not entitled to my blood." So they got very disturbed and sent me to a colonel, in my underwear. You walk through the whole thing in your shorts. It's very degrading. I walked into the colonel's office in my underwear and he's in full-dress uniform. I sit down and tell him, "My blood is my blood. It's not yours. If you want to stick a rusty needle in my arm, you will have to do it by force." The guy was shaking in his chair. This had never happened. He folded, and let me through. They didn't get my blood.

Then they sent me to the x-ray booth. They wanted

to pass an x-ray through my entire body. I said, "Sorry, you can't pass x-rays through my body without my consent." Again I went back to the colonel in my underwear and I prevailed. But at the end of the day I was pronounced physically fit and acceptable for the United States Army.

So I attempted to flunk the mental examination by figuring out the right answer on every question and answering incorrectly. That was a rather large booboo on my part. Of course I scored zero, and that was a statistical impossibility. A blind monkey who took the test and marked the A, B, C and D boxes would have scored twenty-five out of a hundred. The resident psychiatrist pointed this out and began threatening me. They were going to stuff me into cannons and shoot me across Vietnam. Put me out in the frontline cannon-fodder units. The psych very maliciously and hatefully threatened me, "You know, I can put you on the bus tomorrow." So he sent me in for the mental test again. And I scored probably the first hundred they had ever seen there. They were rather amused at me. I was a novel phenomenon for them.

I got my classification I-A. I was pronounced perfectly fit for the Army. I subsequently discovered while reading the regulations that if you were five feet eight inches and weighed a hundred and seven pounds or less, you were unfit for the Army. At the time I weighed a hundred and fifty. I had to get under a hundred and seven. So for six weeks I starved myself. I ate nothing. Once a day I took a cup and put into it dried brewer's yeast and powdered milk, and then poured a little bit of milk into that and made a paste. I ate the paste with a spoon. Then I took a couple of vitamin tablets. That was my staple through the whole thing. At the end I was a skeleton. I felt that if I jumped up I wouldn't come down! I felt fantastic. I felt absolutely fantastic. But before I got on the scale I still wasn't sure my weight was low enough. So I got a short haircut—short as possible. I clipped all my fingernails. I kept going to the bathroom to get out every drop. I even spit a couple of times to make myself light as possible. Then I got on the scale and weighed a hundred and five. So the Surgeon General certified me I-Y. I got a deferment—a three-month deferment! Big deal! For all my efforts all I got was a three-month deferment.

I obviously couldn't go on starving myself like that four times a year and still survive. So I had to try other things. I tried moving from address to address. I moved from Los Angeles to San Francisco and back in a regular shuffle—having all my papers and files switched every time to cause administrative mayhem and prevent me from being drafted. I bought some time that way. I went to UCLA for a very short time. That gave me a II-S deferment. But I quit UCLA —I couldn't stand it. I checked out going to Canada when it got desperate. I went up to Vancouver and looked at it and that was disgusting.

Finally I was I-A, very vulnerable and expecting to get drafted, when they had the lottery, and the pill with my birthday, June 8, 1948, was the very last pill to be pulled out of the bowl. I was number 366. That permanently protected me from the draft. Interestingly, it was not until that moment that I realized the psychological burden that I had been bearing for several years. Until it was lifted, I didn't realize that my whole life style, my whole mentality was cramped and distorted, twisted by fear of the United States government. The fear of constantly having to evade and dodge, to defend myself against people who wanted to kill me, and wanted me to kill.

Skip Baumgarten: The Actor

•

Reilly Ridgell:
He was the big, joking, jovial funny man from Chicago.

William Quivers:
Fat. Skip was fat.

Lee Grossman:
I remember him being an actor. Everything about Skip was theatrical, dramatic. He could put people on, and was very good at it, very entertaining. I enjoyed that. I remember him starring in *The Madwoman of Chaillot*. He was the Ragpicker. I also recall him playing poker in drama class with David Wallace. I wasn't in the class, but I used to cut gym to play cards with them.

Skip came to our high school late, and my impression is that he shouldered his way into the crowd and just took charge. He came on very strong. He's huge. He's probably six feet two or three and two hundred something. It's easy to picture him in a straw boater and striped blazer, as the barker at a carnival.

Bob Searight:
He made a big splash when he came to Pali, and he was kind of the center of attention. He was rich, and kind of extravagant in that way. He was real nice,

but sometimes you had the feeling that he wasn't saying what he really meant.

Candy McCoy:
I remember going to Skip's house one night with some other people. His parents had just moved into this new house. It was an incredible place with every possible accouterment, including a shower that had like ten shower heads, so that you stood in the middle and were showered from all directions.

Jeff Stolper:
I went to a party once and Skip was there. The guy was so sophisticated, so subtle in his jokes that I was laughing the whole time. He had everybody cracking up. I really liked Skip.

I was in drama class the time we were putting on that play about Helen Keller—*The Miracle Worker*. This one guy who'd been in drama all along was trying out for the main part of the father. He had it all sewn up, until Mr. Drury brought in Skip, who was relatively new to the school. Skip went up there with his big powerful voice and did a whole job on the drama department. Needless to say, he got the part as the male lead.

Lynn Marble:
Everybody liked Skip because he was a big, funny guy. But I thought he was tremendously unhappy inside. He definitely had a presence, a very strong presence, but I think he was miserable being fat. Near the end of senior year, he seemed to become more and more unhappy, and so I lost track of him. I have no idea what's happened to him since.

●

Except for a mustache and perhaps a few extra pounds, Skip's appearance has changed very little since high school. During our visit he sat back in an easy chair in his Santa Monica apartment and lit one cigarette after another as he entertained us with his memories. He delivered his lines with the careful pacing of a night-club comic, except for those moments when his infectious laughter got the better of him and he had to pause to catch his breath. The apartment was fashionably decorated with carpets, paintings and sculpture. All the lines in the furnishings and decorations were long, low and sleek; it seemed obvious that Skip was looking for a spare, lean feeling in his surroundings.

•

Nobody I knew in high school had a positive self-image, other than Lany Tyler maybe. That just didn't come in high school. It wasn't offered. Sometimes I thought I was clever. I thought I was suave. Suave meaning good at words. I'm very oral. My mouth has always had a great amount of appeal to me. Want a cigarette?

My first affair in California was with this comely dancer from the drama department. It became very passionate. We went together to the senior prom. We did the jerk, the frug, the box step. I did a hell of a box step. I could do it in four or five different directions. We did a lot of close bear-hug dancing. That was good. You could wrap your arm around and nobody knew. After the prom I took her home. She lived in a small home near the school. She said she was going to take off her formal to get comfortable so we could talk, but she came out of the bathroom naked. Boy, I couldn't believe that this was happening! There she was, with her parents asleep approximately eighteen feet away. We went into her room and the head of her bed was on the other side of the wall from the head of her mother's bed. We made love anyway. I was so scared that when I left I pushed my car out of the driveway and halfway down the street. I didn't want to start the motor near the house because I was afraid I'd wake her parents and I'd be caught.

Grad night was at the Beverly Hilton Hotel, and we

also went together there. The graduation present from my dancer was that she rented a motel room down the street. We showed up for grad night, left after about ten minutes, and spent the entire night at the Westward Ho Motel. A few weeks later she went away to school. She wrote me continuously, and, cadishly, I never answered her letters. That produced so much guilt in me that I was never able to talk to her again.

I was pretty disoriented when I left Pali. Things just hadn't gone right. I was in the lower half of the graduating class, which was very bad for my self-image because I always thought of myself as being bright. I had no idea what I wanted to do. Going to college was never really a question, but I was very lackadaisical and didn't apply anywhere. So I had to enroll at Los Angeles Valley City College. I was very embarrassed about going to a junior college. When people asked me where I went to school, I used to say "Valley" and hope they thought I meant Valley State.

Within a year I was very lonesome. My weekends were taken up working for my father, selling jewelry. I became fatter, and kind of despondent. So in the second year I got involved in theater arts, and once again I was kind of whooshed into the mainstream. It was very similar to my experience at Pali. I finally made up my mind that I was going to become a professional actor. The pressure from my family was immense. "It's not a good job for a Jewish kid. From one day to the next you don't know if you'll be able to eat. Not good." Some of it was true, of course. I could see that there were a lot of very talented people who had been at it for ten years but still didn't have a job. They were so dedicated that they were willing to *starve*. When I thought of that possibility for myself, I decided to quit school.

I went to work for my father full time. I started off working in a jewelry store, and within a short period of time I was managing a chain of jewelry stores. I was very much into making a lot of money. I was twenty,

twenty-one years old and I was making twenty-five thousand dollars. I was investing and playing around in the stock market. I was living pretty high on the hog. I had a very expensive apartment. A maid five days a week. I had all my clothes made for me.

Then came the period when I had to concentrate on beating the draft. My weight fluctuated wildly. At first I had to gain, and then I really slimmed down for the first time. You know, after you eat as much as you have to eat to put on thirty pounds in six weeks, you kind of get tired of food. Eventually I was down to a hundred and seventy-five and for the first time in my life I began to feel I was okay. I also began to feel that I didn't have to stay working for my father.

I might add that as I made this decision, David Wallace, who had been out of my life for some time, appeared again and turned me on to marijuana. I think that was his bag for a while. Like he was Johnny Appleseed. The only person I think he never reached was Michael Medved. So anyway, I quit work and went up to Berkeley, which really turned me around quite a bit. I moved into a household where there were all these women into women's liberation. I was constantly referred to as a *pig*. And I had just lost all this weight!

From Berkeley I went to Europe, where I was going to travel for a month. I ended up being gone for around fourteen months. I rented a small farmhouse on the island of Malta and spent a lot of time writing intro- spectively, trying to cut through the bullshit I'd been living with.

When I had first left the country, I was convinced that I had enough money saved up to live on for ten years. I had about thirty-five thousand dollars invested in the stock market. But in 1970, while I was gone, the stock market plummeted to new lows, and by the time I returned from Europe my thirty-five thousand had been magically transformed into twenty-eight hundred dollars.

With that situation in mind, I tried going back to work for my father, but that lasted less than a week. At this point I hooked up with some old friends and we began traveling around the United States. We spent about a year at it. We stayed on communes, in people's homes, mining towns, Indian reservations, large cities, wilderness areas—it was pretty varied. Our biggest responsibility at that point was deciding what to do with our time. We used to devise games and reasons for traveling. We tried to increase our knowledge about the New Left, and what was happening politically throughout the country, and what was happening in the counterculture. We became very aware that we were privileged. My parents were wealthy and I always had the knowledge that if anything went wrong, I could count on them. I never really had to, but in the back of my mind, I think I could do what I did because I knew that I couldn't really get into too much trouble.

I returned to Los Angeles and decided I was more interested in education than in going back to work. So I started UCLA in the spring of 1972. By the time I got to the first midterms I was smoking after having quit for two and a half years, and by the time finals came I had gained forty pounds—I was back in school.

In the summer of '72 I was lured away once more and went with some friends to Miami Beach for the Democratic and Republican conventions. I was gassed in the streets and arrested in front of Republican headquarters with around twelve hundred other people. At that time Nixon had just been nominated for another term as President. When the police got to me, I gave the name of Peter Kropotkin, the famous anarchist. The amount of fear and uncertainty around Miami Beach was just tremendous. It was very obvious that there were government people infiltrating every meeting.

After leaving Miami I traveled around for a while and ended up on a farm in Indiana. From there I returned to Berkeley, and Berkeley is a very unusual place. It's a very political place, and I immediately got involved working with a group of people who were into rent control. I was working fairly diligently in trying to organize various neighborhoods and communities to show them what it was about. There was also a film festival going on. We saw all the movies. We'd watch about fifteen hours a day each day for ten days.

Paranoia is something people who are involved with politics in Berkeley have to live with on a daily level. I was new, and the paranoia really began to freak me out. There was a faction of militants who wanted to move to direct action. I'm sure that increased my feelings of tension, so that when weird things began to happen it really bothered me. I had my notes stolen several times. I was aware that I was being followed. Today, in light of Watergate and dirty tricks and CIA involvement, it might not seem so outlandish. But at the time I probably dealt with it poorly. The whole scene of underground currents and secretive things just got to me. I freaked out and decided to leave Berkeley. I didn't want to play any more, and I wanted to remove myself from the playing field.

When I came home I went into psychotherapy, and at least that accomplished one thing for me. The psychiatrist I hired wrote a letter which said that he couldn't guarantee that I wouldn't shoot my commanding officer if I ever went into the Army. That seemed to dampen the government's enthusiasm for drafting me, and I finally managed to get my IV-F.

At this point I suddenly became very motivated to return to UCLA and take pre-med courses. I was twenty-seven at the time, and I actually did fairly well. But when I got my degree, I had only an A— average, which of course isn't good enough these days to get you into medical school anywhere. I was trying to decide what to do when I found out that for twenty thousand dollars—actually a twenty-thousand-dollar political contribution—a certain public figure would get me into a good California medical school. My father was very willing to put up the money. He thought it was a fine investment and knew that if I became a doctor, I could pay him back with interest. But I decided that I wasn't willing to go that route to medical school, so instead I got involved in psychiatric halfway houses— places that deal with people who have been in psychiatric hospitals, most often more than once, and have difficulty socializing in one way or another. That's what I'm doing now, in fact. I'm director of two residential-care homes here in California. My father owned rest homes for old people, and I got involved in one of the facilities and changed it into psychiatric aftercare. I'm not a therapist, but we have therapists working in the facility. Both the homes are supposed to be profit-making institutions, and I'm sure they will be. Both are new, recently opened. What we're doing is really pretty innovative. The type of program and growth opportunities and skills that we're offering haven't previously been available in this type of setting. Most of my energy during the day is put into developing activities for the guests that are living in the homes. It's pretty exciting, and I'm enjoying it more than I believed possible.

Until recently I was living with a girl friend, but at the moment I'm living here alone. I don't mind it, but under the right circumstances I'd certainly consider a change in the situation. Any interested persons should send their applications to P.O. Box 49328, Los Angeles, CA 90049.

There's no question in my mind that if I had graduated from high school in 1955 instead of '65, I would have gone off to a university and joined a fraternity. I would have gotten into a lot of heavy beer drinking, and a couple of panty raids. Gotten pinned, engaged, and married. I'd be living now in a suburb somewhere.

The fact that I've avoided that—that I didn't settle into one thing—has made me very happy. I've had a lot of experiences that have definitely given me a better understanding of how to live my life. That's rather lofty, but it's sincere. I look forward to a lot of different experiences. I enjoy the idea that I have absolutely no conception of what will happen to me ten years from today.

•

We asked Skip if he had any regrets about his life as he looked back on it. He paused for a moment, blowing smoke rings into the air before he answered.

•

There was one fellow in our high school class who made a comment to me once. He said I grew up too fast. All through school I was working for my father every weekend. My friend said that I missed a great amount of my adolescence. When I look back on it now, that may well be true.

I also have one very specific regret about high school. I'm sorry I never got to go out with Margie Williams. Never got to know her. Just looked at her a lot. Margie Williams and Lany Tyler: those were the marks of status at Palisades High School. I never knew the guys who went out with Margie Williams, but I knew that I envied them a lot.

Margie Williams: The Cheerleader

•

Judy Tomash:
She was a cheerleader, very cute, turned-up nose. She had bleached-blond hair, and it was always perfect. She wore it a different way every day: flip,

266

pageboy, up, down, in. She used to ask extremely dumb questions in class. She was naïve. She didn't keep it to herself when she didn't understand something. She would entertain the class for fifteen minutes trying to get someone to explain something to her.

Sally Lobherr:
She was one of the first girls I met when I came to Palisades. I was really scared and I went to the bus stop the first morning and Margie was there. She was so cute and bubbly! And she was really nice. She lived in my neighborhood. She had boyfriends coming out of her ears. She'd always giggle and she'd always laugh. She gave you the impression that she was really dumb, but she got good grades, so I knew it wasn't true. Sometimes it seemed like she was sort of insecure. But she was so popular and always went out with so many people that it didn't make any sense.

Mark Holmes:
I liked her, and I thought I was going with her for a while. But then I found out that another fellow thought he was going with her too. With Margie, I was wearing my emotions on my sleeve and she had the ability to make me feel hurt and make me feel upset. I remember her doing the same thing to a lot of people. There's a song, something about a girl saying "I love you," and then saying to someone else "I love you," and it's all a big game. From my standpoint, that fit Margie just really well.

Lany Tyler:
Margie and I were actually best friends in high school. I knew her in a different way than I knew most people. We shared a lot of insecurities with each other, personal problems. We spent a lot of nights at each other's house. We car-pooled to school. We were cheerleaders together. She was as close as I could be

to any female in high school. We had a warm, female camaraderie.

Margie was lively, giggly, spunky. All the boys liked her. Whatever fantasies the boys had about her, or whatever the rumors made her out to be, she was certainly not promiscuous. Margie and I actually had a lot of similar sexual impulses. We were both very flirtatious and vivacious and loving and frustrated a lot of the time.

Skip Baumgarten:
She was cute. Blond and cute. Good tan. Great legs. Small breasts. She was much too cute to be available. Nobody cute was ever available. I often wondered what happened to the cute people after school. They were never around when you wanted to walk home.

●

During the first hour of our visit with Margie, she seemed extremely nervous about the interview and wouldn't allow us to turn on the tape recorder. "I'm not an intellectual," she kept insisting, "you've come to the wrong place." But after we helped her put away a huge load of groceries, and watched as she tucked in her youngest child for his afternoon nap, we went into the den and Margie began to settle down. She leaned back in the recliner, sipped at her orange juice and talked about high school. With her carefully composed features, streaked hair and snug-fitting high-fashion jeans, she seemed like an attractive and well-preserved matron from another generation; we constantly had to remind ourselves that she was in reality no older than we were.

●

Sometimes after school I'd go out riding with different friends. We'd go down to the beach to watch our boyfriends surf, or we'd just sit in the car and talk. Most of the time I came straight home and ate up everything in the ice box. Everything! I liked grilled cheese sandwiches, scooter pies, ice cream. The regular stuff.

I had some problems with my skin, and I was very conscious of it. I'd load myself up with make-up, and then I'd put on red cheeks. I had my hair ratted out into a flip, so I got the nickname "Bozo" from my friends. I didn't mind it too much because it was attention-getting.

I was glad to be a cheerleader, but there were some rough times with that. You had to be on stage all the time. You had to look your best and act your best. You had to act lively even when you didn't feel lively. You had to be *on*. It was really tough. If you were walking down the halls and didn't say hello to somebody in a bubbly way, it was *whisper, whisper, whisper!* "What's wrong with her? She's not *on* right now. What a snob!" You know. You'd get a lot of comments. You weren't allowed any kind of depression or anything. In my senior year I did have some depressions . . . a few emotional problems that have since been worked out.

At one point I had a little group of fans, mostly guys, who used to sit in one section and watch me cheer. They would holler out, "We love Margie." It was like their own special cheer. One time I was rotated down to the other end of the line, and this whole stand, a group of thirty or forty, got up and moved down with me. That filled my ego. I still remember that. After the game they all picked me up and carried me off the field. I don't know what it was about me. These guys were not real winners. I probably wouldn't have gone out with any of them. But I was friendly to them, and joking around with them. I think they needed that, and so they liked me in return.

I went out with a lot of different guys so I wouldn't have to get involved with any of them. I was very backward as far as sex was concerned, and I wanted no part of it. We used to get together, Lany and I and a couple of other girls, to talk about virginity and what it meant to us, and the fact that we would always be virgins. We liked having that bond together. It was a secret bond. If some guy was to make moves on one of us, then whoever it was would call up all the friends the next day and tell them what he did. After that, we'd all give him evil looks. Whoever that guy was, we would spread the word around that he was very fast and to watch out for him.

I had this thing where I never wanted to be hurt, so I never could get involved. I was a real "ball buster," putting it mildly. I'd like to get the guy just where I wanted him emotionally, and then I would say okay, I have to go home now or I won't go out with you again. I had some urge to hurt guys. I don't know what it was. It was really terrible. If they started to like me too much, I wouldn't go out with them any more. Or I'd try to get them to like me and I wouldn't like them back. You know, those stupid little games you used to play. All for no reason.

Thank goodness I went to Pierce College right after high school. I had a great sociology professor there. She was the one that got me to stay in school. From that point on I decided to become a little more serious about life. It snowballed from there.

I've gone to Pierce College, Santa Monica City College, Cal Western in San Diego, and then UCLA for two and a half years. During that time I also worked for a dentist. I worked at Bullock's department store, a little dime store, did all kinds of things.

Actually, since I graduated from high school, twenty years have passed, not just ten years. I am now thirty-seven years old, not just twenty-seven.

My last year in college I met my husband. He is eleven years older than I am. He's in the real estate business. He'd been divorced about five years when I met him. He had two children, Scott and Steven, who were living with the mother. He missed them a lot.

At first I guess it was very sexual—we had a great sexual attraction. The first night I went out with him I knew I wanted to marry him. I had never had any feelings like that for anybody before. It just came over me: This is the guy I want to marry.

I like being married to an older guy. It has more endurance. It's like a father figure. He's such a kind, good person to me. He's very outgoing. Extremely witty. I mean, he should have been in show business, he's so funny. He's an extremely good father. Throughout his whole divorce, he was so good to his children. Calling them; seeing them. So loving, it touched me to think that someone could be like that. To this day, he's just a great father. Maybe he's not so great with the babies—he doesn't want to change the Pampers or heat the bottles—but he plays with the kids constantly. He manages a little-league team. Takes an interest in everything they do. He's the first to volunteer to take the kids to a sports activity or whatever.

About six months after we were married it became evident that Allen's children would be better off in a home with a mother and father full time, rather than a single-parent household. We were fortunate enough to get them. We were so thrilled to have them in our home! I was excited on one hand because I was going to be a mother, but at the same time I was very naïve about what it meant. I was twenty-three. One boy was five and the other was seven. They reacted very positively to me. I found that if I became the dominant figure in their life, it made everyone's adjustment easier. By the end of three months they were calling me "Mom."

As the months wore on I found out what the responsibility of having children entails. I'd never done a lot of laundry, a lot of cooking, a lot of driving to schools, cub scouts, helping with homework. I had a hard time in high school with geometry—how was I supposed to help these kids with the new math?

The oldest son had a slight reading problem and I had to find a good tutor for him.

Each day brought something new. My mind was not preoccupied with myself, and I love that. I really do. In that first year I got pregnant and then Gary was born. What a terrible baby he was! He cried day and night. He was colicky. It was a very rough summer. You don't feel that great, anyway, after having a baby. I had the two older boys at home, and we were remodeling the house. The workers were coming in and out. Then the older boys got sick for about three weeks with whatever kids get—colds, flu.

Thank God the next baby was easier. All he did was eat and sleep for the first ten months. Then he woke up one day. I think it was around Christmas time that he decided that he was a person. Since then, he's been the terror of the house.

I need an outlet. I find I can't do a lot of reading because I'm always interrupted. I'll sit down with a good book and the kids will come through, having a problem. I'll have to put the book down. So I find that I have to get out of the house for a couple of hours and play tennis and vent my frustrations on that tennis ball. I always feel healthy afterwards. I have other hobbies that are also rewarding. I do needlepoint, French flower beading, patchwork pillows, decoupage. I take a lot of photographs and cut them and mount them. I arrange collages. I love the beach and I love walking the children. Every afternoon we're outside, swimming in the pool or playing ball or going bicycle riding. Last summer, almost every evening the three older boys and I would take a long bike ride. The baby would stay home, but I had a seat on the back of my bike for Gary. The two older boys would ride their own bikes next to me.

When Allen comes home, the kids just pounce on him. Allen and I don't have that much time alone.

When the kids are in bed, that's our time. But by that time I'm tired. It's been a long day.

Last summer we went up to a beach house for three full weeks. But it was with the kids. It was a wonderful vacation, but I still had to clean house and cook dinners. The last vacation we had just the two of us was two and a half years ago when we went to Hawaii. We've been talking about another vacation, but that's still up in the air.

A lot of times I get really frustrated with my life. About every six months I say, "What am I doing? I'm working myself to the grave. Nobody appreciates me." You know that routine.

I've thought a lot about what I'll do when the baby is in kindergarten. There are a lot of things I'd like to do. I'd like to go back to school and get my teaching credential, but there are no teaching jobs, so what am I going to do with a credential? I'd also like to have my own store. I'd like to have my own craft shop.

My old high school friends can't believe it when they see me. They can't believe that I have such a settled life. They can't believe the responsibility I have. People used to cut down the typical household, average family, the station wagons, the car pools. It's all a means to an end. The goal is raising the children. You can cut it down because it does get boring. But there's also something very rewarding about it and I'm very happy. They can have all that bullshit they throw around about the typical, average house. I feel that I'm on top of things. There is no one I'd want to trade places with. If I had to do it over again, I'd do it the same.

•

While we were talking, Gary, Margie's four-year-old, came in from outside and joined us in the den. He was wearing white shorts and a tiny white tennis shirt, and he watched the proceedings with polite fascination. Eventually he became restless and reached over to the scrapbooks and photo albums from high school that Margie had taken out to share with us. After these were rescued and placed beyond reach, Margie settled once more in her chair. We asked her if she ever felt nostalgia for the old days at Palisades High School.

●

Kind of. I'm reliving my life from the early sixties right now. I used to love listening to the Beach Boys. Now the Beach Boys are coming back. It's really funny. My twelve-year-old just loves them. I hear those old songs and I just freak out. I think, My God, those songs were big when I was in high school! You know, "Surfer Girl," "Surfin' Safari" and all the rest.

I spend a lot of time at the beach these days. Walking on the beach with my kids. Playing in the sand with them. Like frolicking, forgetting my troubles. Forgetting whatever is on my mind. You know, it's a neat feeling.

Cynthia Morton: The Grind*

•

Skip Baumgarten:
Cynthia was an original. She was like no one else at Palisades High. I remember the way she dressed. Every day it was some kind of plaid skirt, and a button-up sweater. She used to wear saddle shoes—saddle shoes and bobbysox. She didn't care what people thought. She was sort of a mystery. She'd sit on the school bus staring straight ahead with her hands folded on her violin case. Usually the seat next to her was empty, but if anyone sat there, she wouldn't talk, anyway. When we got to school she'd take her books and violin case and walk straight to class. Once she got to class it was all right. The teachers loved her and she always did well.

Jean O'Brian, teacher:
Very, very eager for success and concerned that she do well and achieve—not only achieve, but improve. I had the feeling she was under pressure at home, but she held herself together quite well at school, as far as I know.

Judy Tomash:
Nervous as could be. She had curly hair and those

---

* A pseudonym has been used in this chapter and various details have been altered to protect the privacy of the subject and her family. The basic facts, however, are accurate as reported here.

pointy glasses that made her look like an old lady. She was immature in the ways of high school girls. She's not the girl you'd expect to find at the prom.

Donald Golden:
I remember Cynthia as an obsessively hard-working student. Always worried about tests—she got so nervous you could feel it. She wasn't popular at all, but that didn't seem to bother her as long as she brought home straight A's. I imagine today she's some sort of scientist, probably in advanced research.

Lany Tyler:
It wasn't that people disliked Cynthia, but I think sometimes they resented her because she always got such good grades. I thought she was nice, and a couple of times I tried to talk to her, but she seemed so nervous and shy that I think she preferred to be left alone. She went her own way, doing very well in school, until the concert of the school orchestra at the end of senior year. I remember being very shocked at that. Cynthia was the violin soloist and she was really wonderful. She played with so much feeling and emotion and warmth! I couldn't get over it. I kept thinking, Here is this really sensitive person, who's been with us all this time, and nobody's ever bothered to notice her before. It just shows how little we know each other in high school.

•

We called Cynthia's parents to ger her address, but they refused to give out information over the phone. After demanding to know all the details of our project, they insisted that we come talk to them before paying our visit to Cynthia. A meeting was scheduled at the Morton home in Pacific Palisades, but at the last moment Mr. Morton called us to cancel it. He told us that his wife had been in an emotional state all day: the idea of spending an evening talking to strangers about Cynthia's situation was simply too much for her. Mr. Morton apologized, and urged us to come to his office the next day to meet with him alone. He felt strongly that Cynthia's story should be a part of our book, and he promised to help us in any way he could.

On an overcast September afternoon we drove to the bank in Marina del Rey where Mr. Morton works as branch manager. The bank is located only a few blocks from one of Gary Wasserman's enormous clothing stores, and on the same street as the swank restaurant in which Suzanne Thomas worked as a cocktail waitress. Mr. Morton, however, steered us to a different place for lunch: a cavernous, dimly lit dining room with Polynesian décor. We asked him if he wanted to talk "for the record," and he urged us to bring out our tape recorder. The table was illuminated by a candle in a fat red cup with a plastic fish net on the bottom; Mr. Morton fidgeted with the warm, soft wax and at one point inadvertently extinguished the flame. From the very beginning, he seemed to anticipate most of our questions.

•

I don't think we ever put pressure on Cynthia to do well in school. She put pressure on herself. We just wanted her to be happy. I know it was hard for her, being the middle child in a family of five. Her two older sisters were always attractive and popular, and Cynthia thought she could never be like them. She was quite normal, there was nothing wrong with her physically, but for some reason she never had confidence in her own looks. She wanted to get attention and recognition in some other way, and I guess the way she chose was school. Of course, we approved. I was very proud of her. I'd never been much of a student myself, and it was really a pleasure to see my daughter doing so well. I remember when we went to open house, the way those teachers used to rave! The problem was that Cynthia herself never believed it. The more the teachers built her up, the more scared she got that she was going to fail.

We *did* worry about her in high school, my wife in particular. She kept nagging Cynthia to take more care with her appearance, with her clothes, but Cynthia would never listen to that. It was like that whole business was beneath her dignity, too stupid to consider. She didn't want to compete with the other girls in terms of dressing and appearance. When the senior prom came around, my wife insisted that Cynthia go. She even went so far as arranging a date for Cynthia with a son of one of the neighbors. Cynthia absolutely refused, and I thought she was right. I stood up for her.

When Cynthia finished high school and went on to Stanford, things started getting better right away. The classes were easier than she had expected, and I think people accepted her values more. She gave a violin recital her first year and she made a lot of friends in the music department. When she came home for Christmas vacation we had a couple of long talks—better talks than we ever had before. It was just wonderful to see her. Her brothers and sisters couldn't believe it. She was smiling a lot, talking about school, and just really excited about everything. I remember going to bed that night and saying to my wife, "You see? You've been so worried about Cynthia. There's really nothing to worry about any more. She's coming into her own." I really thought she was going to make an important contribution someday.

I know that for the next few years she continued to do well in school. Cynthia is a brilliant girl. We were all proud of her academic achievement, but it was like she couldn't take any pride in it herself. The first warning sign was when she started going around with a whole different crowd of people—musicians mostly —and you could tell she was changing. She started wearing jeans and sweat shirts like everybody else. When she came home she ran around without a bra, which made her mother really furious.

She had gotten involved with a boy up there, and at first we held him responsible for a lot of Cynthia's problems. Now when I look back on it, I suppose that's not fair. He was just living his own life, and Cynthia made her own choices. I know he was the first boy she'd ever been involved with. He played the piano. He had dropped out of school and was working in night clubs and places like that, earning his living playing jazz. I don't know for sure whether they were sleeping together, but I imagine that they were. For a while they were living with a bunch of other people in a big house in Palo Alto. That place was just filthy. We went up there once to visit and my wife had to hold her nose when she walked through the kitchen. Cynthia kept saying she was happy. She was still doing well in school, but I don't think her grades were quite up to what they used to be. She had switched from science to English, and I always thought that was a big mistake. Of course there were no jobs for English majors, but I don't think she cared. She had already started acting strange. She was doing things like mountain climbing and motorcycles—things that had always scared her to death when she was younger. It was like she was pushing herself to be some other person. I don't know how much of it had to do with drugs. Later on I found out she was smoking a lot of marijuana, but I guess all the kids were doing it at that time.

It wasn't until she graduated and came back to LA that we realized that our daughter was really in trouble. We had persuaded her to start graduate school in library science—which was something practical that she still seemed to enjoy. Her plan was to get her master's degree, then find a job in the country somewhere and live on a farm with her boyfriend. She started at UCLA, and they got an apartment together. We pretty much accepted it, but it wasn't a comfortable situation. Cynthia's sisters saw her more than we did, and they told us that she was taking a lot of LSD. She and her boyfriend went on LSD trips together. I guess it was like a dare—to see how often they could take it and how much they could take. That kind of experience has to do damage. It has to. I know that a lot of other kids did the same thing, and maybe they came out of it okay. For some reason it was different with Cynthia. I don't know.

I think it was really her boyfriend who triggered the first breakdown. It wasn't intentional, but he hit her pretty hard. He had gotten his draft notice, and he decided to run away to Canada. He told Cynthia he wanted to go alone. She couldn't understand it. She was stuck all alone in that empty apartment. We don't know exactly what happened. Maybe she took some drugs. All we know is that one Sunday she was wandering around the Palisades when the police picked her up. They said she was walking in front of cars and things like that, and they booked her for being under the influence of LSD. The funny thing is that Cynthia said she hadn't taken anything. To tell you the truth, I believed her, but it was already too late. When they took her to the jail she really lost control, so the court ordered her to spend two weeks at the county hospital. Maybe we should have fought it at the time, but we didn't. We thought it might even be a good idea for her. But in the hospital things only got worse. They kept her there for ten months, and after that she went to a board-and-care home. I think they were honestly trying to help her. She received a lot of shock treatments and was on tranquilizers most of the time. I think the pain of her boyfriend's leaving, and the humiliation of the position she was in, just made it impossible for her to function or to help herself. I remember when we used to visit her. Sometimes she would be so heavily sedated that we'd sit there for two or three hours before she was even able to talk. It was terribly painful for us, but we were convinced that she would get better soon.

When they finally released her, the doctors said she

ought to be fine. She seemed okay to us, except sort of quiet and slow. I guess she was tired. The first night after she got home we all sat down to dinner. Cynthia was smiling and glad to be back, but it was like she didn't have the energy to eat her food. The doctors said she had been through a severe nervous breakdown, but now she was out of it.

After a couple of weeks we helped her get an apartment near UCLA because she wanted to be on her own. She wanted to go back to graduate school as soon as she was feeling better. I guess it was about this time that she got interested in religion. There's a big group of Jesus freaks at UCLA—religious fanatics— and somehow they got hold of her. She became obsessed with it. For weeks, all she would talk about was Jesus and salvation. She talked constantly about heaven and hell. She wouldn't speak at all to her mother because my wife is Jewish and that meant she was damned. Cynthia had a television set in her apartment and she told us that the TV was giving her messages, telling her what to do. She was seeing a therapist at this point, so what were we supposed to do? One day she just walked out of her apartment and disappeared. I think she walked and hitchhiked all over the state. She didn't even know where she was going. My wife and I had taken a lot, but this was something we couldn't handle. We thought Cynthia was probably dead. My wife was hysterical. Then after a month the police got in touch with us. Cynthia had been arrested in San Francisco for swimming nude in a fountain.

After that she went back to the hospitals and it was a terrible time. Just terrible. I just wanted her to get better, but the courts were making all the big decisions. Cynthia had to stay in these institutions and hospitals, even though she said it was killing her. We didn't know what to do. We had no idea how to help. We were spending fabulous sums to make sure she got the best care she could, and we are not wealthy people. I have four other children, and we have limited means. The lawyers told us we had only three choices: to keep taking responsibility for Cynthia; to give her responsibility for herself, when she clearly couldn't handle it; or to make her officially a ward of the court.

When it came to the hearing, Cynthia insisted on fighting it. It was just too painful for us to face. She defended herself and said she wanted to be on her own. The hearing officer made the judgment in her favor. Cynthia didn't seem angry at us or upset, just happy when she got out. She went to stay with her younger brother, and she told him, "It was easy. All I had to do was lie when they asked if I heard voices." She was still talking about Jesus all the time, and trying to preach to everybody. The doctors told us it was better if we stayed away. Then after a while she started wandering around again, and this time we were pretty much resigned.

●

We recalled the spring day in Berkeley in 1972 when we spotted a familiar face in People's Park. A plump, dirty girl was sitting cross-legged on a sleeping bag, begging food from students as they passed her by. When we approached, we greeted Cynthia Morton, one of the academic stars from our old high school class. We offered to help her with money, but she refused to take it. She said that money only polluted her spiritual life. Her only possessions were her sleeping bag, a well-worn Bible, and the sweat shirt and overalls she was wearing. She told us she recognized us from high school, but then got up and walked away.

During the next few weeks, Cynthia became a familiar sight on the Berkeley streets: a sad barefoot clown who refused to wash any part of herself. At one point she tore the lining of her battered sleeping bag so that she was covered with feathers every morning when she awoke. The tiny white feathers, stubbornly clinging to her curly hair and to every inch of clothing, won her a local notoriety; strangers laughed as they passed her in the street.

•

It's been three years now that Cynthia's managed to keep herself out of trouble, and we're actually very hopeful for the future. She's not seeing any doctors right now, and we think that's for the best. She's living in San Diego at the moment because I think it makes her too nervous to be close to us. We try to help her out financially when we can, so she can have a nice apartment and have a decent life. Her mother goes down there once a week to help her clean up and to bring her some groceries. We love her very much. The last few times we've seen her it's been encouraging, but in the past, whenever we got our hopes up, there's been some report or some phone call or some other kind of contact that just smashes us down again. When I'm really depressed, I think that Cynthia is never going to get better . . . that she's always going to be like this.

I don't understand it. I honestly don't understand it. It must be fate, or something like that. There's no other explanation. There's no history of mental illness in our family or anything like that. I'm not embarrassed to talk about it because I don't think anyone is to blame. We did our best, and we do have four children who are healthy and happy. Maybe we did make mistakes, and if we did, I hope that other parents will learn from them. I also hope that young people will read this and avoid some of the mistakes that Cynthia made. I think the drugs were a mistake . . . a big, big mistake. I also think her overdependence on her boyfriend was a mistake. But who knows? I can't get inside her mind and I can't explain what happened. We've read a lot of books and talked to a lot of doctors, but it's still a mystery. All I know is that we love her very much, and we believe she's beginning to help herself. We're glad you're going down to see her, because it's good for her now to look back on the past. I hope you'll put her story in your book.

•

Cynthia had no telephone in her San Diego apartment, so we sent her several notes to let her know when we were coming. Mr. Morton had told us not to expect a response, but to drive down there anyway at the designated time.

Struggling through freeway traffic on our way south, we worried that we would arrive later than expected and that Cynthia would be upset. Even though we pulled up exactly on time in front of the pink stucco apartment building a block from the beach, we were still nervous as we knocked on the door. There was no answer. It was a hot, pleasant day so we walked down to the beach, passed the time with a dip in the ocean, then returned to the apartment. Still no Cynthia. We decided to wait in our parked car in front of the building. At six o'clock Cynthia's squat, kinky-haired figure suddenly appeared in our rear-view mirror. She was carrying a guitar case, and was out of breath from her frantic pace. She fumbled with a huge ring of keys at the door and went in without noticing us. We breathed deeply, watching the twilight on the quiet street, and then went to the door and knocked. Cynthia opened it immediately. Before we could say a word, she warned us that her only interest was Christianity and that she refused to talk about anything else. Yet she allowed that we might have been sent to teach her something new about the Bible, and agreed to let us in if we promised not to "throw spears" at her.

Cynthia's studio apartment was dominated by the unmade bed that had been pulled into the center of the room. Among the tangled sheets and blankets were several slices of white bread and some half-eaten candy bars. The floor was covered with candy wrappers, dirty clothes and used paper towels. Cynthia sat down on the bed, picked up her guitar case and clutched it to her. We asked her if she still played the violin. She shook her head violently and said, "No, you're talking about me, and I only want to talk about the Bible." She set down the guitar case on the bed and took a tiny dog-eared Bible out of the back pocket of her jeans. She thumbed through it rapidly. We asked Cynthia to read to us, but she kept flipping the pages in silence. Then she glanced up for a moment and a knowing smile suddenly lit her face. "I know it now. You're Jews, aren't you? You might as well admit it."

We told her she was right. Cynthia snickered, then laughed aloud. She put the Bible back in her pocket and slowly turned her body around until she was facing away from us. "I'm sorry that you came so far for nothing. But I'm not going to waste my time talking to Jews." We asked Cynthia if she wasn't half-Jewish herself, but she didn't answer. Then we asked her if she thought Jesus would like the way she was acting. Cynthia told us it was time for us to leave; she had to go to church. We offered to give her a ride, but she refused. We all walked out together, but as soon as Cynthia had locked the door behind her, she ran off at full speed. We called after her, but she lurched on down the empty street without looking back.

We had been with Cynthia for less than ten minutes, but we were badly shaken by the confrontation. On the drive home we tried to occupy ourselves with plans for future interviews, but the conversation kept coming back to Cynthia, and the ways we were not like her . . .

About a month later we received an unexpected phone call from Cynthia's father. Only two days after our visit, while preaching the Gospel on a major boulevard in San Diego, Cynthia had run into the middle of oncoming traffic in an effort to harangue a passing police car. She had been taken away by the authorities and incarcerated in a county mental hospital. Shortly thereafter she appeared before a judge who deemed her "gravely" disabled and declared her officially a ward of the court. She was currently under intensive care at one of the major state psychiatric institutions.

Recalling Cynthia as she had been in high school, we wondered if her problems might have been predicted. Certainly she had been high-strung and nervous, but there were many other students at the time who seemed to face more difficult situations. We thought of poor William Quivers, the first black student in the history of Palisades High School.

•   ^

William Quivers: The Invisible Man

•

Margie Williams:
A black guy? You're kidding! He must have used make-up. Tons and tons of white cloud make-up.

Jon Wilson:
I don't remember any black guy in our class.

Bob Searight:
Was he a foreign-exchange student?

William Quivers: The Invisible Man

Donald Golden:

I remember the rumor that a black student was coming to our school. The gym teachers were quite elated because they assumed they were going to get a star athlete. Then Bill Quivers showed up and he was just a slight, quiet, industrious type who was completely into studying. He wasn't into athletics at all.

Lee Grossman:

The advance publicity on Bill was that his father was a doctor and that Bill had been top student in his school in the South. It was an all-black military academy somewhere in Virginia, I think. But when he got to Palisades, he had an incredibly difficult time. He really struggled through. It makes sense. He was suddenly dropped into the most hostile environment conceivable. He was in a lily-white school, a largely reactionary school. A lot of people made one shot at being nice to him, an opening nice gesture, and then, having met their social obligations, let it go. That's where I was at. He wasn't unfriendly, but he was very withdrawn. It's hard to be friendly and loquacious when you're in terror.

Reilly Ridgell:

He always carried around ninety thousand books and slide rules. He was always studious, always reading, but I don't think he was making it that well at Palisades.

Skip Baumgarten:

One day in class we were all supposed to give reports on different aspects of the space program. I remember William Quivers chose to talk on Re-entry from Space. He was obviously nervous, but he got up in front of that class and gave the most technical report I've ever heard—in high school, college, anywhere. I've never heard anything like it. It got to the point where everybody was sitting there with their mouths open, thinking, My God! What is he saying? Of course, he could have been making it all up and we wouldn't know. Finally, after about fifteen minutes, the teacher interrupted him and said, "Quivers, I think you've lost your audience." I have no remembrance of William saying anything at all in high school after that report.

Lynn Marble:
Oh, my word, I felt that his situation was such a tragedy! It was at the time they were worrying about segregation and placing token Negroes in various situations. I don't know why he was in the class, but I had the feeling that he was being bruised, and that it wasn't my place to ask or intrude.

Jeff Stolper:
I remember right around graduation he had a very small mustache. Not a mustache, really, but a few dark hairs on top of his lips that were getting pretty noticeable. At that time they gave me such a hassle about graduating with what they called long hair that I couldn't see how they managed to let him through.

Lany Tyler:
I had the feeling that everyone wanted to be his friend. I know I wanted to be his friend, but I didn't want to be too obvious about it. I was afraid of being too friendly because it would seem like I wanted to be his friend just because he was the only black at the school.

●

We had no idea where to contact William Quivers. No one from Palisades High had seen him or heard from him in the ten years since graduation, and we learned that his family had long ago moved out of the Los

Angeles area. We heard a rumor that they had relocated in Atlanta, but when we called Atlanta information, we found that they had no listing. Faced with what appeared to be a hopeless situation, we decided to try for a long shot: we would call information operators in each of the nation's twenty largest cities to see if we could find a number for William Quivers. We got as far as Boston when we turned up our first lead: they had a listing for a William M. Quivers living in Cambridge. When we dialed the number, a slow, high-pitched voice answered at the other end.

"Excuse me, is this William Quivers?"

"Yes."

"Is this the William Quivers that went to Palisades High School?"

There was a moment's pause. "You mean Pali High in Los Angeles? Yeah, that's me."

It turned out that Bill remembered us well and seemed to be genuinely glad that we had called. He agreed immediately to the interview we proposed, but warned, "I really don't have a whole lot of memories from Palisades High School."

We made plans to fly to Boston, and arrived on a sweltering Sunday morning near the end of summer. The temperature rose above 110 and the streets were deserted: fortunately, Bill's apartment was efficiently air-conditioned. The rooms were large but surprisingly bare. The living room had no posters on the wall and no rug on the floor: it was completely empty except for a brown vinyl couch, a stereo, and an impressive pile of *Playboy* and *Penthouse* magazines stacked neatly in one corner. Bill was dressed in a gray short-sleeved shirt, loose-fitting brown pants, and slippers. His mustache and goatee had developed impressively since Palisades High School, and his hairline had begun to recede. We found William to be a gentle, friendly person, and not nearly so reticent as we had remembered him.

•

I was born in McDonough, Georgia, which is about thirty miles south of Atlanta. There's a lot of white blood on my mother's side of the family, and my father's mother was a full-blooded Cherokee. I'm sort of a smörgåsbord of the racial composition of the country, and I kind of like that.

My mother is a librarian and my father is an M.D. His specialty is pediatric cardiology. We moved around a lot while he was getting his training, his residency. Right now my parents are living in Baltimore, where my father's head of pediatric services at Provident Hospital.

Before we came to Los Angeles, I was going to a military school near Richmond, Virginia: St. Emma's Military Academy. It was a Catholic school, and the only completely black military school in the country. The first year there was pretty good. But then, the second year, things started to go downhill and I almost got kicked out. I was fighting a lot, believe it or not. I was generally in my rebellious mode of conduct. I was really sort of disappointed with the place because it wasn't what I had pictured a military academy should be. It got so bad that my folks had to come up one weekend and tell me to cool it. They told me we were going to be moving to Los Angeles, and I just had to hang on for a little while.

When I first heard about Los Angeles I was a little apprehensive. I'd never lived outside the South before, and I'm not one to adjust quickly. But then I thought about it a little longer, and the more I thought about it, the more I liked the idea. I'd heard so much about Los Angeles and I was anxious to see it. "Go west, young man, go west . . ." I wanted to check it out.

When we got there, the first thing on my parents' mind was to find a school for me. We were renting a home in Brentwood, and Palisades was the closest high school, so we made an appointment to see the principal, Dr. Aigner. We went down to see him, and in talking to us, he said, "Of course, you will be the first black, and probably the only black student." I said to myself, "Damn!" I was numb for a while. It was a hell of an adjustment, coming from an all-black school to an all-white situation. So I thought, Okay. Here you are. You're a pioneer now, kid, so you're going to have to be on your toes, p's and q's. Just hang on in there.

I compared myself to James Meredith in Mississippi and that thing. I can understand what he went through. So I said, "If he can do it, and others have done it, so can I."

It turned out better than I expected, really. My situation was actually better than some of the other kids', who seemed to have it rougher than I did. The administration more or less looked after me. I'd pass the principal in the hall, and he'd say, "How are things doing?"

I put a lot of emphasis on academic work. I thought it was important that I do that. I would do a good six hours of homework at night. Academically, there was quite a difference between St. Emma's and Palisades. Like night and day. I was in Advanced English, and Math Analysis, which was pretty advanced. I found out immediately that I had somewhat sizable gaps in my background, and I had to work that much harder to keep up, to keep from drowning and going under.

Outside of going out sometimes to view the sights and things, I didn't venture away from home that much. I didn't go out on even one date. I didn't feel sufficiently secure to even contemplate something along those lines.

I remember I had this green sweater. Sort of a security blanket kind of thing. 'Cause I'd had that ever since grade school. It was just an old button-up green sweater. I still have it. I wear it. I wore it quite a bit at Palisades.

Maybe people had a stereotype, but I didn't quite fit

into that. The music I was listening to was mostly classical things. At that time I was into my Stravinsky. Stravinsky and Mozart. I thought the Beatlemania was silly. For the life of me, I couldn't understand why all these girls were just screaming and yelling all over the place, fainting, that kind of nonsense. I still think it's a bit ridiculous.

I remember when the people from *Time* came around interviewing. I felt that since I was there, they should have talked to me some, to at least get some kind of perspective on my point of view. Maybe that's a little ego thrown in there, but I did think that at the time. Not that I would have said anything worth printing, but they didn't even try. They probably didn't know I was there.

I guess I was easy to miss sometimes. But even though I was quiet, I did get involved in a couple of things. I was vice president of the Math Club. Outside of that, I mostly kept to myself and read a lot. I was more or less trying to fit in. I didn't want to stick out like a sore thumb. I remember when they said they were going to take the class picture, I was thinking about it and worrying about it, until one day they marched all the classrooms onto that central quad, and there I was, right in the middle. I thought, There's no way to hide from this!

After graduating from Pali, I went to Morehouse College in Atlanta. It's a black college. That's where Dr. King went to college; it's his alma mater. It's one of the so-called black ivy-league colleges. It has a good deal of prestige among black people when it comes to that sort of thing. I had a good time there. It was quite a change. I really relaxed. After Palisades, I must admit that I felt a bit shell-shocked. I needed a period of convalescence. So I went to Morehouse, majored in physics, and graduated with honors in 1969.

I found out relatively early in my senior year that I was accepted for graduate school at MIT. I said, "Yippee! MIT!" So I came up to Cambridge and the first year went smoothly and what not. I took all my courses and things, and did quite well. Then, second year, I made a few friends. I got along. I was a teaching assistant, which means I sort of taught undergraduates there. I had an office. We'd all get together in the office to do crazy things like throw plastic tops off coffee cans out the window—little Frisbee kinds of things. We played basketball with pieces of paper. It was fun. Just having a good time.

I had a social life, but nothing really serious, in the respect of having steady girl friends. I've had a few close friends over the years, but I wouldn't call any of them *girl friends* or anything like that. I've spent all my time going to school.

In my third year of graduate school I did my master's thesis. It was called *A Study of Inclusive Reactions and the Original Archetypical Model,* whatever that means. It was a good thesis. I got an A off of it. Then I got this fellowship from IBM. They have this program where they give fellowships to black students in the sciences. I was the first one to get it at MIT.

By my fifth year at MIT, I had become sort of disillusioned. I was all by myself. I was the most advanced black grad student in physics at the time. Others were just entering, and three others had gotten their Ph.D.'s just a bit earlier, so I really didn't have anybody to study with. There were no black professors to work with me on research. I was tired of MIT. I'd been there five years; I'd been through nine years of straight school since high school.

I decided to transfer schools. I transferred over to Northeastern, which is in Boston. But about this time, along came my ulcer, and that definitely put a crimp in my plans. At first there was just a pain in my stomach. And burning sensations. So I thought maybe I'm just really tense about something. So I was going around taking a lot of antacids, which didn't seem to be having that much of an effect. So I consulted my father on the phone. He said, "Come home. You probably have an ulcer." That's how I found out about it, and I've been under treatment ever since.

It's healing now. My biggest problem is learning to relax. I still have spasms and they can be kind of rough. It burns. Like somebody is dropping acid on your stomach. I take medications and all, but I have to relax.

I tend to keep a lot of stuff inside rather than expressing myself. Of course, for a long time I wasn't eating right, either. I was eating at McDonald's for breakfast, lunch, any time. I have to watch what I eat now. I can't eat really spicy foods, or anything with a lot of bulk.

Ever since last March I've been on leave of absence. Mostly I've just been resting. I spent a lot of time at home, because my parents were kind of concerned about me and wanted to keep a close eye on me. There was some talk of me possibly getting a job at Morehouse as an instructor, but I decided that wouldn't be what I want to do. So I'm looking at MIT again. I plan to go back in the winter quarter.

If I do get better and go back, it'll probably take two more years to get my Ph.D. I'll have it when I'm thirty. Then I'd like to get a job with the Brookhaven National Lab in New York, or National Accelerator Lab, or maybe the Stanford Living Accelerator.

•

We asked Bill if he thought that being black was an asset, or a liability, in looking for this kind of work.

•

It's an asset. Yeah, very definitely. Ten years from today I hope you'll be able to describe me as "William Quivers: Distinguished Black Physicist." Hopefully, I'll have my Ph.D. by then and a fairly secure position in the field. It's possible to earn a good deal of money, but I didn't go into physics to get rich. Maybe I'll take some academic thing where I can split my time between teaching and research.

I think the atmosphere on campuses has been a little colder in the last few years. During the protest years and what not, I got involved in some of the marches and joined these groups and a certain kind of closeness would develop. We had fun there. We met new people and got to know them and built friendships. Now everybody is busy doing their own thing; there's just the head buried in the book and all that kind of stuff. Just trying to get by, get out.

I got to MIT at just about the right time. They were still interested in getting minority students in a very definite way. People were just starting to see that blacks can do other things outside of dancing and singing and manual labor, or hitting some ball over a fence, or shooting some ball through a hoop, or carrying some other little funny-shaped ball across some long windy field. You see, we have academic talents as well. We're getting a chance to develop more as individual human beings and more as a race. It's good for the country because the country's got that much more brain power. We're becoming more visible. The more visible we become, in spite of the unavoidable racial clashes, it's going to be good in the long run. Black folks are here to stay, and we're going to do what we have to do to survive.

At Pali, I felt I was probably invisible. A lot of it was my own feelings, personal kinds of things, more my hangups than anyone else's. But I can recall when I left Pali I was hoping that they would get some more black students in there to sort of open the school up. I really felt that it was a closed system, and unless it opened up, it was doomed to die, to just stagnate and drop by the wayside. I'm glad to hear that the school has changed.

When I first started MIT, I kept thinking back to my experiences at Palisades. In a way I'm glad I had Pali behind me because I could see where a lot of the other black kids at MIT were facing an all-white environment for the first time. They were having all kinds of problems, which I didn't have. I kept saying, "Thank God for Palisades."

I was really surprised when you gave a call the other day, saying that you were writing this book. I thought, This is good. Maybe I'll find out what some of my other classmates are doing.

Confrontations

•

William Quivers:
I didn't get involved in anything political until I came to MIT in 1969 and joined the Black Students Union. Up until that time, all my attentions had been geared toward my studies, but the events of those years opened my eyes. I got involved in a few marches and protests.

Today the climate has changed—you hardly see that sort of stuff any more. I miss it because it was fun. You know, I felt *useful* for a change. I miss the good old days.

Debbie Gordon:
After I came up to Berkeley, I think I got involved in every demonstration, some way or other. I never got arrested—but was close at People's Park.

I just loved People's Park! It just made my heart warm—the idea of all these different kinds of people going out and building a park! I remember when I heard that the authorities were going to destroy it. I was driving and the news came over the car radio. The park had been blocked off. They had shot demonstrators on Telegraph Avenue. One person was dead. And I was furious. I mean, I was screaming and crying. That enraged me! That week, classes were pretty much canceled, because I had sympathetic teachers who wouldn't teach in that kind of atmosphere. So everyone went down to the demonstrations. I remember running down Virginia Street, across Milvia, running from the police, running through the buildings on campus getting gassed—and standing there when a tear-gas helicopter went over . . . and being incredulous! Good heavens— that's really a helicopter spewing tear gas!

Lee Grossman:
Being politically active was one of the things that helped me to maintain my sanity. I remember when I was a student at Santa Cruz, the regents of the University of California—including Governor Ronald Reagan—held one of their monthly meetings on our campus. At that time the big issue was the student demand that a new college be named after Malcolm X. On the day of the meeting, we all gathered around the area where the regents were supposed to be. The campus was swarming with plain-clothes policemen. The plain-clothes men all wore paper clips in their lapels so they could recognize each other—so naturally, all the students put paper clips on *their* lapels.

The regents were supposed to be meeting in closed session, but a couple of hundred of us jammed into the room. Reagan himself managed to avoid us, but at one point we gathered at the door to the room he was in and trapped him. We started chanting, "We want Reagan, We want Reagan," so he was pretty much forced to come out and face us if he wanted to avoid the use of massive force.

As it turned out, most of the students were much too polite to the son-of-a-bitch. They asked questions and Reagan responded with his usual windy rhetoric. As I recall, I was sitting cross-legged on the floor about three feet away from him. I waited for him to pause, and then I said, in a relatively normal tone of voice, "Reagan, why don't you stop the bullshitting and tell the truth." I'd like to say he bristled, but that doesn't quite capture it. It was stronger. He turned colors. He shot me the most incredible look I've ever been looked. He started to answer me with a finger-wagging speech that began, "Now listen here, sonny boy . . ." But that's as far as he got before the general bedlam broke out.

Michael Shedlin:
For a while I considered myself a Marxist intellectual because I was reading radical books and writing some articles. But I didn't get into any political activity until I moved to Berkeley in '68. The first day I got up there, there was a demonstration in sympathy for the Paris students. A huge riot the first day! A joyous sort of running through the streets and fighting with the cops. It really looked great. It was so neat that it swept us right into it. So we started to get involved in a certain amount of organizing, like for a rent strike, and fighting at People's Park and striking at Cal. It was really exciting shit.

I was never directly shot at during any of the demonstrations, nor was I ever badly clubbed. The worst that happened was that I was nudged and kicked by police. We used to come out when the action was in the streets and we could run at the police and throw something at them and run away and not be trapped. It was relatively light, but it was important for us in 1969 to be realizing that you could actually rebel against the government. And it was fun.

Jon Wilson:
When I got back from Vietnam I had orders to go to Texas, and when I got there they put me on riot-control training. This was 1968. The Democratic convention was coming up in Chicago. About eight hours

a day we practiced riot control, with gas masks on and bayonets on our rifles, going "Hut! hut! hut!" I wasn't up on politics. I didn't even know who was running for President. All I knew was that they were having a convention in Chicago. The hippies were rioting. We were being trained to go and take care of them.

I didn't want to go. I didn't want to go out on the streets of Chicago to bust heads of people who were like my old friends back home. But I was afraid of being court-martialed. They made me go.

They flew in ten thousand of us on Air Force transports. We sat in a barracks and waited for about a week or ten days, and then they shipped us out again. No Army troops hit the streets in Chicago. It was the National Guard and the police who went in. But the rioters knew that ten thousand troops had landed at O'Hare, and things calmed down after that.

David Wallace:
At the height of the Indochina war, I refused to pay my federal telephone tax as a protest against the government. After a year this missing tax snowballed to a grand total of seven dollars and forty-seven cents. This sum disturbed the IRS so deeply that they sent an agent to my home several times, but I always managed to avoid him. Finally a lawyer told me that I had better settle my debt to society—otherwise the government would probably seize my property, including my car. I finally agreed to pay, but instead of giving them cash, I wanted to give them exactly seven dollars and forty-seven cents' worth of books. I bought four books: Thorstein Veblen's *Absentee Ownership, Ecotactics* by the Sierra Club, *The Peter Principle* and *The Rich and the Super-Rich*.

The next day my girl friend and I drove down to the new seventeen-story Federal Building to present the books. We had prepared a neatly gift-wrapped package with the sales slip and a note Scotch-taped to the top. The note said, *"Attention Mr. Yokamura"*—he was the

IRS agent in charge of my case—*"This is the payment for David Wallace's War Tax."* At the time I had long hair and a beard, and the elderly woman at the counter in the IRS office seemed disturbed by my presence. When we put the books down on the counter, she asked us to wait for a moment while she got Yokamura. But we decided it was better not to wait there for his reaction, so we walked out before he emerged.

We took the elevator all the way down to the first floor, and as we walked toward the exit, two security guards came running full tilt in our direction. "Are you David Wallace?" they shouted. I said, "Yes." Then they took me by the arm and said, "You'd better come with us." At this point I noticed that people were streaming out of the building. Secretaries from every office were coming down the elevators and hustling out the lobby. I turned to one of the guards and asked him why this was happening. He said, "It's because of you." They had cleared the building and sent for the emergency bomb squad from Fort MacArthur. They had taken our "bomb" and locked it inside a bomb vault constructed especially for that purpose. Meanwhile they took us and locked us into the basement office of the head security guard. We waited in the room for an hour. Then, through the paper-thin walls, I heard two new men arrive and identify themselves as FBI agents. One of the security guards was explaining the situation. "The suspects entered the IRS office, placed the package on the counter, said, 'This is a bomb,' and walked out." The FBI agent said, "Well, if there is no real bomb, we'll question the girl and let her go and book the guy for disturbing the peace, or something like that." I was horrified.

At this point my girl friend began to lose her patience. When the G-men came into the room, she told them, "This is ridiculous. Just bring the books here and *I'll* unwrap them." The FBI men just stared at her and said, "You're a very brave young woman."

Finally about a dozen more FBI types entered the

room where we were being held. They reeked of disappointment and disgust. It turned out that the bomb squad had arrived and successfully "defused" our books. One of the G-men magnanimously informed us that the Attorney General had decided not to press charges and we were free to leave. On the way out, my girl friend and I shook hands with all the guards and agents. We thanked them for an educational morning and for giving us the chance to spread the word about the antiwar movement.

This still left my unpaid debt of seven dollars and forty-seven cents to the U.S. government. The IRS agent, Mr. Yokamura, came around to my house some weeks later to return the books and to try once more to collect the money. It turned out that I was out of town at the time, but my parents gave him the cash. I was so angry at them for capitulating that we didn't speak for several weeks.

Harvey Bookstein:
One day at Valley State I was walking across campus to the administration building when someone came up to me and told me that the administration building had been taken over by blacks and Chicanos. I turned around and ran the other way.

Judy Tomash:
In the summer of '67 I started going to a lot of peace marches. I went to the big demonstrations against President Johnson at Century City. That same year I decided to sit down in front of the Oakland Induction Center, along with three hundred other people. The idea was to get ourselves arrested. We had to wait there all day before they came and took us away. It was horrible and it was wonderful. At the time I thought, Oh, they'll arrest me, and I'll stay in jail for twenty days. I didn't know how oppressive it would be. It was heavy duty. It totally changed my life . . .

Judy Tomash: The Joiner

•

Sally Lobherr:
Judy Tomash! She was always happy and excited and jumping up and down about nothing at all. I wonder what happens to people like that?

Skip Baumgarten:
Judy Tomash was social. Judy Tomash was organization. Judy Tomash was . . . well, large breasts. I think she joined every organization on campus that would accept girls. Athenians, Delphians, Health Club, School Spirit Board, the whole thing. She was even our foreign-exchange student to Brazil.

Lee Grossman:
She had the nicest pair of jugs I had seen up to that time. But that wasn't her most striking characteristic. Her most striking characteristic was that she was very sweet. She was also very friendly to me, and a girl being friendly to me was such an unusual thing in those days that it absolutely changed my awareness of myself. I think we actually went bowling together, or did something equally risqué.

Debbie Gordon:
Oh, Judy! Very vivacious and outgoing. Big eyes, big life, waving her arms! If she hadn't been so cheerful, I'd have thought she was from New York.

Judy Tomash: The Joiner

Mark Holmes:
I remember her as a beautiful Jewish girl who was on
her way to something fine. A good brain, good values,
a good personality. My father made me aware of Jewish
people as being separate. He would ask me who I was
going out with. If it was a Jewish name, he would gri-
mace. You know, he didn't like that.

Jeanne Hernandez, teacher:
Judy was very bright and very womanly. I remember
thinking that in later years she would become a member of Hadassah or some other women's service group.
She was a completely conventional girl. She had a
strong desire for approval from her peers, and without
question, from her teachers.

•

We heard through the grapevine that Judy had recently
moved with her one-year-old son to a remote corner of
northern California. When we reached her by telephone, the excitement in her voice was unmistakable,
despite the faulty long-distance connection. She seemed
delighted with the chance to talk about her past, and
told us she had been spending much of her time recently sorting out the confusion of the last ten years.
In fact, she was leaving the next day on a two-week
yoga retreat, but afterward planned a visit to her parents' home in Los Angeles. We agreed to meet her
there, and one balmy Sunday joined Judy and her parents around the Tomash swimming pool. We waited
while they finished a discussion of Judy's personal fi-
nances, and then set up our tape recorder. Judy, who
was wearing a purple halter top and red bikini bottom,
asked for a minute to "compose herself" before we
began the interview. She closed her eyes, meditated
for a few moments, then nodded to indicate she was
ready. Throughout the interview, Judy's parents walked
back and forth between the pool area and the house,

checking up periodically on the progress of our conversation.

•

For most of high school I really felt out of it. There were two ways to make it in the high school structure. One was to be really bright and the other was to be really beautiful. I tried for both and ended up in the middle. I could have some close friends and have a good time, but I could never be Lany Tyler.

But in senior year I did get chosen as the American Field Service exchange student, and I got to spend twelve months in Brazil. In a lot of ways it was a traumatic experience. When I got back, I felt pretty out of it. I had become so immersed in Brazilian culture that when I called my dad I couldn't speak English on the phone. And I had to go back to high school where everyone was going to football games and organizing proms and doing the same things that I had finished with a year before. It made me feel sort of isolated, and raised a lot of questions in my mind.

Jean O'Brien, teacher:
I don't think Judy ever reclaimed any sense of a national identity after she came back from the AFS experience. She had always been eager to please; she was very, very friendly. A pleasant, idealistic young woman. But when she came back, she was hollow. Hollow, hurt, devastated. Almost as though she saw the United States from another point of view and could never accept being an American.

After I graduated I went to the University of California at Santa Cruz. I was very solitary that year. It turned out that one of the few people I saw was Lee Grossman, my old friend from high school and junior high. I remember walking in the woods with him and talking about philosophy. He explained Sartre to me,

Being and Nothingness, and made it all seem very clear.

That summer I worked in a Headstart program and became very involved in the whole peace-march circuit and antiwar activities. In October of '67 I decided to let myself be arrested as part of the protest at the Oakland Induction Center. There were three hundred other people who were arrested that day, including Joan Baez. My parents understood what I was doing, and I think they respected me for it.

I was in jail for twenty days in the same room with seventy other women. I nearly went crazy! For one seven-day period they fed us nothing but bread and evaporated milk. We were given a list of thirty-six rules: how to tuck in our blankets, where to place our pillow, how to put our shoes at the foot of the bed. We were rarely allowed to change our clothes, shower or change our sheets. I learned what it's like to be in a situation where someone else has all the power, and you have nothing . . . nothing, and they have everything.

I also had my first exposure to lesbianism. There were three or four regular prisoners who had become men. They wore their hair a certain way, walked a certain way, wore their uniforms with their handkerchiefs in their pockets, and they had boys' names. One of them was really cute—you could see getting a crush on her.

I remember on the last day they gave us all our mail. I opened up a letter from my younger sister and the colors just burst out. She had written on stationery with flowers and butterflies. I hadn't realized that I had missed color so much.

After I got out of jail I moved in with a guy. It was my first real love relationship, but we didn't get along. All the time I was becoming more and more disillusioned. I knew I had done everything I could to stop the war, but no one paid any attention. The war was marching forward, so in 1969 I quit school. I traveled around Europe and the Middle East for two years and spent some time in a kibbutz in Israel. By this time I had become a vegetarian and I was already interested in Eastern religions and reading heavily.

When I got back to the U.S. I lived for a while on a farm in Connecticut, and at this same time I began taking drugs. I took everything that came my way: LSD, mescaline, psilocybin and peyote. It was not good for my body, but I don't regret it. I'm glad I was part of the hippie movement; I think it changed me a lot.

I started doing a lot of yoga, and after a while I stopped taking drugs. I met a man who had just gotten back from India, where he had been living with a yoga teacher. This man was a musician and an astrologer— an interesting person. He had run away from home when he was fourteen and he never finished high school. I started traveling with him, and I started my period of craziness. Intense craziness. I had had my spiritual awakening and I didn't know how to balance it with the rest of life. I was extremely blissful. It was wonderful, just wonderful. I gave everything away— all my possessions. I was oblivious to everything except my own joy. But it was crazy in that I didn't have touch with reality. I had lost touch with the fact that all of us are God—not just me.

●

We vividly recalled a chance meeting with Judy during this period. We had not seen her for eight years when we ran into her at a religious lecture in Berkeley in 1973. She was sitting cross-legged in her chair, rocking back and forth with a blissful and inscrutable grin. Her eyes were unfocused and we feared she might be in some sort of trance. We approached her, greeted her warmly and tried to strike up a conversation. But this proved impossible: though she turned in our direction and her eyes registered recognition, she continued to smile and sway without saying a word.

•

So then I went to India for three months, and stayed with Ram Das—a former Harvard psychology professor who changed his name and brought spiritual teachings to thousands. His guru was there too. It was very wonderful. Unfortunately, I got hepatitis while I was there. I came back and stayed with my folks. I felt they were ungodly because they didn't talk about religion. They thought I had lost my mind, but they took care of me while I was sick. I guess I was just down on them for no reason.

When I got better, I started traveling around northern California. I was still with the same man. I didn't know what to do. I was very much lost. Mostly I just did yoga. Then I decided to go back to school, and I gradually came out of my crazy period. My family gave me money while I went to school. A modest amount, just enough to live on. So I finally graduated and got a degree in religious studies and psychology. That pleased my parents. I felt so happy! I went to graduate school and got a teaching credential. For a while I taught second grade in a small town. But then I became pregnant, so I quit teaching.

My son, Suresh, was born at home. His father delivered him. Naturally, I started giving a lot of energy to my child, and the father just couldn't cope. He'd always been spoiled. He was like a big baby. So when there was a real baby, there was no room for big babies. He found another girl right away. She moved in and the four of us tried living together for a while. I wanted to see if I could work through jealousy and learn to love my sister as a sister. I couldn't. It's a great idea, but in real life it's very different.

Now I'm living by myself with my boy. Financially I'm blessed. My folks gave me a trust fund which provides me with about two hundred and fifty dollars a month. That's what we live on. I mostly practice yoga. I have a teacher whom I love and trust. I'm affiliated with a group that teaches yoga. I do some writing, some reading, some spinning of wool. But mostly I take care of Suresh, who is one year old. Suresh means "Lord of Gods" in Sanskrit. He is a very wonderful boy and he brings me much joy. I am very happy.

•

As the sun went down, Judy's parents brought Suresh out into the patio. A smiling and very active child, he amused himself by playing in the water, crushing pieces of fruit, and defecating on the concrete. Judy excused herself and went over to play with her son. We saw her smile at him, and this smile was different from the blissful smirk we had seen two years before. It reminded us of the high school Judy, and we felt a wave of nostalgia for those days.

Judy returned to the lounge chair, nursing her baby. We asked her why she felt such a strong attraction to Hinduism, in view of her Jewish background.

•

I'm sure that it is my past lives that have drawn me to it. That's what's drawn me. The saints that we're studying now are Christian, Moslem, Buddhist and Hindu. I'm also trying to study Cabala, so I'm not entirely cut off from Judaism. I've thought about it often, I've made contacts with rabbis, and I've tried. I went through some guilt. But it just wasn't happening there for me the way that it's happening here. It's different with Hinduism—I don't have the negative associations that I have with Judaism. All the emptiness that I experienced as a girl I'm sure exists with the average Hindu family in India. But I don't have those associations. I didn't grow up with it.

●

It was dark by now and getting cold; Judy picked up her son and led us inside. We paused for a moment, waiting for Judy's parents, but they remained behind —Judy's mother reaching down with paper towels to pick up the feces, and her father hosing down the patio, cleaning up the mess that their grandchild had left behind.

●

Lany Tyler: The Homecoming Queen

●

Judy Tomash:
Lany Tyler was the most popular person in the school. I got to know her in twelfth grade when we had a class together, with Mrs. Hernandez. I kind of wanted to dislike her, but I couldn't—she was so genuine. She really was a friendly person—not a smile, not a façade.

Jeanne Hernandez, teacher:
She was lovely-looking. Small. Dark. Intense. I remember her as being, even though she was dark, a

"fair-haired darling." Whatever organization it happened to be, Lany was right there. The name was all over campus. Everything was Lany Tyler. If she ran for anything, she won immediately. She never lost an election. If she favored anyone in particular, that young man was in seventh heaven because he'd gone out with Lany Tyler.

Skip Baumgarten:
I had a crush on Lany Tyler. She was neat. She was spirited. Boy, she was really all-American, apple pie. That was Lany Tyler.

I remember she was chosen head of the Girls' League. I sent flowers to her when she won. She called me up to thank me and tell me how wonderful it was, and invited me to the dance that was gonna celebrate whatever it was she had won. I got all excited—until I found out she wanted me to take her twenty-two-year-old sister. So I took Sue Tyler. She's a nice girl. Kind of quiet, into music. But nothing like Lany!

What were the marks of status at Palisades High? Lany Tyler and Margie Williams. If you messed around with them, it was okay.

Jean O'Brien, teacher:
She was Student Body Everything. Cheerleader. A good student. I don't know how she did it all. She took vitamins, I guess.

Sally Lobherr:
It got sickening that she won everything! For cheerleader she was fine and for Girls' League president she was super. She was that type of girl. But I didn't think she was the type for Homecoming Queen. Still, if anyone deserved it, Lany Tyler deserved it because she did so much.

Her secret? I think she was nice to everybody. Even if you were a weirdo, she would smile and say good morning to you, whereas a lot of us, myself included, would be embarrassed to be talking to someone who wasn't on our level. But Lany wasn't afraid of anything. She was very self-assured.

Reilly Ridgell:
Miss Queen! Lany was supposed to be one of the prettiest girls in the school, and she thought that, I guess, and everybody else thought that. She sat in front of me in geometry class once and she didn't turn out to be as stuck up as I thought she was. She always had a smile, a constant smile. I remember one time sitting behind her in geometry. I was pointing out split ends in her hair because I was bored with whatever was going on in class at the time. I said, "There's another one!," and she'd say, "But I just cut my hair!," and then all of a sudden the teacher caught us, and made some remark about amorous intentions between the two of us. It kind of embarrassed me, but Lany just laughed it off.

Lee Grossman:
Lany was one of the first girls that I was at all interested in. I had a general sense of making a fool of myself whenever Lany was around. I don't know what it was that aroused my interest. I was about to say her breasts, but I noticed her before she had any.

Lany was very interested in being popular and she was successful at it. My mother has a theory about her popularity. My mother's theory is that she got a lot of votes from other girls who didn't consider her a very serious threat. Back in high school, I always thought she was a knockout. She had a remarkable figure. But in retrospect, there may have been something to my mother's theory. Lany wasn't pretty. She's not unusually bright. She was certainly into that whole school-spirit thing. I would have predicted that she would have gotten married in her second year of college. She would have had as many kids as possible in a hurry. She would have settled down to a dull, anonymous life while her husband went out and adjusted claims for Aetna.

Margie Williams:
Lany was my best friend in high school. She was a model student. She had the model personality, and the model figure, hair. Everything about her was beautiful. Not just on the outside, which everybody knew, but on the inside. She was friends with everyone, regardless of what group they were in. She would take time from whatever she was doing and talk to you if you had a problem. What a friend! I mean, one in a million!

I remember going to the beach with Lany. She had a few slumber parties at her house, and I remember those good times. Probably all we talked about was boys! In school, we were cheerleaders together.

We've lost contact over the years. Once or twice a year we will get together and pick up where we left off from high school, like those years in between never existed.

Carol Shen:
Lany was sort of the female counterpart to Mark Holmes, I think, in terms of the role she played in high school. Except that you always had the feeling that Lany was terribly bright, which—well, nothing against Mark, but . . .

Mark Holmes:
Yeah, I do remember dating Lany Tyler. First date, we went to the Bay Theatre. I remember asking what her dad did, and when she said he was a gynecologist, I didn't even know what it meant. I remember necking with her in the Bay Theatre. We stayed through two movies. At that point we were, what, fifteen?

At the end of junior high we both got voted Most Likely to Succeed and Best All Around. We were liking each other at the time and people were kind of pushing us together. Then, when we got to high school, I sort of found out that I didn't really like her. It was a strange sensation.

I saw her once in the last part of high school. We had some meeting up in the Pali library for something we were organizing. I drove her home. I remember feeling really nice, like here is somebody who's really nice, who I really like. Nowadays I drive by Moreno sometimes, where she used to live. I think of her. My thought is, Well, she had a lot going for her.

Candy McCoy:
Lany was a person of absolutely endless energy and competence. She was a magnetic personality, and genuinely well-loved. I can't imagine anyone having negative feelings about her.

Gary Wasserman:
She was not terribly attractive, but I actually enjoyed being around her because of her personality. She was a very bubbly girl. But she wasn't even close to being one of the most popular girls at Palisades High School.

•

As we looked over the comments on Lany Tyler, we had to shake our heads in disbelief. Gary Wasserman notwithstanding, the recollections from her classmates amounted to a tidal wave of respect and affection. This response made us all the more curious to see what Lany had done with her life. After winning that sort of success and adoration in adolescence, what can you possibly offer the world as an encore? Our experience with Mark Holmes and Brock Chester had taught us that extreme popularity in high school can be a heavy burden to carry into later life.

Lany Tyler May lives today in New Jersey with her husband and her five-year-old son. Fortunately for us, they decided to spend the summer in their small beach house in Venice, California.

They were just settling in when we paid our first visit. It was an unseasonably cold day, with a heavy fog rolling in off the Pacific. Lany served us mint tea and cookies, and then had a chance to sit down, catch her breath from unpacking and recall some of her high school ambitions.

•

I may very well have wanted to be the first woman President. I also wanted to be the first woman astronaut. The only problem was that I was sort of a klutz. I wasn't a very good cheerleader. We had a cheer we did on a bench, and I fell off the bench once in the middle of the cheer. And once we were running to the goal line to cheer over a touchdown, and I tripped over one of the sideline wires. I fell down and scratched my face. I generally ended up with a few bruises. At the time I thought it was worth it, but I began to realize that outer-orientation is a tough job. It was just awful to be a cheerleader on those days when you don't feel like cheering. And no one feels like cheering all the time—not even Lany Tyler!

In high school, I never liked the way I looked. I worried that my nose was too big. I'd look in the mirror and think, She ain't no great shakes! I slept on twenty rollers every night so that my hair would curl just right—but not too much. I was constantly worried about getting fat. When I felt good about myself, I considered myself voluptuous. But the media tell you that girls should be skinny, and I could see *Seventeen* magazine as well as any other girl. I remember seeing pictures of myself as Homecoming Queen and thinking I was just outrageously fat for a Homecoming Queen.

I was really torn up about that, because Homecoming Queen was the one thing where I could never convince myself that I was well qualified. I thought it should go to some very gorgeous, very regal girl. I rationalized all my other offices by telling myself I was really doing a good job. But Homecoming Queen was pure vanity.

It was a student-body election. I figured there weren't too many people, other than myself, that everyone in the school would know. By that logic it was almost inevitable that it would be me. I probably could have been student-body president too, if I'd wanted it. But I think I always stayed within the role of the girl—I never usurped that much to think of myself as student-body president.

I was very deeply committed to virginity. God knows why, but I was. My adolescent diaries are chronicles of sexual guilt—over nothing! It wasn't until I was twenty or twenty-one that I finally lost my virginity—the year before I met Lary. That's grotesque!

Yes, I won the award at graduation for Most Outstanding Woman in the class. But there were so many women smarter than me! I graduated twentieth in a class of five hundred. I knew I was bright, but I didn't think I was brilliant.

As it got close to the time of getting acceptances and rejections, I realized that colleges weren't looking for nebulous all-Americans with nothing special to offer. About the only thing I was qualified to be at that point was a professional cheerleader! As it came out, I was refused nearly everywhere I applied. The Ivy League totally turned me down.

So I went to Santa Cruz, and those first two years were very important to me. Santa Cruz helped me to be less outer-oriented. There were no more football games and student activities to run to. I had a deep commitment to doing well in my classes, and for the first time in my life I was intellectually involved.

Judy Tomash:

I always used to wonder what made Lany the most popular girl through all those years in junior high and high school. Then when I went away to college, I can remember sitting in the Santa Cruz library and there were three boys in the booth next to me. They were looking at someone and talking about her, about how cute she was and how nice she was, and wouldn't it be great to go out with her. I looked over to see who they were talking about, and it was Lany Tyler. I thought, Here I am at Santa Cruz, and I might as well be back at Palisades High School! Lany Tyler is still the most popular girl!

I liked having men like me, and going out was important. But it wasn't the most important thing in my life at Santa Cruz. I had spent so many years trying for the identity I thought everyone expected of me, but now I was trying very hard to find an identity on my own.

After two years I was going a little stir-crazy, and I decided to do my junior year abroad. I went to Japan, and spent most of that year trying to become Japanese. I came home with an infatuation for a Japanese man that I thought I might marry. I wanted to spend my senior year in Los Angeles, near my family, because I thought I might be going back to Japan after graduation. But within a week after I got back, I managed to fall out of love with my Japanese samurai, and transferred to UCLA to study American history.

My whole experience in Japan had sparked me to try to rediscover who I was within my own national and cultural context. That was what motivated me to go on to graduate school. It wasn't so much a direct career orientation as the fact that in my last year as an undergraduate, I was only beginning to study things that seemed worth pursuing. It would have been foolish for me to quit just because I was graduating.

Lary May was the least boring of all the men I

met at UCLA. He was already in graduate school in American history—the field I was planning to enter. He was twenty-eight. His parents had been divorced when he was very young; he had never really known his father, he'd been a troublemaker who was kicked out of his high school.

My parents were just horrified by Lary. He didn't make an effort to impress. He was not what you would call well-groomed and clean-cut! He's always been something of a rebel, and he loves to argue. He certainly wasn't the type of man I would have expected for myself in high school. Lary never swept me off my feet, which is why I began to trust the relationship.

The year after we got married I had Michael. It was a perfect time to have a baby. I don't think I could have made it through graduate school without it. Grad school is by definition very narrow, very intense. But for me the years were punctuated by the excitement of being married, the excitement of having a child.

Of course, I was very busy. I was doing part-time teaching at one of the state-university campuses, and then I was doing my doctoral dissertation. My dissertation is about marriage and divorce in the first few decades of this century. I was interested in men and women and what they expected of each other. The manuscript is about two hundred and eighty pages—relatively short—but it did get me my Ph.D. I'm revising the dissertation this summer, and after that I hope it will be published.

It was last fall that I got the job offer at Princeton and we moved East. My title at Princeton is assistant professor. It's one of the incredible ironies of my life that the Ivy League turned me down at every juncture of my education—including graduate school—and then finally hired me to teach.

I'm part of a women's group at Princeton, and we get together every few weeks. It's just a number of women faculty members who like to sit around and

317

sip sherry and talk about what it's like to be a woman teaching in that situation. I consider myself a feminist, but I feel that I can take as much of the standard woman's role as I want—and there's a lot of it that I want. I'm happy that I'm a mother, and I'm happy that I'm married. Lary and I share everything. He has changed as many diapers, given as many baths, done as much cooking and everything else as I have. Our careers are also the same.

What I like to think is that the façade I had in high school hid a lot of what was deepest in me, or maybe not developed. I would like to think that this part of me is now much more on the surface, and that I only rely on that other personality—that outer-oriented, cheerleader personality—in moments of stress, like job interviews.

In high school, I was accessible to everybody because I was so afraid that somebody might not like me. I wanted to be loved, universally. I'm much less concerned with that now. I'm much more jealous of my time, my personal life, and I simply don't let people intrude on me the way I used to.

Of course, I had some wonderfully romantic moments in high school. I remember particularly the night of the Homecoming Dance. At three o'clock that morning I danced with my boyfriend in the living room of my parents' home, with my shoes off and my crown on. Like all romantic moments, it was totally destroyed when my angry mother came out of the bedroom and said, "Do you realize that it's three in the morning? Get to bed!"

●

As Lany smiled, we wondered if she would temporarily sacrifice the dignity of her academic position for the sake of the upcoming ten-year class reunion. "What would it take," we asked her, "to get you to dress up in a short blue skirt and your old sweater with the big *P* on it, and to wave some pompoms and lead some old-time cheers at the class of '65 reunion?"

Lany laughed. "It would take either a million dollars—or a *lot* of wine!"

We left our visit with Lany feeling pleased. It occurred to us that the same positive energy that had allowed her to master so completely the Palisades High environment had recently been applied to mastering academia, her dissertation, her role as wife and mother. That was the real consistency in Lany's life—a remarkable ability to gracefully take command of every situation—to be on top of things, to smile and to enjoy herself.

When we returned to Lany's house later in the summer we brought with us a transcript of this interview, plus a special surprise. "Close your eyes for a minute," we told her. "We brought someone out here all the way from Kansas City." Following us up the stairs was a slight, bespectacled figure with cowboy boots and closely cropped brown hair.

"My God!" Lany said as she opened her eyes. "It's Jamie Kelso!"

•

Jamie Kelso: The Idealist

•

Time *magazine, January 29, 1965:*

"I enjoy three things," says Jamie. "Being in a book-
store with $10 in my pocket, a rainy day at the
beach, and insight in terms of finding insight in myself." Like many Pali students, he does not especially
enjoy his home life. "I'm kinda hoping to make a
more meaningful person out of my mother, but it's
hard work." Meaning is Jamie's favorite word.
"What do good grades mean?" he asks. "And what
if I go along, get married, have a good job and
raise kids? Do we know what it is all about? Are the
people around us really alive?"

Skip Baumgarten:
Jamie Kelso used to eat lunch alone. He'd eat alone
and read a book. Actually, I think that's what he ate.
He ate thin paperbacks for lunch. He was probably
very intense. You don't eat too many paperbacks
without getting intense.

Donald Golden:
He always had an armload of books—unusual, strange
books or long novels. He was always straining his
eyes through thick glasses to read them. Always aspir-
ing to some grand philosophical feeling or system. I

liked hanging out with him and I liked his family.
It was a very different atmosphere from what I had
at home. Their house was always a wreck, which I
really liked. It was a loose kind of scene, with lots of
yelling and shouting and all kinds of excitement that
I had never experienced before.

Jeff Stolper:
In elementary school, Jamie used to be a couple of
grades below us, but then he was so smart that they
skipped him two whole years. I think he was the only
person in the history of Palisades Elementary School
who ever did that. It will never be done again, because the administrators don't approve of skipping
people any more. Everybody knew how smart Jamie
was, but he never gave you the feeling he was con-
ceited about it.

Lynn Marble:
I had a big crush on Jamie and I felt very motherly
toward him. I felt that he didn't have a very firm
grasp of reality, and had to be protected from the
giant fall from naïveté. We lived on the same street.
Sometimes I'd wait until I saw him walking to Pali
High, and then drive by with my car and offer him a
ride. He was always flustered, completely undone by it.
He was like a small child, I thought. All of us girls
worried about Jamie. We felt like we had to protect him from the evils of the world.

Lee Grossman:
He was our high school's prime example of *Welt-
schmerz*. Jamie was the troubled intellectual. I remember him standing in front of an English class trying to
get across the experience of nausea in Sartre. It
seemed that he went through the same sort of identity
crisis that most of us went through—only Jamie did it
earlier. He came out of it differently. He's gone a lot
of weird directions since high school.

Mike Medved:
My clearest memories of Jamie center on the hour we spent together in the San Clemente jail. We had gone to San Clemente one weekend in senior year to camp on the beach and hike in the hills. We took a Greyhound to get there, and once we arrived we found that no camping was allowed. We set up our sleeping bags, anyway, built a little fire and stayed up all night reading by candlelight. I was reading Dostoyevsky and Jamie was going through Bertrand Russell's *History of Western Philosophy*. Just two typical campers.

First thing in the morning we were awakened by a police officer. He told us we were camped there illegally and we'd have to leave. After some discussion Jamie lost his temper and threw his book at the policeman. It was definitely a mistake; *The History of Western Philosophy* is a very massive volume. The police officer hauled us in and they held us in the jail for questioning. It was only after they talked to Jamie's father on the phone that they decided to let us go. Mr. Kelso told them that Jamie had been an eagle scout—which was true—and that seemed to do the trick.

Jean O'Brien, teacher:
Don Quixote. I wonder if he got off the horse, or if he found the windmill. Maybe he's still looking. I saw him once several years after he graduated. He was up on Sunset hitching a ride, and I looked and I thought, My God! Inside, you're twelve! It seemed as if none of his experiences had left a mark on him. He had the same face. Is it still the same? Open, inquiring, a little wide-eyed at times . . . He's like a sieve—you know, stuff goes through and doesn't stop. But he's a brilliant kid. Marvelous mind. Grasps the abstract, but he can't create a relationship to the real world. I was hoping he'd go into philosophy and put it down somewhere so that someone could read it.

●

We had seen Jamie only once in the years since high school. During a brief visit to Los Angeles in the winter of 1971 we called his parents and learned that Jamie had joined the Church of Scientology. He was living communally with fifty other scientologists in a ramshackle house in downtown L.A. When we paid him a visit one cold night, we waited in the seedy entrance hall while Jamie's "commanding officer" summoned him from upstairs. The entire house seemed to be administered along military lines. Many of the young people who came bustling in and out the various doorways were dressed in freshly pressed sailor suits. Along the walls were numerous framed pictures of "the Commodore"—L. Ron Hubbard, scientology's founder. Finally Jamie marched down the stairs, wearing thick rimless glasses and a confident smile. He led us into the dining hall, where we sat alone at a long table and talked for ten minutes. We learned that Jamie was part of the Sea Organization, or Sea Org, the elite corps of the scientology movement. Those lucky enough to qualify spent all their waking hours in missionary activity, in return for which room and board were provided by the movement. As part of his commitment, Jamie told us he had signed a "billion-year contract," binding himself in this and all future incarnations.

He spoke quickly and nervously, but the smile never left his face and the intense green eyes smoked and glittered behind his glasses. He toyed with the sugar bowl, spilling some of the sugar onto the table and forming it into little mounds between his fingers. He told us he was very happy, and that he wanted to share his happiness with his friends. He wanted us to leave him an address so that scientology literature could be sent to us in the mail, but we declined the offer. Our conversation had just about run out of steam when one of Jamie's superiors came into the dining hall and called our old friend back to "work detail" upstairs. We said good-bye and wished him well.

Four years later we tried to contact him again in the course of preparing this book. We assumed that the best way to do that was to call the Sea Org, since Jamie still had some time left to serve on his contract. But when we placed the call, the operator at the scientology switchboard had to transfer us to four different officers before we found one who admitted any knowledge of Jamie.

"That's a name we're not supposed to talk about," said the brisk, efficient voice at the other end of the line. "He ran away two years ago. He deceived us, won our confidence, and then he blew. If you succeed in locating him, I hope you'll give us his address."

We had no intention of reporting Jamie's whereabouts to the Church of Scientology, and we began our own quiet investigation. Jeff Stolper gave us some useful leads.

•

Jeff Stolper:

It was about a year and a half ago when I saw him. I was walking with my wife and both kids up in the Palisades. Some kid was walking along and it looked a lot like Jamie. I came up and said, "Hey, do you remember a kid named Jamie Kelso?"

He said, "Man, I've been trying to forget that guy for a long time. That's me, Jamie. You're Jeff Stolper, aren't you?"

I knew all along it was Jamie—I was just putting him on. He told me that he was self-employed, doing some kind of inventing. He was living out in the Midwest somewhere, keeping pretty much to himself. That would fit Jamie perfectly. I would guess that he could never tie himself down to a job where he had to work for somebody. Inventing seems more like him. If you want to find out where he is, you should talk to his brother, who owns Kelso's Café up here in the Palisades.

•

After enjoying delicious cheese omelettes one afternoon at Kelso's Café, we got Jamie's phone number from his younger brother. We called Kansas City immediately. Jamie picked up the phone, and after the briefest exchange of greetings and pleasantries, was ready to talk philosophy at long-distance rates. We suggested instead that we get together for an interview. Jamie told us that he had been thinking about a trip to Los Angeles, anyway, and our project provided him with just the excuse he needed.

He arrived in LA wearing cowboy boots, jeans and a black Western shirt. He was exhausted from his 40-hour bus ride, but when we handed him a copy of the old *Time* article about our high school, he became so animated that we began the interview without delay. He snickered particularly at the purported connection between Candy McCoy and "Jamie Kelso, 16, a skinny near genius who studies only those subjects that interest him, mostly political science and history."

•

That article was totally and completely false! Every quote from me was a fabrication. Every estimation of me was inaccurate: "near genius"—using the word "near." They called me skinny. But I was pudgy, at least stocky. I had a romantic affiliation with Candace McCoy? Absolutely false. You know I didn't rate socially. So this allegation about Candy McCoy was like a super-camp put-down of me. I was made to look like an incredible fool. The whole teenage sex thing is so blatantly absurd! In junior high and high school there was not the faintest notion that sex belongs with the building of a family. It was a completely divorced, alienated world where sex was an end in itself. Very weird. Sex has never been a big deal for me, anyway. In fact, sex without romance is something I just find to be an oddity. A good glass of grape juice is more interesting.

My father is a designer and inventor. He invents anything and everything. He is a completely self-made individual who faked it without degrees and diplomas. While I was growing up, his income fluctuated wildly because he was a lone entrepreneur. Neither of my parents are intellectuals. The outstanding thing that they did in regard to my intellectual development was that they left me completely alone.

By age sixteen in 1965, I had long known that I possessed an incredible mind. I knew I was more intelligent than any of the teachers at Palisades, or any two of them. I suffered enormous stress trying to make sense of the nonsense peddled at that government brainwashing pen. But I hadn't studied, I didn't have the vocabulary, I didn't have the trappings of education. So when one of these teachers would spout this sophisticated trivia, I had to play along to maintain face. As an example, all the English teachers proclaimed the virtues of James Joyce. You know—"*Ulysses* is a masterpiece, a great book." I read the book. It's trash. It's garbage. It's crap. And I know it! But I couldn't say that because I didn't have the assurance to go back to class and just face the teacher and say, "This book is crap. Period. End of report."

I think probably a lot of people remember my lecture on Sartre in Advanced Placement English. Inside my own head, I was in a crisis. Existentialism is of course a fraud. Jean-Paul Sartre is an imbecile. I'm quite aware of that now. But regardless of the virtues or evils of existentialism, it was the first system in which I immersed myself in an attempt to explain the world.

When I got up in front of the class I was so torn up inside that I couldn't see. My eyes were watering. I was close to tears. I couldn't tell what the class thought. They were very quiet. I don't remember any people snickering at me. The teacher let me talk on and on. He sat there like a sphinx. I was really ripped up then. My final grade in the class was F. Flunk. Unacceptable, unacceptable. That was by far the most symbolic grade for me. I would not do homework. I would not turn in papers. In that final semester of high school I was a very changed person. The contradictions . . . I couldn't continue pretending. I couldn't go on writing book reports, taking someone else's evaluation, rewriting it, putting it on paper and getting an A on it. I was just sick to my gills of the crap. I wanted to explore philosophy. I wanted to ask, "Why?"

I didn't even show up for graduation, and a month after that I sold my stamp collection and books, bought an airplane ticket for Copenhagen, and bugged out. I was seventeen, and I wanted to see the world with my own eyes. Living by the seat of my pants, I went to Stockholm, Paris, Nice, Madrid, London, Amsterdam and Rotterdam. My mode of travel was hitchhiking. Accommodations along my route were *au naturel*. I slept in the tombs of the Père Lachaise Cemetery in Paris; abandoned German gun bunkers over the sand dunes of the Bay of Biscay; under an ancient American tractor in a barn with a French farmer's pigs; on the battlefield at Verdun; and on top of the Lion of Waterloo. After a year in Europe I made the rounds in Rotterdam looking for work as a deck hand on a freighter that would get me back across the Atlantic. I persuaded one Finnish captain to take me aboard on his ship's maiden voyage. She was incredibly sleek and beautiful. She sailed for the Caribbean, through the Panama Canal, and from there up the Pacific Coast to Los Angeles, where I debarked.

When I got home I was under a lot of parental and peer pressure, so I enrolled at UCLA. Staying out of the draft also had a lot to do with it. Of course

UCLA, like Pali High, was a branch of the government. And the most concise definition of government is the control of people by force. I was appalled at what was happening. The current thing at the time was Timothy Leary and Allan Watts and the drug culture. I didn't know anyone at UCLA who wasn't using marijuana. Not a single person. The intellectual disintegration was unbelievable. All the professors were using drugs, and it was just an incredible, zombie, Alice-in-Wonderland world of irrational, spinning people. I refused to do my papers and I got F's in classes. Then I left. I quit.

I went up to San Francisco and lived in Haight-Ashbury and became one of the original flower children. This is 1967, when the Jefferson Airplane and the Grateful Dead were free in the Panhandle of Golden Gate Park. At the time I lived from morning to evening in the San Francisco public library, reading all day in the stacks. I had hair down to the middle of my back. Maybe below the belt. Although drugs were universal among the other flower children, that was one thing which I refused to do. I now regard the level of drug use in America's youth as a barometer of the rise or decline of our civilization.

From San Francisco, I tried UCLA again briefly and couldn't stand that, and then went into the religions which I spent the next several years doing. I had emerged from high school with one virtue—and that was that I intensely desired to find out the truth. That was my burning ambition. That was what would bring me through the decade. But with no philosophical underpinnings, I was easy prey for various charlatan solutions to all the world's problems.

I had minor involvements with the Meher Baba fan club, Swami Satchitananda's crowd, the Tassajara Zen Monastery, the Vedanta Society and too many more to remember. But my first serious commitment was transcendental meditation. I got involved through a friend who recommended this particular solution to the world's problems. So I meditated. The entire practice is moronic beyond belief. It consists of nothing more than sitting quietly and repeating a single word millions of times in your mind, morning and evening, several hours a day. My mystic word—which I was never supposed to reveal—was "A-ing." I was living at home with my parents, and meditation became my all and everything. I lived for it. But after two full years of studying the writings and "enlightened words" of Maharishi Mahesh Yogi, I realized that I was turning into a vegetable. I was becoming a very quiet, serene, inert, passive nonentity. Losing all assertiveness, all ambition.

The people who helped me to realize this were with Nichiren Shoshu Buddhism, a very aggressive Japanese outfit. A transcendental meditator is someone sitting in a chair with the outward appearance of doing nothing. But in Nichiren Shoshu you chant at almost a shout. If you repeat the Japanese phrase *"nam myoho renge kyo"* enough millions of times, it will fix up all your problems, yield eternal bliss and realize true Buddhahood for you. You kneel in front of a thing called a *gohonzon*—a scroll of Japanese characters—and it's just bananas. I chanted at least six hours every day for four months. Some days I'd chant for ten hours—going five hours at a time without a break. It was just an absolutely insane thing.

All of these fanatic organizations endeavor to convert the entirety of the human race to their creed, and most of them are rather aggressive in doing so. What we were preying on in these movements is the fact that American civilization, and the average American, has no philosophy and doesn't know where he's going. So when you come at him with a false certainty, saying, "I have the answer, I can help you"—he's a sitting duck.

In Nichiren Shoshu, I spent all day, all night trying to convert other people. I hit all my friends, anyone I knew. Of course, you also go up to total strangers and try to rope them in. I must have gotten dozens and dozens of people to join the movement. Many of them are probably still practicing, and have subsequently roped in dozens and hundreds more.

Once while I was out there looking for converts, I ran into a scientologist who was busy proselytizing for *his* religion. We had a confrontation. I was trying to get him to come to a chanting session, and he was trying to get me to come to a scientology lecture. He prevailed. I ended up going to the lecture, and it turned out that it appealed to me. It was a much more sophisticated practice than Nichiren Shoshu. So I went directly into scientology, and I gave it three and a half years of my life.

Scientology, of course, is ultimately a joke. It is based upon the "enlightened teachings" of L. Ron Hubbard. Its public presentation is very low-key, seemingly reasonable. Who could object to a group that says, "We're for understanding, affinity and communication." It's only when you get to the core of these religions that you find out what they are all about. The scientologists believe that Ron is from outer space. He's come here to save the world. His secret identity is Gautama Buddha. He has researched in detail the full "facts" on the history of man for the last four hundred trillion years. Advanced scientologists, through their application of Hubbard's stuff, gain a full ability to recall their past lives. Ron explains everything. He has an answer for everything.

Once you get into it, scientology is very expensive. They charge astronomical prices for little chunks of training. "Spiritual counseling" costs fifty dollars an hour and up. The people who are giving this training get paid almost nothing. I was one of them—a willing, eager slave laborer. But there is no question that Hubbard himself is a millionaire.

Candy McCoy:
I remember seeing Jamie at UCLA about five years after high school. He used to show up on the plaza in

front of the library, looking just incredibly clean. I remember his short haircut and his rimless glasses. He would go around with a very serious look on his face, distributing scientology literature to people. Most of them wouldn't take him too seriously. They wouldn't want to listen to him, they wouldn't want to be nice. But I felt very protective toward Jamie because of the affection I had felt for him in high school. He had always been a very gentle person. Really a lovely person.

In scientology, they rope you in. I know, because I was a roper. By trial and error you learn the weaknesses of people's minds. You learn tricks that are very interesting. When a person is weak and uncertain, and he plugs himself into an organization where the higher-ups seem to have answers, he has the feeling that he has now joined the "in crowd." He's now on his way up, and his function is to emulate the guys at the top. The big shots. The advanced beings.

Eventually I became part of the Sea Organization, which is the elite of scientology. There were only about two thousand of us throughout the world. We operated rehabilitated mothballed Navy ships. We had a minesweeper and a subchaser—Hubbard's private navy in the Pacific. But most of the time we were on dry land, working for scientology. We would work at least twelve hours every day for no pay. We ate substandard food, lived in substandard houses. People slept in basements, attics, porches enclosed with sheets. There was no personal property. It's all for one, one for all. You are a cog in a machine.

The upper-degree people in scientology are called O.T.'s—which stands for Operating Thetans. What happened to me was that after several years I finally got to the point where *I* was one of the advanced people. I would say that I was among the top hundred people in the world. I was set to go right to the top in scientology. I was in the upper reaches of possibility, and I was supposed to have achieved enlightenment.

But I realized that I had nothing. I had no answers to anything. I had been *had* in a shell game, and now I was actively engaged in conning other people.

There came a day when I woke up and said, "Hey, I'm not a scientologist. This is a joke. What the hell am I doing here?" Normally, if you try to leave they make it very uncomfortable. They go after you and use all sorts of mental arm twisting to intimidate you back into the fold. So I engineered what they call a "blow" to get myself physically out of the organization. With their blessings I got a leave of absence for some kind of super project that I concocted. It was a total phony. When my leave was over, I simply remained out.

What I felt at first was tremendous relief. I stayed in Los Angeles for a while, and it was a pleasure just to wake up in the morning and look at the world. To ask my own questions, and formulate my own answers.

After a while I went out to Kansas City. Kansas City is a very beautiful place. The air is clear and the grass is green. When I first got there I had a number of jobs. Working in stables, working out in the country, doing construction jobs. I managed to make ends meet, but my real activity was to read and research questions of philosophy.

The blockbuster in my research was the Romantic novel *Atlas Shrugged,* by Ayn Rand. It was in the middle of this giant masterpiece that I finally emerged from the shadows of mystic-collectivist dogma and entered the brilliant sunlight of reason and individualism. I have since read and reread every word Ayn Rand has published. She is, without question, the greatest novelist in human history. Until there is a significant minority of people on the earth who understand her ideas, who recognize the nefariousness of Communism or any other form of collectivism, and are willing to take the risks to establish individualism, there is no hope for the future.

So my current, entire purpose in life is writing to salvage Western civilization. With one tenth of my energy I make engravings, etchings and woodcuts. I sell them in order to support myself. But the remaining nine tenths of me all goes into writing. I will write philosophy some day, but all of my attention now is focused on putting the ideals of my universe into romantic novels. My task is to invest the abstractions and values of my mind with the flesh and blood of a hero who lives them all. It is exhilarating in the extreme.

Ten years from today I expect to have written at least ten books which are far superior to anything a college or high school student sees in his literature courses. Those who understand them will recognize that they're masterpieces. I intend to be the greatest American author of all time. A very modest claim.

I have no current girl friend, and I will not get married until I have launched myself as a fabulously successful writer. My pinpoint concentration on one thing is, I am sure, unusual. I have the ability to decide what I want to do, and to discipline every atom of my being to doing it, with no personal upsets, no mental interference, no lessening of desire or drive. It's just a matter of pushing the gas pedal down to the floor and pointing myself in one direction.

I am completely a romantic. The essence of romanticism is the portrayal of reality and life *as it should be*. The idealization of values, of truth and morality. It is antithetical to the naturalistic and degraded *Midnight Cowboy* school of art, of homosexuality, betrayal, cheapness, shoddiness, the anti-hero.

In politics, I would be described as a right-winger. Among my other activities, I am now a member of the John Birch Society, a rather misunderstood organization. The John Birch Society is not a religion and it is not a fanatical organization like these others I have been describing. It is an educational army, and its only weapon is facts. I have worked to combat totalitarian big government, and I've spent much time in that, thousands of hours. I have participated in congressional campaigns, state senatorial campaigns. I've participated in organizational activities for the Libertarian and the American parties. I am running for U.S. Congress in 1976 as an advocate of free-enterprise capitalism.

For the last few years, I have been one of the most active Birchers in Kansas City. The battle of the Birchers, the libertarians, and the right wing in general is to sell the idea of individual responsibility: that no man may initiate force against another. I've engaged in debates and frequent radio forums with the leading lights of the liberal left. The hope is that these guys are dedicated to the truth, not just their ideology, and that they can be reached. I'm intellectually sound. I've been in their camp. You know, I participated in the radical left at one time—demonstrations, marches, the Spring Mobilization of '67 in San Francisco, flag burnings at UCLA, and so on. I have read all their stuff—Marx, Lenin, Trotsky, Kropotkin, Bakunin, all of these creeps and assorted moral worms. It's a long list. Idiots. Dolts. Moral degenerates and mental midgets.

If I could, I would make Ayn Rand President. But in the political sphere today, my first choice would be Robert Welch. He's way too old; you know, he's eighty or something. But Robert Welch would be excellent. He's the founder of the John Birch Society, and he's well known.

Today I live in a small house in the countryside south of Kansas City. I share the house with my brother John, a blacksmith. John, nineteen years old, shoes a couple hundred head of horses here. We are in the process of buying another small, actually medium-sized house. Around us are rolling fields grazed by cattle and horses. Landholdings are in hundreds of acres. Roads are gravel and paved. The dominant architecture is basic fence. This is not quite like the great flat Kansas in so many pictures. Here, where the Kansas and Missouri rivers meet, the land is more hilly and much more wooded.

The seasons are an amazement to someone raised in the semiaridity of the Palisades. Spring is unlike anything you ever see in Los Angeles. The ground explodes with green plants everywhere, and the clouds and sky are the biggest possible. Terrific electrical storms can be so bright as to light the night sky like daylight. And steady winds come blowing off the Great Plains.

The vastness of space and the quiet aid me in focusing my energy on thought and writing. The drama of the seasons challenges the body and the mind. Extraneous matters are forgotten, as my mind conforms itself to the expanse of the land.

My life is designedly simple. There is no distraction from my study excepting the hours spent earning my livelihood. I don't go to movies. The last movie I saw was *Zorba the Greek* in 1965 in Paris. I don't smoke or drink. I use no drugs of any kind. I don't party or dance. The last pop or rock concert I attended was the Monterey Rock Festival in 1967. My favorite eatery is McDonald's where I ritually partake of the Quarter-Pounder, large fries, two o.j.'s and a cherry pie. $1.94 a shot. That's the fanciest meal I eat, and I love it. I keep myself in A-1 condition by daily cross-country running. I spend most of my time in my books, which line the walls of my bedroom. All that I cherish is on those shelves.

There are on planet earth entire subcontinental areas where the idea that you deserve freedom, that you are born with a birthright of freedom and you own what you create—where that idea doesn't exist. There are people that are so close to an animal-like state in their worship of force that it's entirely another world. What's the difference between the Indian subcontinent and America? It's not resources or accidents of history. It's philosophy. And it is our job, the Birch Society's job and my personal crusade, to spark a renaissance; to begin to create a group of people who *think;* to go from animal to human.

I do expect that truth will prevail. In fact, I'm taking bets that inside of twenty years, I will live on a planet where Communism, socialism, Big Brother-ism, collectivism, fascism and all variant systems of terrorizing free men will repose on the scrap heap of history. But whether we win or lose the battle, all of those who have figured out the game for themselves have already won the ultimate victory. That victory is individual freedom, five minutes of which easily outvalues a thousand lifetimes of a mind enslaved.

●

During the remainder of his visit to Los Angeles, we went around with Jamie as he visited several old friends and acquaintances. In every situation he put forward his ideas and proved himself gracious, consistent and persuasive. For a while he even considered a visit to the Hare Krishna Temple and an attempt to "rescue" Bob Searight, but this project never materialized.

After his return to Kansas City, Jamie sent us a large packet of "artifacts" for possible inclusion in this book. There were photographs showing him at various points in his journey, a "Complimentary Notice" from his ninth-grade English teacher, Jeanne Hernandez, and a sample of the etchings which he now sells to earn his living. The etching, executed in skillful and beautiful detail, showed a serene landscape of rolling hills and grazing horses. Also included in this package was Jamie's junior high school annual, from June 1962, which featured a notable inscription by one of his former classmates:

Jamie:

May God be with you. (WHEN YOU MEET HIM). Listening to your social studies reports I get the strange feeling you're a communist. No offense.
FROM A SECRET ADMIRER,

David Wallace

●

David Wallace: The Underachiever

•

Margie Williams:
He was very small, probably about five feet six. Always had his hair parted perfectly, without a hair out of place. That part was so straight, he probably spent two hours on it. He had freckles and straight teeth. He was very quiet, but nice.

Lee Grossman:
David is an example of a guy whose intelligence I underestimated. He didn't excel in the classroom stuff where everybody else got judged. In school, he played cards all the time. Poker mainly. He played bridge for a while. He was also very into handicapping horses, which he started when he was five. He was into statistics, athletic statistics. David's foremost characteristic is that he is a collector. He is a chronicler by nature. He never lets go of anything. That means old papers, old books, old friends.

Jeanne Hernandez, teacher:
David always looked as if he were enjoying some kind of private joke. He very seldom let anyone in on it. When he did write, his métier seemed to be anything sardonic or satiric or in some way critical. He had a very dry, almost noiseless laugh. He seemed to be

laughing into his neck. I kept trying to pull him out of himself, but he resisted manfully.

Jamie Kelso:
I liked David. He was more sophisticated than the rest of us. His thinking and his humor were subtle and complex. David also did not seem to be straining to prove something as people like myself and Medved were. You got the feeling that David felt he had it made. I knew he was the son of Irving Wallace, who was apparently a very prominent author. So I used to call David "Son of Oiving." I imagine that probably rubbed him very badly.

Lynn Marble:
I didn't trust David Wallace because I didn't like the books his father wrote. I felt that if his father was such a crudnik, how could David be much better or have the potential to be much better? I remember sensing David as a little, little boy, like seven years old in comparison to the rest of us, who were seventeen. That was the image I had of him, but I never felt protective toward him.

Ron Conti:
Maybe he wasn't such a great student, but I could tell he was very smart. When the teachers called on him, he would always make everything sound so good! I felt almost embarrassed sitting around him in class. If his hand went up, I was afraid the teacher would look over and see me and call on me.

Judy Tomash:
He was my friend. I liked him very much. Shy, funny, a wiry body and neat hair. He used to drive me to school. I was so grateful not to have to ride the bus. He kept pretty much to himself. His father was famous, and I think that made him more retiring than he may have been otherwise.

David Wallace: The Underachiever

Debbie Gordon:
He had a very dry sense of humor. Sort of sitting back, fancying himself a social critic.

●

Today David lives with his girl friend and their five cats in a wing of his parents' sprawling Brentwood home. We met there for our interview in the last hectic week before the class reunion. Walking down the familiar hallway past the Toulouse-Lautrecs and the Giacomettis, we entered David's office with the broad window facing onto the garden. We had to clear away two cats and a pile of books to make room to sit. There are over five thousand volumes in this one room. David is particularly proud of his collection of first editions of popular literature—including all the number-one fiction and non-fiction best sellers since 1895. Another corner of his office is devoted to food-stuffs, featuring a 60-pound tin of honey and a 100-pound sack of pinto beans. An organic vegetarian for the last seven years, David weighs only 110 pounds—thirty pounds less than he did in high school. He has a bushy reddish-brown beard, which is showing its first streaks of gray. His wide blue-eyed gaze and gentle manner suggest an attentive listener, even when he himself is speaking.

●

As far back as I can remember, my teachers, parents and peers made it clear to me that I was one of the smart ones. I was supposed to perform well and get good grades. There was a "Peanuts" cartoon that I glued to the cover of my notebook. It showed Linus saying, "There is no heavier burden than a great potential." That was me. But I had no interest in academic achievement. I resented homework, hated tests and was usually bored by lectures. I had a B— average in high school, which greatly disappointed and disturbed my parents.

Typical of my experience at Pali was the mock legislature they set up in government class. I was elected to the House of Delegates. Our first act as legislators was to vote that the teacher had to leave the room while we met. He told us that we weren't allowed to do that, and he stayed. I have been mistrustful of governments ever since.

To me, the important things in high school were sports and gambling. Senior year I played a lot of blackjack and gin rummy, and won four hundred dollars during school hours alone. My only other major accomplishment in high school was that I invented a fictional student named Sid Finster and enrolled him in several classes. My friends and I would take tests for him and answer roll calls. Once Sid was even quoted in the school newspaper. In later years a number of people took out a telephone in Sid's name. Unfortunately, Sid never paid his bills, so he ran afoul of the phone company and the IRS and is wanted by the FBI.

Socially, I was very insecure. I remember very vividly my first day in junior high school when I was huddling together with some friends during lunch. Another guy walked over and joined us. He said, "David, you see those girls over there?" And he pointed to a group of older girls who were huddled together much as we were.

I said, "Yeah. I see them."

He said, "Well, I just overheard them talking about how funny-looking you are."

I was traumatized by that. I was short and chubby. Even though I later replaced my fat with muscle, that didn't change my basic awareness of myself.

After high school graduation I went to Europe with a couple of other guys. I was miserable and lonely, so I wrote a long, panting love letter. Unfortunately, I had no one to send it to. So I sent it to a friend who also happened to be a girl. When I got back to the

United States she acted as if nothing had happened, and I was too ashamed to mention it.

In the fall I entered UCLA because it was the closest large university and because I rooted for their basketball team. I still do. But UCLA was a bad experience. I worried obsessively about the draft and felt alienated by the academic competition. I suffered a severe identity crisis and dropped out in my first semester. But in order to maintain my student deferment, I had to enroll at Santa Monica City College. My old friends from high school—especially Michael Medved —were shocked that I ended up at a junior college. At about the same time there were several deaths in our family, and I experienced eight hours of madness. While lying in bed the night before a funeral, I had a vision of a spindly-legged toad monster traveling through a dark forest mutilating people.

Santa Monica College was easy academically, so I never had to spend any time studying. I made friends, I lost my virginity and I started smoking marijuana. I was going to a psychiatrist, and I started meditating. Transcendental meditation with Maharishi Mahesh Yogi. This was 1967. The hippie movement was flourishing, and I thought it was wonderful. I went to a couple of love-ins and peace marches. I took mescaline for the first time and had a strange reaction. I actually felt love for Lyndon Johnson, and that made me fear for my sanity.

In the fall I moved to San Francisco and attended San Francisco State College. At first I was an English student. Then I switched to film, and then I lost interest completely. There was too much else going on. My favorite occupation was to smoke a joint, walk across the street to Golden Gate Park and sit under a tree by a lake and write poetry. Those were the days when people smiled at each other on the street, and there seemed to be hope for a more joyous world. My roommates and I used to go to the Fillmore and push to the front and dance ourselves into oblivion while

Janis Joplin performed on stage ten yards away. Fine times. I remember sitting in the laundromat playing chess with a friend, waiting for our laundry. Six or eight hippies walked by laughing and smoking marijuana. One of them noticed us, came into the laundromat, handed us a lit joint and walked out. This sort of thing was not uncommon.

In November of 1968 the black students at San Francisco State went on strike because they wanted the formation of a Black Studies department. At first I was opposed to the strike because I was a pacifist and I heard that some blacks had beaten up the editor of the school paper and thrown typewriters through windows. But then I attended a mass meeting, and to my great surprise, the striking students were much more articulate and rational than the administrators. I didn't attend another class for the rest of the semester, but I learned more in the months that followed than I did in all of my years of class attending. Every day there were fights and beatings. Students were arrested, reporters were fired for filing pro-student stories, FBI men used up rolls and rolls of film. The worst part of it was that when I visited Los Angeles and told my friends and family what I had seen, they didn't believe me. They had read about the strike in the newspapers and seen it on TV, and they believed the media instead of me. I was hurt.

It was about this time that my friends and I discovered laughing gas—nitrous oxide. It was a much more controllable experience than LSD, but equally intense. We used to have gas parties in which a lot of people would sit around a big five-foot tank getting high on nitrous oxide. In the course of two years we must have turned on a thousand people to laughing gas. We even wrote a book about gas which was published by an underground press.

In my last semester at San Francisco State I decided to make a documentary film about a gas party. It's ninety minutes long, and it shows a lot of my friends getting stoned, passing out, taking their clothes off and trying to make love. At one public showing of the film I distributed gas to the audience, thereby inciting an orgy among the spectators. But generally the film was not well received. It was two years after its completion that it was "rediscovered" and shown at the Venice Film Festival. I went to Italy to see it, but it still has never been shown commercially.

I dropped out of college six units short of graduation and moved to Berkeley. At that point the outside world seemed hostile and violent, so I sought desperately for peace inside. I read a lot of religious and spiritual books and that kept me going—that and some good love-making. I also put a lot of energy into a rent strike which I stumbled upon by moving into an overpriced, dilapidated flat.

I was enjoying myself, but I had no idea what to do next. I was living from week to week by cashing bonds that had been given to me years before by my grandparents. Every time I cashed one I thought of them.

I had become very committed to organic foods and I was hoping to find someone to teach me how to raise fruits and vegetables. In Los Angeles I met a seventy-year-old Sicilian farmer named Chico Bucaro. He wanted to write a book about organic farming but he didn't know how to read or write. We decided to work together and produced a manuscript of two hundred pages. We sent it to my father's agent, who is also a family friend, and he was able to sell the book. Though I made only fourteen hundred and forty dollars on the whole thing, I had my first published volume. Needless to say, my parents were delighted, even though by this time I had changed my name.

People often think that I took a new last name in order to dissociate myself from my famous father. That's not true. In reality, the name change stems from my resentment of arbitrary authority. In Russia my grandfather's name had been Wallechinsky, but when he came to this country it was changed by an immigration clerk who didn't think it was "American" enough. I wanted to take the old name back, and that's the name I use in public now.

In 1970 and '71 I spent most of my time traveling around the country doing some antiwar organizing. I was also thinking about a new kind of reference book that would help to educate people. I prepared an outline, but it was hard to get a publisher. When I was a little boy, my father had always said it would be great to work together on a book someday. We thought we might do a sports encyclopedia or something like that. Now, when he saw me struggling along with the new almanac, he suggested we work as co-authors.

We got a contract from Doubleday and hired two hundred free-lance writers to help us, including six alumni of the Palisades class of '65. *The People's Almanac,* in its final version, is fifteen hundred pages long. I just finished a publicity tour in which I gave ninety-eight interviews. And this week the book hit the national best-seller list. But the most wonderful moment was two months ago—the day the first copy arrived in the mail. I was standing by the window waiting for the postman. As soon as I spotted him, I dashed outside and tore open the package from the publisher. I leafed through the book in a daze. I had worked on this project for four and a half years and at last it was a real book. I went back inside and cried.

I've been living with my parents for the last twelve months. Flora lives here too. She is a former hairdresser and airline stewardess who I met in New York. She comes from a Chicano family and a background that's very different from mine. She slept in the same bed with her grandmother till she was sixteen, so today she's a champion snuggler. We're not legally married, but we are definitely a committed couple.

Sometimes it's a little uncomfortable living here together, but I think it's good for all of us to have the two generations in the same house. The biggest problem, to tell the truth, is our cats. Sometimes they commit indiscretions in my mother's kitchen, and she doesn't appreciate it.

These days, when I want to relax, I go to a book-store, buy some off-beat books, go home, smoke a joint, and read. When we're finished with this project, I hope to celebrate by going to London to buy more books.

When the reviews of *The People's Almanac* started coming in and they were all so positive, and the book-stores started selling out, my mother reminded me of an incident from many years ago. A psychiatrist friend took my parents aside and said, "You know, David is never going to amount to anything because he only does what he wants to do." I guess I am that way basically, but it seems to be working.

Michael Medved:
The Walking Commotion

●

Jean O'Brien, teacher:
Every time I saw Medved, I was annoyed. He was a walking commotion and I think he probably knew it. It was impossible for us to get along. He demanded as much respect as I did, and neither of us would give it to the other. And so we were very careful to stay out of each other's way. What I remember most about Michael was his eyes. Just busy. Busy eyes. He was a mischief-maker, Michael Medved.

Donald Golden:
He was definitely a Palisades institution—like Lany Tyler. Shortly after he came to the school he made

Medved Sounds Off; Calls Football Barbaric

Palisades High's much publicized "Great Rice Paddy Debate" took place last Friday in the Oral Arts building' The debate came on the heels of numerous P. A. announcements and "rice is nice" parades staged by the Dolphin Declamation Society.

The q u e s t i o n, should Palisades High turn its football field into a rice paddy, was argued by Mike Medved, and Murray Cantor, pro; and Richard Shapero and Steve Daniels, con. The two main points brought up by the "pro" team were:

1. Cost. Mike Medved said, "The ultimate goal after the rice paddy is planted is to earn m o n e y from the planting of rice, and with these funds we shall build rice hall. This establishment shall include swimming pools and will be a finely equipped student recreation center. Whereas football costs the student body money, the rice paddy would earn money for the benefit of all students. Equal rice for all!"

The second point brought up by the "pro" side was the human element. Medved stated, "What skills are taught by football? Only the skills of crashing against your fellow man. Football is based on jungle law. Rice planting, on the other hand, would prove to be of inspiration to all students and would satisfy their agricultural needs."

The "con" side brought up three valid points.

1. The planting of rice is reminiscent of Mao-Tse-Tung. 2. Football is traditional to our national heritage. 3. There is a rice surplus in the U.S., and the government will pay us money not to plant rice.

his theatrical bid for attention in a thing called "The Great Rice Paddy Debate." For weeks in advance, there were signs and banners and marches. I remember Lee Grossman made a banner with the American flag and the trademark picture from Uncle Ben's Rice superimposed on the cluster of stars. Some of Michael's followers came to school with bags of rice and started throwing it at people. It was the biggest controversy that had hit Palisades up to that time.

It was important to Michael to get good grades because he wanted to go to a top-notch college. But he had an impossible time with math and chemistry and all the sciences. At one point we took the same chemistry class, and I did all his lab work and prepped him for all the exams and helped him to get through.

Bob Searight:
He was a real character. Real intelligent. I remember they used to have this show on TV where teams from all the different schools would compete in answering questions. Palisades went on one year and we won the championship for all of LA. Medved was the star of the team. I went to the studio one time to see the show in person and I remember he answered every question.

Lee Grossman:
I think maybe his most notable trait was how uptight he was. He was the champion pacer. Looking at his folks, competitiveness is definitely a Medved characteristic. I looked up to Mike a whole lot. It was very important for me to be liked by him.

In high school, Medved particularly dug my mother. He was very impressed with the fact that she was a writer. He was writing. I don't know if he wanted to be a writer at this point. I think he may have wanted to be king. But I do remember some of his writing from that period. There was a long epic poem about the assassination of William McKinley. It was very ambitious, and awful.

Reilly Ridgell:
Who could forget him? In class he was very high-powered, always going about five directions at once. But what I really remember is the way he used to get himself on the PA system. He'd get on for some reason, for some activity, and just talk and talk during morning announcements. He was really funny. He was the Stan Freberg of the Palisades High PA system. I remember he would say things like ". . . and there is only one way, count 'em, one . . ."—things like that. I really enjoyed it, but a lot of people couldn't stand it after a while. It got so that whenever Medved's voice came on the PA system, some of the teachers would turn it off so it couldn't come into their classrooms.

Jeanne Hernandez, teacher:
I remember him with a briefcase in front of him. It was a barrier between the teacher and himself. As a teacher, I'd never had to deal with so much energy. It wasn't easy. Many times he would challenge what I said, many times criticize what I said. I found myself on the defensive a number of times, and I was furious about it.

Jamie Kelso:
It was perfectly obvious that Medved was the only person in the school with brainpower of my caliber. And like myself, he was very intense. We never had a personal friendship, though I went over to his house a couple of times in very formalistic terms. Like little state visits.

Judy Tomash:
I remember him being an oddball. Very tall, very

bright. He wrote a lot. I remember he got into Yale. He was the only one who got into Yale and I was surprised. I thought he was strange.

Excerpts from David Wallace's high school diary;

February 2, 1964:

Today all the boys were talking about the Clay-Liston fight. Michael Medved was collecting his bet money in a little bag.

April 23, 1964:

Medved told me that at 4:17 PM he was being transported to 16th Century England. During Nutrition break someone put a lamb's heart in his briefcase.

April 28, 1965:

Medved hit me in the face with a pie tin of Silly Soap. We spent the rest of the day having Silly Soap fights and spraying Silly Soap on innocent students.

May 6, 1965:

Sixth period Medved yelled out the Yale motto and smashed Jeff Elman with Silly Soap.

May 18, 1965:

Medved was in bad shape today. Deep depression. I think he was serious. He said he had walked from Bluegrass to Chautauqua and back late last night. That's 12 miles. He claimed to have had 62 cups of coffee since 11 o'clock last night.

May 20, 1965:

Medved sat, without moving a muscle, for 14 minutes and 40 seconds. He finally cracked when I said, "Shut up, Reilly!"

May 28, 1965:

I witnessed a fantastic scene at the Medveds'. Mike and his mother had a violent fight about whether or not Mike needed a new typewriter ribbon. For some reason, Mike was furious at his typewriter and wanted to throw it away, but his mother said it just needed a new ribbon. Finally, Mrs. Medved grabbed the typewriter and removed it from Mike's bedroom.

June 4, 1965:

Stayed up all night talking to Medved. Mike is truly a genius. He is the most articulate and eloquent person I've met.

●

Dinner at the home of Michael and Nancy Medved was scheduled for a Tuesday evening. It began shortly after sundown, when Michael returned from evening prayers at the synagogue two blocks away. He burst in, full of energy and good fellowship, with the traditional skullcap attached by a bobby pin to a full head of unruly brown hair. Before the meal was served, we lined up at the kitchen sink for the ritual washing of hands, then returned to the table and remained silent until bread had been broken, blessed and distributed to everyone. The bread in this home is fresh and delicious; Nancy Medved bakes it herself twice a week. A slim girl with black hair and shining brown eyes, she brought to the table plate after plate of steaming kosher food. It took nearly an hour to finish the meal. Then, after tea and cake, Michael and Nancy sang the "Grace After Meals," a joyous Hebrew prayer lasting more than five minutes and delivered at top volume with much banging of the table and rattling of glasses. When we had finished, Michael leaned back, sighed and said he was ready to put himself on tape. We both felt nostalgic at the last of our interviews. After long months of work, our project was nearly completed.

●

By the time I got to Palisades High School I was so used to being a misfit that I almost enjoyed it. My father is a Ph.D. in physics, and when we first came to Los Angeles he was teaching at UCLA. I very consciously looked down my nose at the smug affluence of Pacific Palisades. I was fond of recalling my earliest years, when my father was in graduate school and we lived in a dingy basement apartment in Philadelphia. As part of my bogus poor-boy image, I used to wear the same faded sweat shirt almost every day in high school. It was dark blue, with holes in it, and sleeves that were too short.

Dating was out of the question for me. For one thing, I didn't drive. I failed my driver's examination three times in a row, and I didn't get a license until I was a junior in college. My romantic fantasies were so intense that it was hard to find a high school girl who would respond to them. I had serious crushes on Lynn Marble, Debbie Gordon and Lany Tyler, but they never came to anything.

It was only in my last semester of high school that I was able to turn my notoriety to political advantage. I was elected to student-body office, and at last won a measure of respectability. I won a National Merit Scholarship and was accepted at Yale. I remember that one of my teachers wrote in my senior annual: "I hope the faculty at Yale can handle you better than we did."

The morning before I flew back East, all three of my little brothers started to cry. I was very touched by that, because my treatment of them had always been rather cavalier. Then my mother began crying as she packed up my things. I was her first-born, and the first one to leave home. On the way to the airport we went through a whole box of Kleenex.

As it turned out, the years in New Haven were good for me. For one thing, I felt that I had finally made the big time. Let's face it: Yale is a more impressive place than Palisades High School. I was looking for roots, for a sense of belonging. Yale had been there a long time and it had honorable traditions. I loved the pomp, the pretensions, the Gothic entryways, the fireplace in my dorm room, the civility of the dining halls.

I was a member of the last all-male class at Yale, and that made for some notable social distortions. The prevailing ideal was for a slick, cynical Yalie to import a Vassar girl for the weekend, store her in the Taft Hotel, get her drunk as soon as possible and then make his moves. This held little appeal for me, and I spent my weekends hitchhiking and camping. I refused to touch liquor, and considered even beer a degradation. When drugs arrived in the middle of sophomore year, I isolated myself even further. My training as an oddball at Palisades High School made it easier to resist the trend. I would have nothing to do with marijuana or anything else. My heroes were Tolstoy, Mozart and Prokofiev. Rock music, hip posters, "The Wisdom of the East"—all of that was anathema to me, and it still is. There's no better indication of the strength of my friendship with David Wallace than the fact that it's survived David's ten-year involvement in that unhappy culture.

I had my own private world in New Haven and I was happy there. I was doing volunteer tutoring two days a week with kids from the New Haven ghetto. This is 1966, at the time of the big urban riots, when everyone was talking about race war and Armageddon. I wanted to make some sort of commitment, and through sheer force of will make the problems disappear. I really loved those kids. I became very involved in the world of teaching and social work and spent all my summers in New Haven working in various programs. I remember the summer of '67, when one of my best students was from Detroit, and at the same time we were working together on his writing, his home was burning down in the Detroit riot. It was scary for me, and the only response I could manage was to try to make myself as black as I possibly could. I envied *real* blacks, because of their sense of purpose and solidarity. I hadn't yet realized that the same identification was possible for me, on a much more significant level, with my own people and their struggles.

I suppose it was inevitable that I got involved in the presidential campaign of 1968. The McCarthy people had a heavy recruiting focus on Yale. I was a junior by this time, and beginning to face the realities of the draft and the war: I had only one more year before my student deferment ran out. Like most young men of our generation, my position on the war was shaped by self-interest. I was opposed to the war because I didn't want to fight in it, and I didn't see any valid reason why I should. So with a sense of desperation about our country, and about my own future, I enlisted in the McCarthy campaign during the New Hampshire primary.

I was elated when we did well in that first test against LBJ, and even more elated when Robert Kennedy entered the race. I had been something of a Kennedy idolator since junior high school, when I had spent free afternoons working in JFK headquarters during the race against Nixon. Now, with Bobby throwing all his weight against Johnson, I was convinced there was new hope. We were going to save Western civilization, and I was going to be part of it.

I remember the night Lyndon Johnson announced

his withdrawal. I had developed a fairly steady girl friend at that time, and she was even more of a romantic than I was. After hearing Johnson's announcement on TV, we were both crying for joy and cheering. We went down to the New Haven green with about three thousand other Yalies, carrying American flags and singing "Glory Hallelujah" and "God Bless America."

After that, I was in such a state of euphoria and involvement that school became impossible. I got special permission from my professors to fly home and work for Kennedy full time in the California primary.

During May and the first week in June I spent every waking moment in the campaign. I actually slept on a cot in headquarters a couple of times. It was incredibly exhilarating to be part of something so much larger than myself, to be standing shoulder to shoulder with hundreds of other people who shared my goals, my devotion to RFK. I think Bobby was the last hero I ever had. On the night of the primary I was celebrating our victory at the Ambassador Hotel with dozens of new friends from the campaign. Of course, I didn't mind the fact that there were so many pretty girls who seemed to get involved in politics. We were jumping up and down, acting like kids. I was planning to follow the campaign when it moved on to New York for the next primary. I was still only a lower-level aide, and had not been invited to the smaller ballroom upstairs, where Kennedy was due to make his first victory statement. But with some friends I snuck up there, anyway, and was standing only ten feet away when he came out to give his talk.

Twenty minutes later he was shot in the kitchen. I didn't hear the shots, but I certainly heard the screams. It was strange. The moment you heard that sound of moaning and hysteria, you knew what had happened. You didn't have to ask. The hotel was sealed off for the rest of the night. Crowds were shifting from room to room, sobbing, and people were fainting in corridors. I couldn't go home. Everything was confused and the place was crazy with rumors.

Finally at dawn the police had finished their search for accomplices and we were free to go. I drove down Wilshire Boulevard with the sun coming up behind me. I was listening to a soul station, as they played gospel music and prayed for Bobby. When I finally got back to my parents' house I fell asleep in front of the TV, waiting for news on his condition. They were trying some operation on his brain. The next thing I knew I woke up to hear my father sobbing behind me. He just held his face and said, "He's dead, Michael. He's dead."

After living through that experience, I couldn't walk away from politics. It was as if Kennedy's death, and my presence in that hotel, had put a holy seal on my commitment. Over the next three years, liberal politics became my whole life. I went from one campaign to another, working for antiwar candidates who seemed viable.

I took off just enough time to finish my B.A. and to begin Yale Law School. I had no interest in becoming an attorney, but I wanted to stay around New Haven for personal and political reasons, and the law school offered me a generous scholarship. While struggling through my first-term classes I was also teaching part-time at a Jewish parochial school in order to avoid the draft, and serving as chairman of the Vietnam Moratorium in New Haven. I had hardly any time for sleeping, eating or normal bodily functions. Something had to give, and what gave was law school.

The problem was that by this time my parents were completely sold on the idea of their son the lawyer. I drove home in the winter to explain myself to them, and then, after completing my first semester, I took an official leave of absence from law school.

I was floating free, giving every ounce of my energy to political work. Eventually I wrote speeches for a senator, two congressmen and numerous local candidates. But my best job was as head speechwriter for the Democratic nominee in Connecticut for the U.S. Senate. I was still living in New Haven at the time and commuting to Hartford every day—about a hundred and ten miles round trip. I used to drive home late at night—sometimes at one or two o'clock—with the big Connecticut sky opening up cold and starry over Interstate 91 and the road deserted. I'd sing to myself, delighted with what I was doing. I was only twenty-one, and considered a child prodigy. I was earning good money. If my Senate candidate had won, I would have followed him to Washington, and my whole life would have been different.

But as it turned out, after a series of defeats, I was finally ready to hang up my hired guns. I was tired of writing other people's speeches. I needed a rest. I wanted to grow a beard. I wanted to write a novel, using my experiences in the political world.

Actually, I had written novels before. I made my first attempt in the eighth grade: a completed four-hundred-page tome about coal miners in England. Then in tenth grade there was an uncompleted novel about high school. More substantial was the epic I wrote as a senior project at Yale, working part of the time with Robert Penn Warren. The book, a rambling and overwritten mess, was consciously patterned after *War and Peace,* except after six hundred pages I realized I wasn't Tolstoy and cut it short.

The first step on my resumed literary career was to start living the way I thought a novelist should live. I was supporting myself with a part-time job writing TV documentaries—a job won through political connections. I was sharing an apartment with my girl friend of that time—a Boston aristocrat with yachts and prep schools in her thoroughly non-Jewish background. I spent most of my days hiking, and that became important to me. There are hundreds of miles of trails in Connecticut and I tried to explore them all, looking at birds and trees and keeping a journal of what I saw. It was a welcome change of pace from writing daily press releases about sewage-disposal problems or the governor's latest budgetary requests.

I think the combination of writing and hiking gave me a new perspective on what was important in my life. It's impossible to be in the woods every day without developing some sort of spiritual sensibility. I began reading about Judaism, and was appalled at my own ignorance and lack of affiliation. My previous religious education had been the bland and irrelevant smattering typical of suburban Jews. My exclusive choice of gentile women over the years—though it caused my parents great pain—was a common product of that background. I began to sense that I wanted something better for myself, and I became involved in a tempestuous love affair with a Jewish girl from Rumania. When she moved to California, I decided to follow her and to finish my novel in Berkeley.

I got a tiny apartment and lived out everyone's fantasy of bohemian life by San Francisco Bay. My love affair didn't work out, but the novel was finished in a couple of months. I sent it off to an agent, but while waiting for fame and fortune to come knocking at my door, I had to earn a living. So I went to work as a salesclerk in a classical-record store. I would meet people in this shop on Telegraph Avenue, and at first they'd be surprised that I knew so much about music. Then they'd find out about my Yale background, and I always enjoyed the pained expressions: "What a waste! All that expensive education, and here he is working as a lowly record clerk for two dollars an hour." Little did they know, I thought, that it was only a matter of time before my fate would arrive to drag me off to glory!

Well, that fate never came and my novel never did get published. There were some glimmerings of interest from New York, but on the whole it was very depressing. Fortunately, I was preoccupied with other things by the time my hopes fell through. I was in the process of getting married.

I met Nancy through Jewish activities in Berkeley. A large part of our attraction was based on our mutual rediscovery of Judaism. She is an artist, three years younger than I am, and a graduate of Beverly Hills High School—not such a different environment from Palisades. Within three weeks of our first date we knew we wanted to get married. The wedding was the most joyous experience of my life, with two hundred people eating and singing and dancing themselves into hysteria. Jewish weddings are fun. I heartily recommend them to anyone. Especially if you have the chance to marry someone like Nancy.

But my in-laws hadn't taken me into their family with the idea that I'd be a record clerk for the rest of my life. I didn't want to go back to politics—I wanted some time to spend with my wife—so I thought I'd try advertising. I got a job in a politically minded black advertising agency in Oakland, and very quickly rose from copywriter to a partner in the enterprise. This sounds very impressive until you find out that there was only one other person involved in the firm. Because this person happened to be black, he was able to bring home a certain number of contracts due to everyone's concern with "affirmative action." The deal was that he would get the contracts, I would do all the work while keeping my white face in the background, and we would split the profits.

We handled some interesting accounts—we produced TV recruiting ads for the Oakland and San Francisco police departments, and did political work for candidates of both parties—but generally the job was depressing. I was conscious of how far my own expectations for myself had been lowered. Five years before, I had been involved with blacks in a passion for brotherhood and justice; now I was involved with them in a shoddy commercial rip-off. Years before, I had written political material from a sense of personal commitment; now I was doing it just to make a living.

After we finished the police contract, I got out of the advertising business and began my era of false starts and odd jobs. I got an M.A. in creative writing and looked unsuccessfully for teaching jobs. I wrote a guidebook to classical music that was never published. I applied to graduate schools in history, wrote grant proposals for community-development corporations, served as principal of a Jewish secular school, reapplied to Yale Law School, did professional lecturing for Hadassah Clubs and other Jewish groups, and seriously explored the possibility of running for state assembly from my home district in West Los Angeles. Fortunately, the grass-roots support was less than overwhelming.

It was about this time that an old friend from high school stepped back into my life. One evening David Wallace came over to our flat in Berkeley and talked about his big project, *The People's Almanac*. He wanted me to write for it, but at first I refused. I thought it would be hard on my ego working for David Wallace. He's so much shorter than I am. But David came back several times, and finally I agreed. I ended up writing some fifty articles for the *Almanac*. I did their entire chapter on the Presidency, and have more than two hundred and fifty pages in the final published version.

I never suspected that these historical articles would finally get my stillborn writing career off the ground, but that's the way it turned out. After working together on the *Almanac*, David and I planned this book, and got our advance contract from Random House. Meanwhile I was able to sell another project of my own to Reader's Digest Press. It's a series of biographies of the top aides to each President of the United States since Lincoln. It will be published in 1978.

To people like my parents and my in-laws, the whole idea of a career as a writer still seems shaky and superficial. When I got readmitted to Yale Law School, they wanted me to go back. But I like the life I'm leading now. Nancy and I moved down to Los Angeles to work on this project, and it's the first time I've lived in LA since high school. We're staying in a sunny house near the beach in Venice—a house that we're renting from none other than Lany Tyler. We make our own decisions on how to spend each day. We have time to walk on the beach, to observe the Sabbath, to be part of a Jewish community. It gives me great joy to be living the same values and practices that my great-grandfathers lived. In a sense, my entire journey in the last ten years has been a long and arduous homecoming. I don't know what I'll be doing in the future, but right now I feel at home with the way I live. In a rootless generation, that's the greatest gift of all.

Reunion

•

On Saturday night, December 27, 1975, the Palisades class of '65 held its gala reunion. Exactly ten years, six months and twenty-two days had elapsed since the date of our graduation from high school. The scene of the reunion was a huge banquet room in the Lobster House restaurant in LA's Marina del Rey. For months in advance, Pali alumni had sent their $8 reservations to the treasurer of the reunion committee, HARVEY BOOKSTEIN. Another committee member, JEFF STOLPER, had arranged for a professional disc jockey to play old records from the early sixties as part of the evening's entertainment. The restaurant prepared meatballs, cocktail franks and other hors d'oeuvres, while DAVID WALLACE made a special trip to a produce market to provide snacks for our vegetarian classmates.

Over three hundred people attended this event—a hundred more than expected by the reunion committee. Questionnaires had gone out to everyone on the class mailing list, and the responses offered some intriguing statistics. For example, 61 percent of the women are now married, but only 48 percent of the men, and 64 percent of our married classmates have children. Only half the women who are married described their primary occupation as "housewife"; nevertheless, "housewife" was the most common occupation listed by members of the class. The others most frequently mentioned were "teacher" (13 percent) and "lawyer" (10 percent). Attorneys seemed to be particularly overrepresented among the people who actually attended the reunion, and at times the gathering had the flavor of a Bar Association cocktail party. Fully 9 percent of the survey respondents were still students, including an impressive number of women who had recently returned to school. We were astonished as we reviewed some of the more personal comments and statistics from the questionnaires. An amazing 11 percent of our class admitted to an arrest record, and in nearly all cases this involved either political or drug-related charges. Eighteen individuals from the class of '65 reported histories of psychiatric hospitalization.

Standing by the door at seven o'clock on reunion night, we watched the people as they arrived. It was hard not to notice what a handsome crowd this was. The men seemed prosperous and confident, and the women, in their evening dresses, chic pants suits, or even jeans and T-shirts, looked remarkably attractive and sensual. Several times we heard comments on how much better-looking everyone seemed to have become. The old high school beauties were still beautiful—SUZANNE THOMAS arrived looking cool and stately in a slinky orange dress with plunging neckline, and PATTY FINDLATER, with her radiant red hair, looked stunning even in her plain black sweater and gray slacks. What was surprising was that these celebrated belles no longer stood out as outstanding or exceptional; there were dozens of other attractive women who could rival them. This superficial showing gave an overly optimistic perspective on the class of '65. The actual stories of our classmates were often depressing, but at the reunion we were strongly reminded that around the age of twenty-eight—or ten years after high school—people usually reach their physical prime.

We realized, of course, that the people who attended this affair were not necessarily representative of the entire class. Our more successful and affluent classmates were far more likely to show up at the Lobster House than those who were struggling with poverty or personal difficulties: It was no accident that people like CYNTHIA MORTON, BOB SEARIGHT and JUDY TOMASH were nowhere to be found in the Saturday-night crowd. But MIKE SHEDLIN was there, wearing tennis shoes and a striped T-shirt, with his blond hair hanging down to his waist. He seemed unusually subdued when we spoke with him, and he spent most of the evening sitting in a corner with a dreamy smile, shaking his head in disbelief.

By eight o'clock the room was jammed, and the familiar pungent odor of marijuana was wafting its way through the crowd. Before long the manager of the restaurant became concerned, and an announcement was made by the master of ceremonies that all those who wished to smoke marijuana should please do so in the parking lot. Meanwhile we noticed a half-dozen classmates snorting cocaine about five feet from the bar. Despite repeated pleas from the management, the marijuana joints also continued to circulate. Recordings of "Surfin' Safari" and "Leader of the Pack" played insistently in the background, but no one seemed to notice. There was no dancing; talk was the evening's chief entertainment.

Our friend LEE GROSSMAN seemed overwhelmed by the entire scene as he stalked around with his handsome mop of long hair, looking nearly as shy and awkward as he had in high school. His evening was not helped when one of his best friends from high school whom Lee hadn't seen for ten years ran up, embraced him and greeted him as "Steve!"

We found MARGIE WILLIAMS standing arm in arm with her husband, chatting with a small circle of her former admirers. We came up and talked for a while, answering questions about our book. We mentioned to Margie that SKIP BAUMGARTEN had said that his biggest regret in high school was not having gone out with Margie Williams.

Her husband, Alan Sandorf, nodded knowingly and said, "So *he's* the one!"

"What do you mean, 'he's the one'?"

"He's the one guy you didn't go out with," came the response.

Skip himself came ambling along and took us aside to talk about what we had learned from our project. He sipped slowly at his drink, and his contagious smile never deserted him, but he seemed to be in an unusually serious mood. "Coming to Pali from another school it always seemed very provincial," he said. "There was a whole feeling that Pali was the place it was happening. It was Fantasyland. Just look at this crowd. Our parents worked and struggled to make some money, and they tried to protect us from the grubby realities. We came out expecting the impossible. Everybody was going to be famous. Everybody was going to be rich. I must have talked to twenty different people tonight who have written books and are waiting to get them published. I'm not surprised that people keep switching jobs. When people have such high expectations, most of them are bound to be disappointed." We were listening attentively when another classmate came by and pointed out to Skip the cocktail waitress who had been assigned to our party. She was a gorgeous Amazon more than six feet tall, with a bursting white sleeveless sweater, long braceleted brown arms and a provocative swing in her walk. Skip nodded his appreciation as she passed, and a number of other eyes followed her progress through the room. We saw Jeff Stolper come up to her with a mischievous wink and point out GARY WASSERMAN across the room. "You see that guy?" Jeff said. "You know, he's a millionaire." The waitress thanked him for the information, and hurried off to get Gary's order.

Gary and Suzy Wasserman were both dressed impeccably. She wore a shiny white satin pants suit, while Gary's stylish jacket and vest were cut from a soft beige fabric. He greeted us heartily when we came up to him, and seemed to be enjoying the reunion as much as anyone there. He told us that since our interview, he and Suzy had sold their mansion in Brentwood and bought a more original, more private home on a spectacular sight overlooking the Pacific in Malibu. He invited us to "bring our ladies" and come up to visit the new spread.

Most of the people at the reunion seemed to prefer talking about the present rather than reminiscing about the past, but a former Student Assembly president, now a claims representative for Kemper Insurance, seemed to be an exception. He came up to Harvey Bookstein with a serious expression on his face, and looked down directly into Harvey's eyes.

"Harvey," he said, "one of the reasons I came tonight is that I wanted to apologize to you. I remember the way I used to pick on you on the school bus for all those years, and I wanted you to know, I'm sorry."

Harvey rocked back on his heels and laughed. "That's okay," he said. "I don't even remember you."

The master of ceremonies attempted to quiet the crowd in order to announce the results of the door-prize drawing. Twenty class members had donated various prizes as a way to enliven the evening. The prizes included three speech-therapy lessons, donated by Jeff Stolper; a home-cooked meal, donated by Skip Baumgarten; two copies of this book, donated by the authors; and a can of Coors beer, donated by JON WILSON, the only Vietnam veteran in attendance. We hadn't noticed Jon before, but after his donation was announced we went over and shook hands warmly. Jon is someone we like very much. He told us that he had recently moved into a new house in Santa Rosa and was going back to school at Sonoma State.

As the drawing continued, the crowd gave an appreciative murmur when the MC announced a prize of a "fifty-dollar gift certificate at Gary Wasserman's men's store in the Marina." Jeff Stolper leaned over and wryly observed to us that the $50 should go a long way toward the purchase of one of Gary's ties. The most popular prize of the evening, however, was a free acupressure treatment donated by MARK HOLMES. The lucky winner was Patty Findlater, who indicated that she hoped to use the treatment to help her lose weight and stop smoking. She took Mark aside and asked him a series of shy questions about what to expect. At one point he took her arm and dug into it hard with his thumbnail. "That hurts!" she protested.

"I know," he said. "That's what it will feel like. But it helps you."

DACE ("CANDY") McCOY arrived late in the evening and stayed for only an hour. She seemed bored and uncomfortable and told us, "All these old faces . . . it freaks me out." One of the few people she did approach was DEBORAH GORDON, who had come in from San Francisco for the occasion and seemed thoughtful and serious through most of the evening. At one point, when she bumped into her old high school boyfriend,

Deborah announced dramatically, "I've got to talk to you!," then smiled and gave him a warm embrace.

RON and ANITA CONTI left the party relatively early, and we caught them on their way out. Anita wore a flowing blue maternity dress and it was impossible not to notice the fact that she was seven months pregnant. Ron told us that in preparation for their new addition they had bought a house in the Palisades, and as it turned out, the previous owner had been the Kelso family. Ron and Anita had just moved into the house in which JAMIE KELSO had grown up.

Jamie was unable to attend the reunion, but from Kansas City he mailed us a sheet of comments which he deemed appropriate to the occasion:

For two reasons it was certain that many members of the Class of '65 would become parasites living off their parents or the taxpayers. First, their parents prevented the children from understanding the problem of survival by always solving their problems for them. By age 18, a man or woman's character is largely set. If, up to this age, the parents have freely provided cars, tuition, allowances, vacations, clothes, apartments and entertainment, then they shouldn't be too surprised when they discover that their son or daughter is a moral cripple. The second reason to expect parasites is the unreality of what was taught at Pali. Bearing with us from high school no philosophical substance, and irrationality as method, we were easy prey for the sharpies in the university, and sitting ducks for the spiritual con men of our time.

We wondered what Jamie's reaction would have been if he had been present at the reunion, and whether he would have been able to slip into the unbuttoned spirit of the occasion.

Without question, the most visible and popular person at the party was LISA MENZIES. She was dressed in an extremely low cut flaming orange dress and wore a heavy layer of bright red lipstick. There wasn't a moment in the course of the evening when she wasn't surrounded by at least three or four men. She greeted all her old friends with warm kisses and prolonged hugs, laughed, sang, shrieked and enjoyed the attention of the crowd. She arrived with her hair piled on her head in a heavy bun, but by eleven o'clock she had shaken it loose in a dramatic gesture. The bright hair came cascading down her shoulders in a rich, tawny mane, which, along with her flashing dark eyes, made us think of a rampant lioness. She talked of her promising career as a singer—she had just won an engagement at a local supper club—and invited us to come down and see her show. When MICHAEL MEDVED presented her with an autographed copy of *The People's Almanac,* she rewarded him with a wet and noisy kiss. At about midnight, as she stood by the door, we asked her if she was planning to go home soon. "Oh no," she said. "There are still plenty of people here to make smooshy-smooshy with."

The formal program for the evening concluded with the master of ceremonies shouting at the crowd in an attempt to win a moment of silence to honor the five people from our class who had died since high school. Finally he settled for an imperfect quiet, and read the names over the continuing low buzz of conversation. Three of the dead had been victims of auto accidents; one had died in a plane crash; and of course, the last person on the list was BROCK CHESTER.

After the tribute was finished and the party resumed, we saw Mark Holmes standing alone in a corner. We came up to him and noticed that his eyes were glistening. As we started to talk he held out his hand to quiet us. "Just a minute," he said, sighing, straightening himself and looking away. "I've got to take a while to shake off that aura." Mark looked every bit as clean-cut and handsome as he had in high school. Near the end of the evening he spent twenty minutes talking to

Lany Tyler, his one-time admirer, about techniques of acupuncture. Before she left, Lany told us, "This reunion is amazing! It's like everyone is trying to take care of unfinished business. In high school, most of us were virgins. But now we all know that nobody, but nobody, is a virgin any more. It makes a big difference."

At one-thirty in the morning there were only twenty people left in the room, huddled together in exhausted little groups and talking quietly. At one table Skip Baumgarten sat alone with the beautiful cocktail waitress he had spotted earlier in the evening. He smoked and joked and laughed, while his new friend smiled at him with admiring eyes. "Come over here," he beckoned to us. He introduced us to the waitress. Her name was "Spray." It was time to go home.

But we had one last responsibility before turning in for the night. The parents of one of our good friends from elementary school days had called us before the reunion to ask a special favor. Their son wanted to attend the party, and they were willing to bring him there, but he needed a ride back to the psychiatric board-and-care home in Orange County where he now lives. He had spent most of the evening alone, circling the room with an attentive smile, listening to conversations but offering not a word of his own. He was equally silent during our two-hour ride down the deserted freeways. We rolled down the windows and let the cold night air rush in on us. When we dropped him off at his residence facility, we waited until the guard arrived to open the door. Our friend hesitated for a moment, shivering in his blue nylon jacket, then smiled at us and waved good-bye. It was four o'clock in the morning.

We drove home as quickly as possible, with Michael at the wheel and Nancy beside him, while David and Flora snuggled in the back seat. Thinking back on our project, we got out our battered copy of *Time* magazine with the article about Palisades High School, and recalled their rosy predictions of "a golden era." "Teenagers today," that article concluded, "do not think of themselves as 'knights in shining chinos' riding forth on rockets to save the universe. But even the coolest of them know that their careers could be almost that fantastic." *Time* had been right about our wide-ranging possibilities, but had not foreseen the fact that we might be paralyzed by them. With the experts of the world waiting expectantly for glorious achievements, how could we possibly disappoint them? And so we struggled forward, constantly shifting our choices, plagued by chronic indecision, searching in vain for a fate that might be worthy of us. Our former teacher Jean O'Brien may have been right when she called the period from '65 to '75 "the saddest years of the century." Perhaps that was the real reason for our sense of loss as we looked back. But when in human history have the bright hopes of seventeen ever been satisfied —least of all by the age of twenty-seven? We reminded ourselves that we were still young, and that unwritten chapters lay ahead.

ABOUT THE AUTHORS

MICHAEL MEDVED was born in Philadelphia in 1948, and attended public schools in San Diego and Los Angeles. He graduated from Yale in 1969, attended Yale Law School, and received a master's degree in creative writing from San Francisco State. He has worked as an encyclopedia salesman, political speech writer, record clerk, teacher at Jewish schools, advertising man, TV scriptwriter and professional note-taker.

DAVID WALLECHINSKY was born in Hollywood, California, in 1948 and educated at public schools in Los Angeles. Since completing a script for a cowboy film at age nine, he has been writing steadily, and is co-author of *Chico's Organic Gardening and Natural Living*, *Laughing Gas* and *The People's Almanac*. His most recent book is *The Book of Lists* (with Irving Wallace and Amy Wallace).